SOUTHERN
SCRIBBLINGS

SOUTHERN SCRIBBLINGS

BRION McCLANAHAN

RED MILL

PUBLISHING

Red Mill Publishing
Post Office Box 2713
Phenix City, AL 36868-2713

ISBN: 978-1-7349504-0-3

10 9 8 7 6 5 4 3 2 1

TABLE OF CONTENTS

FOREWORD

"An unarmed man can only flee from evil, and evil is not overcome by fleeing from it."

Jeff Cooper

"Well, he should've armed himself."

Clint Eastwood, The Unforgiven

THERE IS NO DOUBT about it. There now exists a widespread, vindictive, and unholy war against the real, actual, and true history of the United States of America, and the largest offensive of that war is directed at the American South. Those of us who are proud of our storied heritage are not inclined to take a backward step in this cultural and political war. And we know that our enemy has all the resources: control of the media, the political establishment, academia, and an iron grip on popular culture.

But we were "born standing up and talking back."

And there is good news for our struggle. The many millions of us who are now the targets of this ongoing national epidemic of cultural cleansing and political correctness have a new "manual of arms" to consult in our never-ending resistance to this demagoguery. If you are reading this foreword, you have in your hands our best rebuttal. If you are sick and tired of the relentless attacks against our Southern Culture and History, don't be alarmed. The facts, the real story, and the wonderful truth is that the American people are not fooled, and Brion McClanahan's "Southern Scribblings" is Exhibit A in the evidence for our Defense.

In sixty short and incisive essays, McClanahan takes on the canards of the "Progressive Left" and eviscerates them one by one with common sense, humor, and erudition. Along the way, he debunks the myths of Eric Foner and Kenneth Stampp, and makes short work of "the twitter brigades" who spend their days attacking the character of Robert E. Lee. By using specific facts and overwhelming truths, he takes down the politically naive Ashley Judd, praises the humility and grace of Jimmy and Rosalyn Carter, illuminates the dire ramifications of the current political culture clash in Virginia, and re-introduces us to nearly forgotten historians like Virginia's Lyon Gardiner Tyler, John Cussons of Alabama, and Mildred Lewis Rutherford of Georgia.

In a piece about the effort to alter the lyrics of "Maryland, My Maryland", Dr. McClanahan ties the efforts of the misguided proselytizer Christian McWhorter into a knot from which "The Great Houdini" could not have escaped.

Then there is McClanahan's shining prose, reflecting wit, "Like a good Yankee, Franklin Roosevelt drove through Georgia and thought he could fix it" and tossing challenges, "You don't have to be a farmer to be an agrarian. We could all use a little more of the Southern tradition, but it is up to us to take the challenge of 'raising the human spirit' through our "older, more American' worldview, seriously."

And then there are essential wisdoms such as this, "Symbols may be destroyed, but as long as the tradition itself continues to exist, the barbarians cannot win."

Brion McClanahan has shone a clear bright light into the swamp of revisionism, presentism, and political correctness. He has written a guidebook on how to hold off the barbarians. He knows that the South is not going to "rise again" because it never fell. In fact, the South is always rising.

Ben "Cooter" Jones

Washington, Virginia

SECTION ONE
THE SOUTHERN TRADITION

The Challenge of the Southern Tradition

IN 1966, SENATOR Jim Eastland of Mississippi walked into the Senate Judiciary Committee and asked, "Feel hot in heah?"

A staffer replied: "Well Senator, the thermostat is set at 72 degrees, but we can make it colder."

Eastland, puzzled by the response, doubled down, "I said, Feel Hot in heah?"

The staffer now was perplexed and fearing that he might not understand the question suggested that he would lower the temperature.

Eastland shot back, "Damn it, son!" Is Sen-a-tor Feel P-H-I-L Hot H-A-R-T in heah?"

I begin with this story because it is emblematic of the regionalism of the United States. Or at least it used to be. Listening to congressional debates from the middle of the 20th century was like hearing a symphony of dialect. The Kennedy brothers—though hailing from Irish Catholic bootleggers—sounded like they were from an old Brahmin Massachusetts family. Stennis, Russell, Thurmond, Ervin and other Southerners brought their instruments to the show.

I attended school in Delaware, but my eighth grade English teacher was from Alabama. Yet because her husband was a minister and had to move around, she dropped her accent and adopted a flat Midwestern timbre all while assigning great Southern writers or notably anti-Yankee partisans like Washington Irving. You can take the girl out of Alabama, but you can never take Alabama from the girl.

With a few exceptions, it would hard to detect any regionalism among the current crop of 535 members of Congress. As Americans move and consume, we become a less independent and more plastic people dominated by a

Midwestern Yankee Puritanism. Recent studies have shown that children who move frequently are less likely to excel in school or in a social environment. They aren't from anywhere and have no real culture. This is by design. Nationalization creates a crop of drones with an "Americanism" that suggests saying the Pledge of Allegiance makes you an American and that Abraham Lincoln and Hamilton's state capitalist dream are the greatest parts of American history. We have replaced Billy's Grocery, Harvey Lumber Company, and Daniel Appliance with Publix, Home Depot, and Best Buy respectively. Buy your American flag at the Home Depot with your credit card during our Presidents' Day sale in every town USA. Let's do this.

The South always offered a counterweight to this type of "Americanism," but today you can't sound Southern and still be taken seriously, just as you can't suggest that anything from the Southern tradition is true and valuable without being slapped over the head with the book of bigotry. I'm surprised the modern left doesn't walk about like the monks in the Monty Python film the Holy Grail chanting "Pius Mother Planet Earth, Save Us From Our Privilege, Slap." The only thing they haven't done is require a bonfire of the vanities and demand that every heretic throw some traditional vice—the Bible, your guns, precious metals, certainly your Confederate flags—into the fire in a communal cultural cleansing. That's probably coming.

Senator John Stennis from Mississippi said in 1974 that while people in the South "lacked for money, and lacked for worldly things...they got plenty of things money can't buy—like good neighbors, good friends, the community spirit of sharing with the other fellow." Sam Ervin, the last Jeffersonian to serve in the Senate, shared a similar sentiment when he suggested defeat was good for the soul because it shook the glory out. Ervin was from Burke, North Carolina and the spirit of that place and people ran through his blood and bones.

Some interwar Southerners knew that the world was changing, just as their ancestors knew the United States was destroyed by fire in 1865 and replaced with a unitary American empire beholden to Hamiltonian political economy and Yankee social engineering, the very thing John Taylor of Caroline and other "Old Republicans" warned about in the late eighteenth and early nineteenth centuries. Nothing had changed after the War. Robert Lewis Dabney derided the "New South Creed" for its infatuation with progress in all forms. Industrialization was simply the mistress of social transformation and the destruction of tradition. The fusion of big banks, big business, and unconstitutional big government along with government sponsored social engineering made for a Frankenstein that could not be tamed. There is a reason Populist Senator Tom Watson of Georgia titled his newspaper the *Jeffersonian* in the early twentieth century. The continuity between generations, the traditions that shaped the South and her people, were the most important part of Southern identity.

That identity has been remarkably consistent even when it seems otherwise. Take for example the efforts of "progressive" Southerners to tame the evils of Yankee finance capitalism in the pre-World War I Congress. The War saw the complete victory of Hamilton's economic system in the post bellum period. Protective tariffs, central banking, federally funded internal improvements, and corruption signaled Republican rule. Southerners had some success in pushing back against these measures in the 1880s and 1890s, but it wasn't until the Wilson administration that they achieved any sort of legislative victory. The Glass-Steagall Act, the Clayton Anti-Trust Act, and the Underwood Tariff were all part of a broad Southern effort to place a Jeffersonian stamp on the economy. These were undoubtedly "big government" and constitutionally questionable ideas and policies, but to these Southerners, using the apparatus the Republican Party created to undermine what they considered to be the backbone of anti-Southern and anti-Jeffersonian principles seemed natural. Oscar Underwood of Alabama even classified the Federal Reserve as a Jeffersonian inspired central banking system. Henry DeLemar Clayton of Alabama also secured federal loans for farmers in the 1910s, a type of reparations for being punished by poverty after the War.

But in spite of or perhaps because of this crushing economic dislocation, Southerners clung to their history, their regionalism, and their culture and used it as both a shield and a blanket when confronting modernity or in some cases adopting it. For example, Fuller Callaway, a Southern industrialist in LaGrange, GA, told the muckraker Ida Tarbell that he "made American citizens and used cotton mills to pay the expenses." His son Cason Callaway focused his energy on scientific agriculture and eventually made his Blue Springs farm a private nature reserve called Callaway Gardens. He and his wife Virginia cultivated the Jeffersonian agrarian spirit and believed in independent farmers and localism. The family farm dominated their lives, and azaleas, blue spring water, woods, and outdoor recreation were their Southern legacy.

This is something every Southerner took for granted in the 1920s and 1930s. Jimmy Carter's agrarian manifesto *An Hour Before Daylight* portrays his father as a Jeffersonian worried about New Deal regulations on hogs and tomatoes. Like a good Yankee, Franklin Roosevelt drove through Georgia and thought he could fix it. It's no coincidence that the first industrial hog slaughterhouses appeared in the United States in 1930s. Chicken houses followed in the 1950s and soon "industrial farming" was ripping apart the family farm, the backbone of the Southern tradition.

The twelve Southerners who wrote *I'll Take My Stand* in 1930 could not have been more prophetic, but most people, even some Southerners, didn't want to listen to what Mary Cuff, in a recent piece in *Modern Age*, describes as an "untenable" prescription. She writes: "Thus even for those who sympathize deeply with the agrarian diagnosis of modern society's ills—the social alienation and dehumanization triggered by sprawling urbanism, industrialism, and the dominance of technology—there is often the sense that agrarianism is unhelpful as a solution in the twenty-first century." These Southerners have been labeled romantics who hectored about farming and never picked up a plow. Southerners, even in the early twentieth century, seemed to agree. As eleven-year-old Lillian Nettles of Magnolia, MS told a photographer in 1911, "we like the mill work much better than farming." Five of her nine family members worked in the mill.

But these criticisms miss the point. Did "agrarianism" make the man or did the man make "agrarianism?" More directly, was *I'll Take My Stand* an *agrarian* or a *Southern* manifesto? The authors could have called themselves twelve farmers, twelve poets, or twelve writers, but they chose twelve Southerners, and the title is certainly a Southern choice. David Chandler in his book *The Natural Superiority of Southern Politicians* wrote that "the South has produced the pre-eminent geniuses of American political history." That genius was only made possible by Southern culture, the root of "agrarianism." A *Southern* man could still be agrarian and not live on a farm. It certainly helped, but at its core the Southern agrarian tradition was based on an organic rhythm of life, a Christian sensibility of "good friends, good communities," faith, property, independence, and a chivalric code that had honor as one of the highest traits of man and organized society. To be Southern meant that you embraced the old order of Western Civilization as handed down by the Anglo-American tradition and peppered with the cultural mosaic of the various peoples that settled south of the Mason-Dixon.

And as Southerners began to wrestle with the implications of a Yankee victory in 1865, they became consciously more Southern, but that did not change their traditions. The historian Drew Gilpin Faust vaulted into a college presidency at Harvard by, in part, continually insisting that "Confederate nationalism" was inorganic, a creation of racism and white supremacy. But is this true? The evidence points in another direction. Edwin Alderman, the first president of the University of Virginia and editor of the comprehensive *Library of Southern Literature*, told a University of California audience in 1906 that, "when the age of moral welfare shall succeed to the age of passionate gain-getting; when blind social forces have wrought some tangle of inequality and of injustice, of hatred and suspicion, when calculation and combination can only weave the web more fiercely; when the whole people in some hour of national peril shall seek for the man of heart and faith, who will not falter or fail, in the sweet justice of God, hither shall they turn for succor as once they turned to a simple Virginia planter." This Southern tradition had nothing to do with race. It was an expression of the Jeffersonian mind, a critique of the Hamiltonian vision for America.

Turning to the Virginia planter—the "man of heart and faith"—not the industrialist or the shopkeeper, had to be the solution, and that planter brought up on the traditions of his people, the stories of his ancestors, men of action when the time called for it, had to be a Southerner. This was a call to Washington or Jefferson, not Lincoln or Grant, and certainly not J.P. Morgan or John D. Rockefeller. But would America, now in the throes of industrialization, look to the sage of Monticello for answers, and if not, how could a defeated people sell this tradition, or should they?

Literature professor Charles Kent advised Southerners to look inward, to become better Southerners, not coopted Yankees. "It seems," he wrote in 1907, "much more desirable that we should endeavor to comprehend what our fathers stood for, especially in all matters relating to self-government, then study calmly our own situation, and resolutely acknowledge and adapt the principles and policies that seem most constant with our welfare. So far as my own studies allow me to judge, no other people or fraction of a people has a more admirable body of publicists from whose writings inspiration and guidance may be derived."

The Southerners who wrote *I'll Take My Stand* in 1930 and contributed to *Who Owns America* in 1936 took this challenge seriously. *Who Owns America* is, in some respects, a more interesting book. It is more prescriptive and less philosophical, a practical application of the principles the twelve Southerners sought to define just six years earlier, and while not explicitly Southern focused like *I'll Take My Stand*, the Southern tradition dripped from its pages.

The great poet Donald Davidson outlined a plan for regional government that incorporated Frederick Jackson Turner's prophecy that the core of American government was naturally the relation of "section and nation," not "state and nation." Davidson called it a "New Federalism," not be confused with Richard Nixon's bastardization of the term in the early 1970s. He wrote, "For the United States, the ideal condition would be this: that the regions should be free to cultivate their own particular genius and to find their happiness, along with their sustenance and security, in pursuits to which their people are best adapted, the several regions supplementing and aiding each other, in national comity, under a well-balanced economy." This has not happened, he lamented, because the Constitution could not allow it. The result had been the clash of competing imperialisms, with the Northeast the ultimate victor. "The old outcry against Wall Street," Davidson argued, "is an outcry against a regional foe symbolized by a single institution. It means that the towers of New York are built upon Southern and Western backs."

Andrew Nelson Lytle, the philosopher as historian and writer, heaped praise on Franklin Roosevelt for acknowledging the importance of the family farm, what Lytle called the "livelihood farm." He was giving FDR too much credit, for Roosevelt's discovery that the Southern agrarian tradition was vital to American prosperity was like Augustus telling Livy to write glowing histories of Rome in the first century A.D., or in Josiah Baily of North Carolina writing the "conservative manifesto" in 1936 warning about the potential constitutional and legal hazards of the New Deal. In both cases, the empire had already consumed its parents.

Regardless, Lytle insisted that a United States with one quarter of the people engaged as livelihood farmers would boast the most stable economy in its history. The tangible benefits would be seen in the welfare of the general population, what he termed their more "natural living conditions." Lytle continued "this should be the important end of polity, for only when families are fixed in their habits, sure of their property, hopeful for the security of their children, jealous of liberties which they cherish, can the state keep the middle course between impotence and tyranny."

This, however, required the Southern tradition. John Crowe Ransom argued that "the South may be a valuable accession to the scattering and unorganized party of all those who think it is time to turn away from the frenzy of Big Business toward something older, more American, and more profitable." What Ransom loathed and feared most was a South beholden to "foreign ideas." And notice that he used the term "American" along with the descriptive "older." The Southern "agrarian" tradition is older than the United States. The straight line from the "old Republicans" like John Taylor of Caroline to Ransom, Davidson, and Lytle should be easy to see. But that tradition, that "older, more American" vision of America was swallowed up in the post-World War II nationalist orgy and Cold War propaganda. Us against them had no room for regionalism and Southern agrarianism. The machine age and the nuclear age required a Hamiltonian Americanism. We had to beat the commies, but more importantly, beating the commies required a civic religion that also took aim at tradition, the very thing Dabney said would take place immediately following the War.

Which brings us to 2019 and Tucker Carlson's now infamous—at least among neoconservatives—monologue criticizing what he called "market capitalism." This was a clumsy though refreshing attempt to articulate the "older, more American" vision of the twelve Southerners. The establishment panned it as anti-capitalist and foolish, with media darling Ben Shapiro immediately going on the offensive in both print and video.

Carlson mislabeled his enemy "market capitalism." He was really throwing barbs at Hamilton's state capitalist system and the over century long Republican Party led attempt to remake America. That involved an economic, social, political, and diplomatic transformation that replaced of the "older, more American" world of the Southern agrarians with the Lincolnian American empire. Regardless, when Carlson asked for "A fair country. A decent country. A cohesive country. A country whose leaders don't accelerate the forces of change purely for their own profit and amusement. A country you might recognize when you're old. A country that listens to young people who don't live in Brooklyn. A country where you can make a solid living outside of the big cities. A country where Lewiston, Maine seems almost as important as the west side of Los Angeles. A country where environmentalism means getting outside and picking up the trash. A clean, orderly, stable country that respects itself. And above all, a country where normal people with an average education who grew up no place special can get married, and have happy kids, and repeat unto the generations. A country that actually cares about families, the building block of everything," he was channeling the Jeffersonian America that dominated politics and culture until the close of the War in 1865 and that found a voice in fits and spurts in the post-bellum period, particularly from Southerners who knew they told you so.

Richard Weaver offered the best explanation for why the Southern tradition still has currency in modern society in his *The Southern Tradition At Bay*. He wrote, "The South possesses an inheritance which it has imperfectly understood and little used. It is in the curious position of having been right without realizing the grounds of its rightness." The interwar Southern critique of Hamilton's America came closest to doing so, and in the end, we are left with Weaver's conclusion that the Southern tradition offers not an example but a challenge. "The challenge," he said," is to save the human spirit by re-creating the non-materialist society." This is the very challenge Carlson offered his viewers, the twelve Southerners scribbled about, Dabney thundered from the pulpit, and Taylor of Caroline, the most Jeffersonian of all Jeffersonians, insisted we remember when faced with Hamilton's schemes. Weaver concluded by suggesting that "The Old South may indeed be a hall hung with splendid tapestries in which no one would care to live; but from them we can learn something of how to live." You don't have to be a farmer to be an agrarian. We could all use a little more of the Southern tradition, but it's up to us to take the challenge of "saving the human spirit" through an "older, more American" worldview, seriously.

Anything is Nice if it Comes from Dixieland

IN OCTOBER 1901, President Theodore Roosevelt invited Booker T. Washington to dine at the executive mansion. This was an unprecedented move. No African-American had ever been asked to dine with the president, and while neither Roosevelt or his staff said much of the event, it was surely done in the spirit of reconciliation and Roosevelt's desire to be "the people's president." Reaction to the visit was mixed. The pro-Republican press tended to support Roosevelt's unexpected gesture while Democratic organs, North and South, either questioned Roosevelt's intentions or denounced the meeting altogether.

Historians have mostly focused on the Southern response to the event, primarily "Pitchfork" Ben Tillman's vicious statements condemning the dinner as a slippery slope toward the creation and acceptance of a "mongrel race." But less than one month later, William Jennings Bryan dedicated nearly three pages of his personal newspaper *The Commoner* to what one Southern paper called the "peculiar" interview. Bryan was no race baiter. He showed sympathy toward African-Americans and argued that they were as capable of "self-government" as any member of white American society, yet he also believed in the status quo in regard to race relations. Bryan wrote that he:

> ...hoped that both of them will upon reflection realize the wisdom of abandoning their purpose to wipe out race lines, if they entertain such a purpose. Prof. Washington's work as an educator will be greatly impaired if he allows it to be understood that his object is to initiate the members of his race into the social circles of the whites, and he will do injustice to those of his own color if he turns their thoughts away from intellectual and moral development to the less substantial advantages if there are any advantages at all to be derived from social equality.

This was the widely held sentiment of the majority of Americans in 1901, North and South, even by those who, unlike Tillman, saw value in Washington's work and purpose at the Tuskegee Institute and supported his charge to "cast down your buckets where you are." Washington personified reconciliation, the key to understanding both Northern opposition to Mr. Lincoln's War paradoxically encouragement for Lincoln's "with malice toward none" approach to "reconstruction" rather than the "recreation" of the United States.

Reconciliation began before the War ended in 1865 and continued unabated well into the late twentieth century. Northern Democrats and conservative Republicans favored "resumption" of the Union once hostilities ceased and sought reintegration of the South into all aspects of the United States as quickly as possible. Roosevelt himself was part of this policy, as was his predecessor William McKinley. Long before Richard Nixon made the phrase "Southern strategy" popular, William McKinley toured the South as president, even standing for Dixie while it was played in Atlanta, and in his first inaugural in 1897 insisted that "The North and South no longer divide on the old lines, but on principles and policies; and in this fact surely lover of the country can find cause for true felicity." Roosevelt admired the "unreconstructed" views of his Georgia born mother and ordered all confiscated Confederate flags be returned to their Southern homes in 1905. Every president from McKinley in 1896 to Bill Clinton in 1996 courted the South and used Confederate imagery to do so. The South was not some alien section of "deplorables" to be castigated but a valuable and manifestly integral part of the American experience.

Music echoed this sentiment, and as virtually every distinctively American form of music originated in the South, it became the most enduring and conspicuous example of "reconciliation." Southern music is provincial, a reflection of the culture that produced it, and every Southern State has a song dedicated to it in popular culture. The lyrical content of much of postbellum Southern music–regardless of form, style, or genre–can be divided into two categories: affirmation and defiance. Love and respect for people, place, and family underpin both descriptions, and Northerners quickly adopted an affirmationist version of the South through music. Many of these tunes were written and performed by Northerners themselves.

These songs tended to incorporate a superficial understanding of Southern society, but nevertheless portrayed the South and its people in a positive light. The most popular singer in America during the 1910s, Billy Murray of Colorado, often belted pro-Southern songs into gramophone recordings. "Anything Is Nice If It Comes From Dixieland" and "Are You From Dixie ('Cause I'm From Dixie, Too)" were popular tunes in the World War I era. Sunny weather, warm people, good food, beautiful women, and a slow pace were common themes in these Southern themed songs. "Are You From Dixie" was penned by a Polish Jew and a native New Yorker:

Hello, there, stranger! how do you do?
There's something I'd like to say to you
Don't be surprised
You're recognized!
I'm no detective but I've just surmised.
You're from the place where I long to be,
Your smiling face seems to say to me,
You're from my own land,
My sunny homeland,
Tell me can it be?
It was a way back in eighty nine,
I crossed the old Mason Dixon line
Gee! but I've yearned,
Longed to return
To all the good old pals I left behind.
My home is way down in Alabam'
On a plantation near Birmingham,
And one thing's certain,
I'm surely flirtin'
With those southbound trains:
Are you from Dixie?
I said from Dixie!
Where the fields of cotton beckon to me.
I'm glad to see you,
Tell me how be you
And the friends I'm longing to see.
If you're from Alabama, Tennessee or Caroline
Any place below the Mason Dixon line
Then you're from Dixie,
Hurray for Dixie!
'Cause I'm from Dixie too!

No one considered the theme or lyrics to be insensitive or odd in 1919. Jerry Reed recorded a slightly different version in 1969 where it became one of his biggest hits. The highest paid radio act in 1928, New York's "Happiness Boys," often sang Southern themed songs, with "I Would Rather Be Alone In The South" one of their most recognized tunes. Anything was better than being in New York, but the South, with its climate, women, and food, represented a marked influence over anywhere else in America.

And this characterization of the South was not confined to white American society. Louis Armstrong's "When It's Sleepy Time Down South" was a moderate hit in the jazz era, but later became his signature tune. The language would be considered "racist" today, but the song was penned by Armstrong and three other African-American song writers, one of whom was a leading song writer of the Harlem Renaissance. Armstrong even performed a short film of the tune in 1942 clad in plantation costume while sitting on cotton bales at a Mississippi wharf. No one, white or black, blinked an eye, while one of the dancers in the film, Nick Stewart, was a pioneering African-American actor.

Ah, the pale moon's shining, the fields below
Darkies crooning songs soft and low
You needn't tell me, boy, because I know
It's sleepy time down south
The soft winds blowing through the pinewood trees
Folks down there live a life of ease
When old mammy falls upon her knees
It's sleepy time down south

Oh, steamboats on the river a coming, a going
Splashing the night away
You hear those banjos ringing, the darkies singing
They dance 'til the break of day
Dear old southland with his dreamy song
Take me back to where I belong
Right here in my mammy's arms
When it's sleepy time down south

Detractors would argue that this song and film were made for a white audience and as such had to conform to white sensibilities. That is the same critique of reconciliation. But this is a misrepresentation of both. Armstrong recorded the song nearly one hundred times in his career and it chronicled the Southern diaspora of the early twentieth century. Nearly twenty million white and black Southerners moved away from the South following the War, and Armstrong capitalized on a latent longing for a better environment South of the Mason-Dixon, even among African-Americans. It was their home, too, and all forms of Southern art in the postbellum period included peaceful and positive interactions between white and black Southerners. Northerners often imaged the worst of Southern society, and certainly the highly publicized acts of violence against African-Americans added fuel to the fire, but while nasty, illegal, and unjust, these were the exception not the rule. As the historian C. Vann Woodward pointed out in his *The Strange Career of Jim Crow*, Northerners had no room to lecture the South on racial injustice. Segregation was born in Northern cities before the War, and the North was never immune to racial violence. Some of the worst lynchings of the postbellum era occurred in Northern States. That also added to the desire among some members of the African-American community to go home.

Perhaps the most iconic reconciliationist song was Phil Harris's "That's What I Like About the South." Harris was not born in the South, but no one provided a better image of the region and her people than the popular comedian best known for his work on the Jack Benny Show and for voice work in Disney films. "That's What I Like About the South" captured the spirit and fun of the region. Who wouldn't want to go there after hearing this:

Won't you come with me to Alabamy
Let's go see my dear old Mammy
She's fryin' eggs and boiling hammy
That's what I like about the South

Now there you can make no mistakey
Where those nerves are never shaky
Ought to taste her layer cakey
That's what I like about the South

She's got baked ribs and candied yams
Those sugar-cured Virginia hams
Basement full of those berry jams
An' that's what I like about the South

Hot corn bread, black-eyed peas
You can eat as much as you please
'Cause it's never out of season
That's what I like about the South

Aahhh, don't take one, have two
There's dark brown and chocolate too
Suits me, they must suit you
'Cause that's what I like about the South

Well it's way, way down where the cane grows tall
Down where they say "Y'all"
Walk on in with that Southern drawl
'Cause that's what I like about the South

Down where they have those pretty queens
Keep a-dreamin' those dreamy dreams
Well let's sip that absinthe in New Orleans
That's what I like about the South

Such positive views of Southern society reached millions of Northerners in the early twentieth century. The South became a popular vacation destination and by the post-World War II period a permanent destination for Northerners looking to escape the problems of New England, the Midwest, and the Mid-Atlantic States. But what Northerners could never understand is that you can take the Yankee out of New England, but you can never take the Yankee from the man. Southern society was an organic creation of the people and their culture, and the weather never determined how the Southern people would develop. What Northerners liked about the South would be erased by Northern culture as they moved to a warmer climate. New England has been transplanted to Charleston.

By eliminating the real culture of the people and the place, Northerners are unwittingly eliminating what made the South a bastion of culture for much of American history. There is a reason writers, artists, and musicians loved spending time with Southern people, why H.L. Mencken considered Southern culture to be the most admirable in the United States; it was not infected with the plastic consumerism that dominated the Deep North in the twentieth century. This is what the Fugitives warned against. What Northerners loved about the South could only be preserved if the South remained as it was, imperfect and undeniably human. To Southerners, Hank Williams, Jr. said it best in the 1970s: "If Heaven ain't a lot like Dixie, I don't want to go." That had been the case since the English began populating the Southern colonies in the seventeenth century. "Anything is nice if it comes from Dixieland."

Lyon Gardiner Tyler and Southern History

Presented at the 2017 Abbeville Institute Summer School.

THE ATTACK ON the so-called "lost cause" myth in American history is nothing new. Beginning in the 1950s and 60s, historians like Kenneth Stampp began a concerted effort to undermine the dominant historical interpretation of the War, namely that the War and Reconstruction had been stains on American history, that the War could have been avoided, and that slavery was only a peripheral issue in the entire conflict. Stampp privately wrote that he could never be a "negro-hating Doughface" like James G. Randall or Avery O. Craven, men whom Stampp considered to be some of the worst historians in American history. Why? Because unlike Stampp Craven and Randell did not buy the neo-abolitionist narrative of the events leading to the War. Craven, in fact, placed the War at the feet of a "blundering generation" too foolish to accept compromise to avoid bloodshed. He had no love for Southerners, but he was equally hard on Northern abolitionists. To Stampp, the War had been a moral crusade from the beginning, a conflict that began when Southerners realized the institution of slavery was doomed and the only recourse was secession. Abolitionists were the morally righteous men in white hats destined to save America from the evil slaveocracy. It did not matter that most American viewed abolitionists with suspicion in the antebellum United States, or that their tactics were less than peaceful. What matters is that they won, and the South should be viewed in a far less sympathetic light than the "blundering generation" school accepted.

This is what Stampp had to say to his mentor, William B. Hesseltine, in 1945: "I'm sick of the Randalls, Cravens and other doughfaces who crucify the abolitionists for attacking slavery. If I had lived in the 1850s, I would have been a rabid abolitionist. When the secession crisis came I would have followed the abolitionist line: let 'em secede and good riddance....But once the war came, I would have tried to get something out of it. I would have howled for abolition, and for the confiscation and distribution of large estates among negroes and poor whites, as the Radicals (some of them) did. I would have been a radical because there was nothing better to be. I couldn't have been a conservative Lincoln Republican and rubbed noses with the Blairs and Sewards; and I couldn't have been a Negro-hating copperhead. My only criticism of the Radicals is that they weren't radical enough, at least so far as the southern problem was concerned." Stampp, along with Eric Foner and others, are often cited as the "objective" historians in contrast to the "Lost Cause" pro-Southern ideologues. Who is telling the truth, here?

We would be foolish to think that Stampp occupied a novel place among American historians. The early postbellum period was littered with historians ready and willing to make the South the ultimate villain in American history, the "peculiar" other offset by the superior and progressive North. James Ford Rhodes multi-volume work on American history is indicative of this type of scholarship. Rhodes believed Reconstruction to be one of the worst episodes in American history, but he held men like Calhoun and Jefferson Davis responsible for the carnage and bloodshed of the War and placed the institution of slavery front and center. Rhodes was not a neo-abolitionist and minimized the role of abolitionism in the coming of the conflict, but he rejected the Southern position that the War had been fought for the principles of 1776 and the right to self-government. Other historians, like the German Hermann von Holst, took the same approach, which is why Southerners believed, and rightly so, that the real war was only beginning.

The War that ended on the battlefield in 1865 began anew with the pen not long after the ink dried at Appomattox Courthouse. Southerners understood the stakes. If the Northern view of the War, now so triumphantly supported by Lincoln's assassination in 1865, became engrained into American society, there would be no hope of salvaging any promising memory of the Southern people. They would be traitors identified with an institution that the majority of Americans now found morally repugnant. They knew the real story of America, the fact that Virginia was the most important colony and State in the early federal republic, that the South had led the way for much of American history, that their cause of secession was the same as that of the founding generation, and that there was more than just a smidgen of hypocrisy in Northern self-righteousness in the afterglow of victory. But how do a defeated people retain their memory and their character? More importantly, how do the losers help write the story? And it must be noted that the vicious attacks on traditional Southern history we face today are not novel. Southerners in the postbellum period experienced the same thing.

There were two types of Southern historians in the postbellum period, the amateurs and a burgeoning and productive group of well-trained professionals. Both aimed to craft a history of the South untainted by Northern views. The first group included people like Mildred Lewis Rutherford of Athens, GA and John Cussons of Alabama.

Cussons penned two little books on Southern history in the late nineteenth century. For thirty-two years he had watched as "Northern friends of ours have been diligent in a systematic distortion of the leading facts of American history— inventing, suppressing, perverting, without scruple or shame—until our Southland stands to-day pilloried to the scorn of all the world and bearing on her front the brand of every infamy." The South had sat silently, watching as the North explored every avenue to disparage her people, her cause, and her history. In the short period following the War, Northerners had painted the South as the personification of "meanness," "folly," and "utter and incurable inefficiency." The South was the despicable "other" in the American mind, and as a result "The economist with a principle to illustrate, the moralist full of his Nemesian philosophy, the dramatist in quest of poetic justice—in short every craftsman of tongue or pen with a moral to point or a tale to adorn turns instinctively to this mythical, this fiction-created South, and finds the thing he seeks."

This had broken the unwritten agreement between the two sections following the War. Northerners would acknowledge Lee and Jackson as great Americans and in return the South would consider Lincoln to be the man of hour who saved the Union.

And the South had come to accept it. Her people had been turned against their own history, brainwashed into believing the Yankee version of American history, a history fabricated in the years following the great Southern struggle for independence. Southern children were the targets and as a result "our grandchildren, trained in the public schools, often mingle with their affection an indefinable pity, a pathetic sorrow—solacing us with their caresses while vainly striving to forget "our crimes." A bright little girl climbs into the old veteran's lap, and hugging him hard and kissing his gray head, exclaims: 'I don't care, grandpa, if you were an old rebel! I love you!'" This could have been said today.

Cussons understood one of the great maxims of history by quoting the great British historian Lord Macaulay, "a people which takes no pride in the noble achievements of a remote ancestry will never achieve anything worthy to be remembered by remote descendants." The systematic destruction of the Southern tradition by distortion and lies would render her people impotent in the future. His words were more than quaint "unreconstructed" rants against the government.

They were not "I'm A Good Ol' Rebel." Cussons wielded a philosophical hammer against Yankee Puritanism in an attempt to save the South from self-loathing, guilt, and shame.

Cussons knew the South, the real South, still existed. It had been defeated in war, but the Southern people had much to admire in their history. Her heroes defended a noble tradition and that tradition, if correctly articulated and saved, would place the South at its proper place in the forefront of American history. Unfortunately, his double-barreled assault on Yankee distortion has been mostly forgotten. His two short works defending the South are not placed among the great tomes of the late post-bellum period primarily because not many know they existed. *United States "History" as the Yankee Makes and Takes It* and its more substantial sister *A Glance at Current History* are clear, concise, and more importantly caustic. They are as witty as Bledsoe's *Is Davis a Traitor?* or Taylor's *Destruction and Reconstruction* and while not as meaty as Stephens's or Davis's multi-volume masterpieces on the War and Southern history offer the same defense.

Cussons was born in England and emigrated to North America in 1855. He lived for four years among the Sioux in the Northwest where they named him "The Tall Pine Tree." He moved to Selma, Alabama in 1859 and became a newspaperman as the half owner of the *Morning Reporter*. He opposed secession but when the War began in 1861 he served as a commander of scouts and sharpshooters in the Army of Northern Virginia. He was captured at Gettysburg and after his release spent the remaining months of the War in the Western theater, eventually fighting with Nathan Bedford Forrest. Following the War he founded a publishing firm, owned a large hunting lodge in Virginia, and served as one of the officers of the United Confederate Veterans.

United States "History" as the Yankee Makes and Takes It was a short work designed to illustrate the growing problem of Puritan history in America. The Puritan, Cussons argued, always considers himself to be the moral superior to any other people. From the beginning, Puritans had formulated the false notion that their customs and traditions produced better men and societies than those of the South. For example, the "Yankee" or "Puritan" idea would logically "formulate and demonstrate" the following proposition:

1. Patrick Henry, furnished with a good stock of groceries, failed at twenty-three.

2. A Puritan, even of the tenth magnitude, under like circumstances, would not fail at twenty-three. Ergo: A tenth-rate Puritan is the superior of Patrick Henry.

This, of course, is a fallacy in logic but one that makes perfect sense to the New England mind. Cussons defined the Yankee as thus:

Self-styled as the apostle of liberty, he has ever claimed for himself the liberty of persecuting all who presumed to differ from him. Self-appointed as the champion of unity and harmony, he has carried discord into every land that his foot has smitten. Exalting himself as the defender of freedom of thought, his favorite practice has been to muzzle the press and to adjourn legislatures with the sword. Vaunting himself as the only true disciple of the living God, he has done more to bring sacred things into disrepute than has been accomplished by all the apostates of all the ages....Born in revolt against, law and order—breeding schism in the Church and faction in the State—seceding from every organization to which he had pledged fidelity—nullifying all law, human and divine, which lacked the seal of his approval—evermore setting up what he calls his conscience against the most august of constituted authorities and the most sacred of covenanted obligations, he yet has the impregnable conceit to pose himself in the world's eye as the only surviving specimen of political or moral worth.

Cussons questioned American education, the attempt by the general government–more importantly the Union veterans of the Grand Army of the Potomac–to write a "true" history of the War, and the false narrative that the North had long been opposed to the principles of States' rights, nullification, and secession.

At every step, Cussons defended the men and the cause of the South and lamented that her history was being written by the victors. "The whole story of the war and its causes," he wrote, "has been distorted and perverted and falsely told. Yet at the bar of unbiased history, before the tribunal of impartial posterity, it will become manifest that the vital principle of self-government—the world's ideal, and what was fondly deemed America's realization of that ideal—went down in blood and tears on the stricken field of Appomattox. It was there that Statehood perished. It was there that the last stand was made for the once-sacred principle of 'government by free consent.'" The old republic of the founding generation was buried by Puritanical self-righteousness. Cussons predicted the inevitable outcome:

"Potential classes are now longing for a change; they are earnest in their desire for what they call "a strong government." And it may be that their yearnings will not be in vain. The corruption of a republic is the germination of an empire. A period of domestic turbulence or foreign war would render usurpation as easy as the repetition of a thrice-told tale. Political speculations would then reassume their old names—incivism, sedition, constructive treason—and the familiar remedies would be applied—press censorship, the star chamber, *lettres de cachet*, and bureaus of military justice."

In the final chapter of *A Glance at Current History*, Cussons addressed the relationship between the Indian tribes and the general government and compared the plight of the Indian—harassed, chased, threatened with extermination—with that of the South during and after the War. He recoiled at their treatment and bristled at attempts to make them "good people." How would it sound, he asked, if the Indian said in response to the bloodthirsty General Philip Sheridan that, "There is no good Yankee but a dead Yankee?" Like the South, the Indian had a noble heritage that was being trampled by an invading army. Cussons believed the two shared a common cause.

Like Cussons, Rutherford was not a trained historian, but also like Cussons had a firm grasp of the Yankee problem in postbellum America. Rutherford, however, was a leading figure in the establishment of the United Daughters of the Confederacy and was the historian general of that organization. It is true that Rutherford made mistakes in her histories, and she is often castigated for her "romanticized" version of the antebellum period, particularly of race and slavery (positions that are unfashionable today but were bolstered by the professional historians of the time), but Rutherford also made several good contributions to Southern history most often by using the words of Northerners to support her arguments. Her often vilified *Truths of History* is a collection of primary documents designed to defend the Southern view of government and society with Northern voices. This is an artful tactic that can still be used today.

Rutherford took seriously the concern of author and diplomat Thomas Nelson Page—another vilified figure from the New South—that "In a few years there will be no South to demand a history if we leave history as it is now written. How do we stand today in the eyes of the world? We are esteemed ignorant, illiterate, cruel, semi-barbarous, a race sunken in brutality and vice, a race of slave drivers who disrupted the Union in order to perpetuate human slavery and who as a people have contributed nothing to the advancement of mankind." Again, could not the same words be written today? Rutherford insisted that Southerners study their own past to combat what we would call cultural Marxism today, or the Yankeefication of American history. And Southerners responded. The late nineteenth and early twentieth century witnessed a resurgence of interest in Southern history, particularly from native Southerners. Most, including Rutherford, wanted to place the South as the pivotal section in the founding of the American "nation." As Northerners ran around telling students that the

Pilgrims invented American democracy and all great intellectual, cultural, and technological innovations came from the North, Southerners pushed back, with a new breed of professional historians leading the way.

The South in the Building of the Nation series was published in 1909 as both a counterweight to the Northern mythmaking of American history and an affirmation of the South's role in the establishment of the United States. The title gives away the intent of the project. Southerners were not content to be the backwater of American civilization, the "peculiar" others; they were the primary builders of that civilization, from the founding period to the early 20th century. The series can be viewed as a companion to the *Library of Southern Literature* and like that series the editors and contributors to *The South in the Building of the Nation* were a veritable who's who among Southern historians in the early twentieth century. Several university presidents and leading Southern historians participated with no historian born or bred north of the Mason Dixon among the list. Some recognizable contributors and editors include Franklin L. Riley, the founder of the Mississippi Department of Archives and History, U.B. Philips, for a time the pre-eminent American historian on slavery and plantation life in the South, George Petrie, the first Alabamian to earn a Ph.D and the founder of the Auburn University history department, graduate school, and most importantly for many in that state, the Auburn football team, Walter Fleming, a member of the "Dunning School" of Reconstruction and the editor of the important but now out of favor *Documentary History of Reconstruction* among other works, Samuel Chiles Mitchell, president of several universities across the South including the U. of South Carolina, Edwin Mims, professor of lit at Vanderbilt and primary advisor for almost every one of the fugitive agrarians, Douglas Southall Freeman, the distinguished historian and author of multi-volume biographies of Lee and Washington, and two important presidents of the College of William and Mary, J.A.C. Chandler and Lyon Gardiner Tyler, the latter of the two being the focus of a later portion of this talk.

Like many of the histories produced during this period in the South, *The South in the Building of the Nation* is often ridiculed for its open racism and glorification of the Old South, but these attacks are often leveled by people who have never read any of the volumes. Like U.B. Phillips and the Dunning School of historians, they are often flippantly discarded by establishment historians and graduate students while much of the fundamental material has not been disproven only re-interpreted by later generations. That is the key to understanding the current situation. The fight is against *interpretation* not *fact*, and as any honest historian will tell you, most of history is just that, interpretation. The progressive historian Charles Beard, for example, never said he had *the* interpretation of the Constitution, it was *an* interpretation. This is why graduate students used to study historiography. Now they study fashionable trends without digesting who wrote history or why a particular history was written. That is often as important as the material itself. There are, of course, exceptions to this rule. One of the better is John David Smith's *Slavery, Race, and American History* where he criticizes "contemporary scholars" who "pay insufficient attention to the contributions of their intellectual forefathers, especially those with whom they disagree ideologically...."

It is true that most, if not all, of the contributors of this series were "racist," but so was most of America in 1909. They had commonly held views for their time, but the charge of racism is an anti-intellectual statement designed to smother or blacklist a currently unfashionable belief, study, or program. Many of these men were progressives who also viewed the South as important part of American civilization moving forward. One contributor, Peter J. Hamilton, served as a federal judge in Puerto Rico; another, Colyer Meriwather was an American advisor in Japan; and Mims became an outspoken opponent of lynching in the South, and later served as president of what is now called SACS, a regional accrediting body for Southern colleges and universities. Several of these men held leadership positions in colleges and universities across the South well into the mid-twentieth century. The history contained in these volumes is perhaps the best expression of the Southern mind in the early postbellum period. That alone should make it worthy of study, but that would also require a careful examination of the material without the lenses of presentism, something the current academic profession seems almost unable or unwilling to do. In short, these volumes cannot simply be written off as some quaint "lost cause" fabrication of American history or a "white supremacist" polemic. They are a serious academic exercise in a solid narrative format, a thorough and at times critical examination of the South's role in the American experience and an attempt to understand all facets of Southern history, political, cultural, and economic with the evidence available to them.

Two volumes, in fact, are dedicated to Southern economics, something that had not been comprehensively studied since the late antebellum period. One section on "Free Contract Labor in the Antebellum South" plowed new ground in telling a sympathetic story of free black labor before the War, a field that in 1909 was virtually non-existent. This section, by the way, was written by Alfred H. Stone of Mississippi, a man now regarded as one of the more virulent racists in the South but in his day was so well received as an economic historian that he was appointed as a research associate at the Carnegie Institute of Washington. The aforementioned Smith wrote a very good essay on Stone in his *Slavery, Race, and American History*.

Yet, while Phillips, Freeman, and Fleming still receive attention from the modern academic community, even if insufficient, one of the contributors to this series, Lyon Gardiner Tyler, has been either ignored or ridiculed by the modern academy and the public at large. The reason? Tyler did not confine his efforts to academic history. He would often engage the popular press—and by engage meaning take them head on when they were wrong—and write histories intended for consumption by the masses. In other words, Tyler took seriously his role as a historian for the people, not just academics. This is what the late Shelby Foote used to tell anyone who would listen. Historians need to learn how to write.

Tyler was the second youngest son of President John Tyler's and as such a fervent son of Virginia. In addition to holding the position as the President of the College of William and Mary, Tyler spent much of his career writing popular histories of Virginia from the colonial period to the present day. He wrote and edited "Tyler's quarterly historical and genealogical magazine," which is a fine collection of stories related to all elements of Virginia history. Some of these works were little more than pamphlets for mass consumption. For example, his "Virginia First," also published at the Abbeville Institute website, is a collection of fifteen points designed to place Virginia at the forefront of American history. As he wrote in his first point, "THE name First given to the territory occupied by the present United States was Virginia. It was bestowed upon the Country by Elizabeth, greatest of English queens. The United States of America are mere words of description. They are not a name. The rightful and historic name of this great Republic is "Virginia." We must get back to it, if the Country's name is to have any real significance." The rest of the little essay follows this trend. Virginia had the first representative government, the first thanksgiving, was the first to declare independence, the first to agitate for independence, the greatest of the early American statesmen and leaders and gallant sons who served with distinction throughout American history. Tell that to the tour guides at Plymouth and they will give you a curious look of bewilderment. Don't you know that Plymouth was the first at everything?

Tyler was also responsible for an essay that ran in *Time* magazine in June 1928 entitled "Tyler vs. Lincoln." In April of that year, *Time* ran an article comparing Abraham Lincoln to John Tyler. As you might image *Time* found Tyler to be lacking, calling him "historically a dwarf." It must be understood that modern Lincoln worship and disdain for the South did not begin in the modern age. L.G. Tyler responded in a splendid little rebuttal. Tyler wrote that "real history cares nothing for the blare of trumpets and the shouts of propagandists...." He then surgically sliced apart the Lincoln myth in a way that few historians have been able to do. Tyler wrote, "In conducting the war Lincoln talked about "democracy" and "the plain people", but adopted the rules of despotism and autocracy, and under the fiction of war powers virtually suspended the Constitution. This surely cannot be said of John Tyler, as president, who, though of parentage much higher in the social scale than Lincoln, was a much greater democrat, since he professed faith in the Constitution and would not violate it, even at the dictation of his party."

Tyler attacked Lincoln's career as a lawyer by claiming that Lincoln made dirty deals and underhanded moves to secure victory for his usually well financed clients. This extended to his political career where Lincoln so vigorously pursued office that he cared little as to how he obtained a seat in Congress, or ultimately, president. Whereas John Tyler assumed the office of president after several brilliant terms as a United States Senator, Lincoln was nominated because he was slick and was able to appeal to everyone and no one at the same time. In other words, Lincoln was a politician and Tyler a statesman. Tyler sought peace and avoided war with Mexico during his administration through expert diplomacy with both the British and the Mexican government, something Lincoln entirely avoided in the time leading to the disastrous conclave through arms between the North and South from 1861-1865. Lincoln professed peace but never showed the resolve to see it through. Tyler, even in 1861, sought peace until it became clear that the Lincoln administration had no interest in a bloodless solution to the conflict. Tyler correctly shows that Lincoln's entire program was directed toward war from the minute he assumed office in March 1861. This would be considered "Lost Cause" mythology today—and several of Tyler's critics have labeled it that—but the evidence is clear that Lincoln went headfirst into war when other options were on the table.

Perhaps the best part of Tyler's piece is his explanation as to *why* the tariff issue was important in 1861. It was not because, as several modern historians like to suggest, the South paid more in tariff revenue than the North, but because the newly crafted Southern tariff would be less than half of the tariff of the general government, thus creating a competitive economic environment that the North would lose. Lincoln was not concerned about "losing his revenue" because Southerners were out of the Union and thus could not buy Northern manufactured goods. He was concerned about "losing his revenue" because the miniscule Confederate tariff would undercut the North and shift trade to the Southern confederacy, thus destroying the Northern economy. We should stop saying "Southerners paid 80 percent of the tariff" and start outlining the real economic motivation behind Lincoln's insistence that the South remain in the Union: Northern financial interests could not compete with a vibrant free trade federal republic on their doorstep. Again, this is written off as a "lost cause" myth and establishment historians can sit on television and make stupid statements like, "No one was talking about the tariff" in 1861 when as Tyler clearly shows they were.

But this is only scratching the surface of Tyler's supposed "lost cause" mythology. According to the critics, Tyler's most substantial contribution to the "lost cause" myth was his 1920 *A Confederate Catechism*. The *Catechism* received quite a bit of press in May of this year with several mainstream and leftist media outlets running pieces on its modern influence or lack thereof. The *Catechism* is still used by some SCV camps as an educational piece and certainly has historical worth. Critics won't agree, but remember, the current assault is over interpretation. The *Catechism* does outline several points that critics view as both illogical and ahistorical, not the least of which is Tyler's minimization of slavery as a cause of the War. It is also denounced because of its format, but most modern academics equate catechisms to solely religious functions, not realizing that many "history textbooks" used a catechism format in the late 19th and early 20th centuries. Mathew Page Andrews, for example, used a catechism format for his very popular United States history textbook, a work that was adopted by hundreds of schools across the United States. Rote memorization was the standard method of historical learning until the 1960s when it fell out of fashion. Better to learn theories and trends than actual people, places, dates, and events, unless of course those people, places, dates, and events correspond to a revised version of America.

Tyler contends that the Northern invasion of the South started the War, that Lincoln purposely broke the peace between North and South when he invaded Fort Pickens—not Sumter—that Lincoln did not wage war to "free the slaves," that the South had long been the "milchcow" of the North and that secession was true "government of the people, by the people, and for the people." These positions are simply heresy to the Lincoln mythmakers, and accordingly Tyler, like the Southern historians of the early 20th century, has come under attack for being a liar, a mythmaker, and worse a racist.

This explains why the New South needs more attention. Could every one of Tyler's 20 points in his *Catechism* or his 15 points in *Virginia First* be validated? Could modern historians learn from L.G. Tyler, or how about Cussons, or Rutherford, or the dozens of professional historians like Phillips or Fleming, or pro-amateurs like Stone? I think the answer is definitively yes. More importantly, can the New South be as vital to the understanding of the Southern tradition as the Old? Did men like Dabney and Mencken or even the Agrarians fail to entirely understand the influence of the Old on the New? Could the New have prospered without some of the ways of the Old, and was the race question the only element of Southern history in the 20th century that made it unique? In other words, were Southerners just good racist Northerners? In essence, the narrative goes take away race and Southerners are as bland, corrupt, and money hungry as a New England Yankee, only more violent and with less real culture. It was only race that made them unique. That would seem to be the assumption, but I think a tremendously incorrect one.

My goal in these two lectures has been to pique your interest as historians, philosophers, writers, and scholars in the New South, to seek to understand this period and save it from the clutches of the carpetbagger dominated "Southern studies" programs that now dot the landscapes of the Southern academy. Their goal is to condemn and "contextualize," to sell a myth to the American public that these Southerners were corrupt and deceitful without remorse or compunction for the sin of secession and sectionalism. Those are modern value judgements, and their myth is even more whimsical than the "lost cause." As Alfred Stone wrote in *The South and the Building of the Nation*, "Southern history, as told by Southern people, may be full of myths and ill-founded traditions; but, as it has thus far been written by historians of other sections, it is replete with interpretations and conclusions almost fantastic and apparent efforts of the imagination."

New South Voices of the Southern Tradition

Presented at the 2017 Abbeville Institute Summer School.

AS SCHOLARS DEDICATED to exploring what is true and valuable in the Southern tradition, we are most often drawn to the antebellum South and the early federal period, the days when Jeffersonian federalism and political economy reigned supreme and Southern statesmen were regarded as the best in the land. We still fight the old battles, taking our time to explain the morality of secession and nullification, the depth of antebellum Southern literary and religious figures, the Jeffersonian critique of industrial capitalism, and the unquestioned superiority of Southern legal scholars and political theorists like St. George Tucker, Abel P. Upshur, John Taylor of Caroline, and John C. Calhoun. Antebellum Southerners, as Eugene Genovese pointed out, have an important place in the historical record, not merely as subjects of condemnation as the modern profession so often proclaims, but as real intellectuals whose "finest aspects of their thought, shorn from the tragic commitment to slavery and racism, constitute a searing critique of some of the most dangerous tendencies in modern life." We wield pens instead of rifles and charge the ramparts for historical glory, waving our flags and hoping that we will not meet the same fate as Pettigrew's men at Gettysburg. Unfortunately, the cultural Marxists stand on Cemetery Ridge, supported by the huge cannons of the Lincolnian myth, the professional academy, and their allies that control American pop culture and media.

This is instructive for Southern historians, particularly those who refuse to subscribe to the presentist narrative that saturates the establishment academy. I am not suggesting that we concede the field, surrender, and retreat to our homes, but we should not die in vain glory, either. The old battles are still worthwhile, and we can find avenues to parry their attacks, perhaps even mount an oblique assault. An Institute of Northern Studies dedicated to Northern hypocrisy on a variety of antebellum issues—slavery, secession, racism, history, literature—would be splendid. This has been and continues to be our goal, to chip away at the "treasury of counterfeit virtue" of Northern self-righteousness. This is often enjoyable—indeed it can be quite exhilarating—but by focusing most of our energy on the antebellum period, we leave other parts of Southern history open to the ravages of the modern historian, a group which views every subject through the lens of race, class, and gender.

The postbellum period in Southern history has suffered the most for this. The historian George Tindall, often considered one of the deans of the New South field, wrote that "Part of the trouble with the years after Reconstruction has been the apparent lack of dramatic appeal." This is true. Modern Southern historians looking for a topic are naturally drawn to the conflict of the antebellum period. More often, they look at the antebellum era and the War as an opportunity to either gut or support the "lost cause" narrative. For example, current Harvard University President Drew Gilpin Faust crafted an image of rowdy riotous women in the South during the War to combat the "myth" that women enthusiastically supported the Southern cause. This, of course, belies the historical record, but Faust made a career out of her attempts to destroy the so-called "lost cause myth." She is not alone. An entire library could be filled with books dedicated to the eradication of the "lost cause." The modern political and cultural anti-Southern pogroms are merely an extension of this trend.

At the heart of this historical debate is not the Confederacy itself, but the memory of the antebellum South, or in other words the collective remembered past of the Southern people. Faust, like other anti-"lost causers" in both the historical profession and the mainstream educational, political, and cultural establishment, is not really concerned with Southern history *per se*, but with how Southerners and Americans at large *interpret* and *remember* that history. Their goal is political not intellectual. Charles Dew, whose *Apostles of Disunion* is now required reading for graduate students across the United States, openly admitted as such when he wrote in the preface that he intended his work to be a polemic against the "neo-Confederate" movement. That is a political not a historical statement.

This is why Richard Weaver chose to write about the postbellum South in his seminal *The Southern Tradition at Bay* subtitled *A History of Postbellum Thought*. Weaver understood that is where the real battle was taking place, as Southerners came out of the War with the intent of defining the South and defending their cause. Making the term "lost cause" a pejorative tied to race and slavery has not only altered our perception of the antebellum South but has critically wounded the study of the New South as well. It was the New South, after all, which supposedly made the whole thing up. They lied. These, then, are the great questions of our age. Who were the "New South" leaders, what did they want, was their conception of the Old South rooted in wishful mythmaking or honest history, how did they ultimately affect American politics and culture, was the "solid South" based entirely on the principle of "white supremacy," and most important, can the study of the New South provide examples of the Southern tradition, meaning was there a continuity between the Old South and the New?

This question of continuity can be addressed in several ways, but the two most pressing issues are cultural and economic, with culture comprising political culture as well as the general habits, attitudes, and ideas of the Southern people.

The New South is often regarded as a transitional phase for the Southern economy. When Henry Grady visited New York in 1886 and gave his famous "New South" speech, he championed "new ideas and aspirations" in the South. These included most conspicuously railroads and factories in place of cotton fields and cash crops. That image of an industrializing South stuck. The South, it was argued, would only be rescued from the crushing poverty brought on by the War through economic diversification. We often attach the "New South" moniker to economic transformation. Certainly there were Southerners before the War who pushed this message. James De Bow's *Review* argued that the South needed to diversify its economy to keep pace with the North. A few industrial centers took root, most importantly Columbus, GA, Augusta, GA, and Richmond, VA, but most Southerners did not see the necessity in investing money in factories or railroads when they could become very wealthy growing cotton, sugar, or rice. And the good, navigable rivers of the South seemed to make railroads an expensive and wasteful economic adventure. The same held true for factories. Large plantations were a certain avenue to wealth; factories were not.

Historians have debated the wealth of the Old South, but studies in the 1970s conclusively proved that the South was not poor before the War and wealth was distributed across a wide swath of society, not concentrated in a few "oligarchs" who ruled the region. There were more "middling" landowners and a more vibrant "middle class" than the traditional image of Southern life portrayed. What transpired after the War, of course, was crushing poverty for the entire region, and it seemed that the South had to adopt new economic models to dig itself out of the Yankee imposed economic mess. What might be surprising to most, however, was that the South remained predominantly agricultural well into the mid-twentieth century. Most Southerners, black and white, were still farmers. Only 15 percent of Southerners were engaged in manufacturing in 1910 and by 1930 70 percent of the South was still rural, compared to 44 percent for the rest of the United States. Cotton production doubled between the 1870s and 1890s, as did production for other cash crops including tobacco. Farms did begin to diversify. By the 20th century, the South was the leading exporter of fruits and vegetables and both wheat and cattle production increased exponentially.

There were warning signs that this would soon change, hence the agrarian manifesto *I'll Take My Stand*. The Southerners who penned that marvelous collection of essays were concerned that the way of life they had all known and accepted as the bedrock of stable civilization, land and agriculture, was slowly being chipped away by mechanization. Nearly ninety years later, their prognostications have been proven correct. Today Southerners are more concerned with Wall Street stocks than the cotton price. But this talk is not concerned with the broad transformation of the Southern economy nor with the micro-economics of the region, but how Southerners coped with this transformation within the context of *being Southern*.

The Agrarians were *Southern* first and foremost. Their worldview was pegged to a way of life entirely unique in the American experience. They came from a region steeped in history and culture, which is why they reacted so harshly to H.L. Mencken's characterization of the region as the Sahara of the Bozart. Mencken, of course, was not entirely disparaging the South in his famous or infamous essay. His was a lament of what once was. As he wrote, antebellum Southern civilization was "the best that these states have ever seen." But Mencken missed the vital link between the old and the new, the continuity that held the past to the present. The South may have been changing, but it was a uniquely *Southern* change, and as the Agrarians pointed out in scathing commentary, Mencken did not understand nor recognize the jewels the South produced after the War. She was still a vibrant section, which is why modern students of the South, particularly those interested in saving Southern civilization, should pay more attention to the New South.

Southerners were still consciously *Southern* in the postbellum period. This may seem like an obvious statement, but we have to remember that their identity was constantly being attacked and disparaged by Northern forces. Reconciliation had not yet arrived in the 1860s and 1870s and even into the early 1900s, the South was often still the conspicuous other in American society, the section of traitors and the economic and social drag on American progress. Southerners sought to salvage their identity from the ruins of war. More important, Southerners wanted to show the *American* people that their region was *vital* to the *American* experience. And Southerners aimed to place their own stamp on this idea of progress. Genovese called this the "slaveholder's dilemma" in the antebellum period, the coupling of the belief in progress with a labor system that was characterized as medieval. In the postbellum period, Southerners aspired to show their Northern counterparts that their civilization was as "progressive" as the North. Simply put, they clamored for acceptance within the context of their own unique identity. It was not cultural assimilation they desired but real *diversity*. This has been despairingly called "the New South Creed," a "myth" that helped spawn the "lost cause" myth. Those who tear down the "New South Creed" do so in the same way they attack the "lost cause." The Creed was a myth perpetrated by Southern advocates who lied about the real conditions of the South in order to attract foreign capital, meaning Northern investment. This ultimately involved the establishment of Jim Crow segregation—a system C. Vann Woodward pointed out was created in Northern cities and then copied in the South with much resistance from the "redeemer class." So how much of this was true? Was the South a cultural wasteland after the War? How did Southerners *Southernize* industrialization? And how did the South view its past?

There are so many questions to be answered in the New South period, and yet too few of us spend any time investigating and studying that era of Southern history. My focus in my talks today will be on three areas that need further development: political and philosophical continuity between the Old and New South; the effort by Southern intellectuals to place the South at the forefront of American culture and history; and Southern attempts to "Southernize" the growing industrial economy in the South.

In the decades following the War, nearly 700 former Confederate leaders served in elected positions at every level of government. One, LQC Lamar, served on the Supreme Court. In some cases, these leaders became Republicans and helped form early Reconstruction efforts, most notably Amos Akerman who held the position of Attorney General in the Grant administration. Akerman was later sacked because he opposed federal aid to struggling Northern railroads. By the 1870s, there were enough former Confederate leaders in the Congress that one California newspaper thought it necessary to print the names of every "rebel" who represented the Democratic Party in Washington D.C. These men—often called the "rebel brigadiers"—would infuriate their Northern counterparts with continual references to the glory of the Old South.

John Warwick Daniel of Virginia—often called the Lame Lion of Lynchburg—epitomized these "rebel brigadiers." Daniel was severely wounded three times during the War. He was shot through the hip during the Battle of First Manassas only to return to combat within the year. He carved a bullet out of his hand with a pocketknife in 1862 and nearly bled to death during the Battle of the Wilderness in 1864. Daniel became one of the most powerful Southern voices in the United States Senate. He served there from 1887-1910.

Daniel supported Winfield Scott Hancock for president in 1880 as the only hope of real reconciliation between the sections and his public career, while often characterized as either rabidly partisan or rabidly racist, displayed a willingness to bury the hatchet and move forward as a unified federal republic. But Daniel never lost sight of Southern political principles or the role the South, in particular, Virginia, played in the early history of the United States. After Daniel's death in 1910, one contemporary remarked:

> *I fancy that John Daniel would have named Thomas Jefferson as the greatest American statesman; certainly his own political instincts and ideals were largely those which Jefferson had caused to prevail. Like Jefferson, he trusted the people of his country, because by close intimacy and wide experience he had found them worthy of trust and believed them also worthy of freedom and political power. His abiding faith in the honesty of his fellow citizens, his rooted belief in their common sense, his trust in the appeal to the educated reason of the voters, his assurance that human society is capable of indefinite advancement in virtue and uprightness, his firm conviction that majorities rule not by might alone but of right as well, made of Thomas Jefferson the typical American and the like qualities made of John Daniel the typical Jeffersonian Democrat.*

There was much truth to this assessment. Daniel was asked to speak about Jefferson Davis's life and character before the Virginia Legislature in 1890, just one year after the former President's death. His purpose was to honor the man and his legacy and to vindicate the South and its struggle for independence. Daniel said, "Jefferson Davis never advocated an idea that did not have its foundation in the Declaration of Independence; that was not deducible from the Constitution of the United States as the fathers who made it interpreted its meaning; that had not been rung in his ears and stamped upon his heart from the hour when his father baptized him in the name of Jefferson and he first saw the light in a Commonwealth (Kentucky) that was yet vocal with the States'-Rights Resolutions of 1798." Davis, Daniel insisted, should have been etched in stone among the great pantheon of world heroes. His cause was that of America.

Daniel asked:

> *Did not the South love American institutions? What school-boy cannot tell? Who wrote the great Declaration? Who threw down the gage, "Liberty or Death?" Who was chief framer of the Constitution? Who became its great expounder? Who wrote the Bill of Rights which is copied far and wide by free commonwealths? Who presided over the convention*

that made the Constitution and became in field and council its all in all defender? Jefferson, Henry, Madison, Marshall, Mason, Washington, speak from your graves and give the answer.

And Daniel emphasized that American history had been defined by the South, from the Old Northwest territory to Texas, Southerners had led the charge to settle North America, to bring America to the West, and by America he meant the principles that defined the South: liberty, independence, and free government. Their cause was that of the patriot who rode to battle against the British in 1776, both North and South.

Modern critics would call this "Lost Cause" mythology, but Daniel displayed a cogency in his advocacy for the South in every possible venue. He was asked to give the concluding oration at the dedication of the Washington Monument in 1885. The speakers of the day included the "Old Icicle" John Sherman, brother of William T. Sherman, and President Chester Arthur. Daniel heaped praise on the New England patriot during the American War for Independence but reminded the audience that Virginia had been first to resist the Stamp Act and had been the first to propose independence. He invoked the great names from Virginia history in an effort to place the Old Dominion at the forefront of the American experience. More importantly, Daniel emphasized that Washington was a Virginian before he was an American. This was no "Lost Cause" mythology. Southern historians in the post bellum period used it to dig at the notion that America had been formed by New Englanders. This was another skirmish in the long cultural war between North and South that began, as Daniel illustrated in his speech, during the English Civil War of the 1640s. David Hackett Fischer's *Albion's Seed* beautifully explains the cultural differences between North and South long before the slavery question was interjected into American politics. Daniel and other Southerners had been saying this for years.

Daniel is but one example of the dozens of Southerners who connected the Old South to the New, who sought to provide historical context for the actions of the Southern states in 1860-61. This may be a myth to those with a social or political agenda, but to the men who survived the War and lived in the defeated South, the "myth" was a powerful reality. Even Henry Grady, so conspicuously tied to the "New South Creed," worked to hitch the Old South to the New. In one high profile political campaign, Grady and his Atlanta *Constitution* supported John B. Gordon for governor in 1886 against August Octavius Bacon, a Macon lawyer, businessman, and statesman. Gordon had tarnished his reputation as a political leader while in the United States Senate—several letters indicating corruption were published in the press—and he was virtually broke in 1886, but the Southern people still held him in high regard for his military efforts during the War. Grady expertly used this to his advantage when he invited both Jefferson Davis and Gordon to the cornerstone ceremony for the Confederate monument in Montgomery, AL in 1886. 5,000 people attended that day, but over 100,000 people, many of whom were former Confederate soldiers, flocked to catch a glimpse of Davis and Gordon when they traveled to Georgia.

Lost in this story is A.O. Bacon, a future anti-imperialist, limited government Senator of the United States. Bacon also served in the Confederate army, but never had the public profile of Gordon. His political career was fairly free of scandal and Bacon was the favorite to win the governorship until Grady interjected Gordon into the race. Bacon personified the continuity between the Jeffersonian principles of the Old South and the application of those principles to the New. He favored diversification of the Southern economy but thought men like Grady had taken it too far. He went head to head with the administration of Teddy Roosevelt over the unconstitutional expansion of executive power and joined hands with a diverse group of statesmen and business leaders in opposition to the Spanish-American War. To the end, Bacon favored the policies that formed the early Jeffersonian republicans. He was recognized as the archirype of the Southern gentlemen, the walking contrast to the new breed of Southern leaders like "Pitchfork" Ben Tillman of South Carolina and even Henry Grady.

As these conservative voices began to die off in the early 20th century, they were replaced by the "progressives." Woodward claims that Southern progressives were at one time Southern conservatives. There is some truth to this statement. One thing that has often perplexed antebellum Southern historians is why these men accepted a strong federal government. The Wilson administration ran roughshod over the Constitution, often with the complicit support of the Southern congressional delegation. The answer, I think, is to be found in their disdain for the Northern elite.

Take for example the great Southern political leaders of the 1910s and 1920s, men like Oscar Underwood, Henry Steagall, and Henry D. Clayton of Alabama, Carter Glass of Virginia, and Arsene Pujo of Louisiana. All supported, at least to some extent, the progressive agenda of the Wilson administration. Underwood helped craft the Underwood Tariff, which included a revised income tax with a punitive top marginal rate. Clayton was famous, or infamous, for the Clayton Anti-Trust Act, and both Glass and Steagall had their names attached to the banking regulations known as Glass-Steagall which were recently repealed by the Republican controlled Congress. Pujo waged a one-man war against central banking and denounced the Federal Reserve as a dangerous institution. Put together, you can see the Jefferson/Taylor resistance to Northern finance capital but without the corollary of resistance to strong central government. These men had figured out that the apparatus the Republican Party put in place in the nineteenth century could be used against them. If they wanted big government, let them have it with a Southern brand of regulation. Northern finance capital and industrialists were the group harmed the most by these regulations. At the same time, Clayton made a strong push for agricultural loans which eventually happened. Punish the Northern elite and help the small farmer. We can quibble with their methods—and even Underwood reversed course in his *Drifting Sands of Party Politics* published in 1928 after he left Congress—but the intent was purely Jeffersonian.

The same can be said for the group of Southerners that led the Congress during the mid-twentieth century, people like Richard B. Russell of Georgia, Sam Ervin of North Carolina, Harry Byrd of Virginia, John Stennis of Mississippi, and even men like Huey Long of Louisiana. They are often denounced for their stand against Civil Rights, but all espoused a form of Jeffersonian political economy and Southern charm that made them irresistible to a broad spectrum of the American public. Ervin kept a published phone number so anyone could call him at home, even the loons who would often keep him on the phone for hours at a time. The Left has long wrestled over admiring his stand against Nixon and his opposition to "no knock laws" while wondering how such a principled defender of civil liberties could oppose federal Civil Rights legislation. Long was instrumental in the careers of the Vanderbilt Agrarians when many taught at LSU. Robert Penn Warren's *All the Kings Men* would not have been possible without the Kingfish, and Long's "Share the Wealth" program had a recognizable Jeffersonian influence in its attack on big banks and government supported finance capital even if its methods shaded toward socialism. David Chandler's *The Natural Superiority of Southern Politicians* published in 1979 outlines why Southerners have been able to control the halls of Congress, but all of these 20th century figures need our attention. What can we learn from them and can we separate their views on race which are not palatable to the 21st century politico from their views on government and finance? I think the answer is definitively yes, but work needs to be done in this area.

The Southern attitude toward organized finance leads to another question. How did the Old South affect the economic life of the New? Certain Southern attitudes toward labor and work permeated the industrializing South. Most historians have focused on the system of sharecropping and crop lien, and rightly so, for it impacted a large swath of the Southern people, both white and black. Most Southerners were still farmers well into the twentieth century so labor patterns in Southern communities were still tied to the land. Lost in much of this work are free black property owners and the impact of economic devastation on both the white and black community. It used to be that Reconstruction was portrayed as a stain on American history, a time when Northern policies were unduly harsh toward white Southerners, particularly in regard to economic activity. Philip Leigh's *Southern Reconstruction*, just published in 2017, has concisely shown the effects of Northern policies on the Southern people. More work needs to be done here. As an aside, the now popular Southern novelist Ron Rash does a good job with the New South through literature. His *One Foot in Eden* and *Serena* depict Southerners wrestling with modernity and the changing nature of Southern society. We can still gain something from Southern literature, but more on that later.

The South, of course, undertook industrialization slowly, and did so in their own way. While many Southern factories adopted Northern labor models and hired women and children to do much of the work, by the early twentieth century such patterns had been modified to adopt a more humane approach to labor. This was born in the paternalism of Southern labor relations before the War. That term, paternalism, is now considered a trigger, but there was a time when studies of antebellum Southern labor discussed whether the South was paternalistic or ultra-capitalist. My thought is that was a bit of both. Southerners made money but even as the establishment historian Julie Saville notes in her *The Work of Reconstruction*, slave labor models were often determined by the circumstances of the plantation and not by some Northern conception of wage labor and the nature of work. There was a rhythm to Southern plantation work that carried over into the New South and into the factories.

For example, a 1950s documentary on the Avondale Mills in Sylacauga, Alabama highlights the paternalistic system so common in Southern factories at that time. Workers were given homes, gardens, schools, public amenities like swimming pools, and a stake in the town. To be sure, this took time to develop. The founder and scion of the Avondale project, Braxton Bragg Comer staunchly opposed child labor restrictions in the early twentieth century, but by the 1920s, much of that was dropped in favor of paternalism. The Callaway Family in LaGrange, GA practiced the same type of system in their cotton mills even in the late nineteenth century. Fuller Callaway remarked that he wanted to organize the mill on "human lines." His motto was simple: "If you are working with cows, you have to think like cow. If you are working with men, you have to think like them. And you must never expect them to do anything that isn't human." Callaway called the poor people of LaGrange the finest people on Earth and later gloated, "I make American citizens and run cotton mills to pay the expenses."

There are countless stories across the South of this type of economic model, and even today the South is the home to dozens of companies that regularly appear on Forbes Top 100 for employee relations and benefits. TYSYS and AFLAC are routinely ranked highly for employee relations. Both are headquartered in Columbus, GA. TYSYS was founded by W.C. Bradley and boasts a "servant leadership" model that is the envy of many other companies. This includes family counseling benefits based on a religious model. Before Google became the standard by which other companies are measured regarding benefits, there were Southern companies that took pride in labor relationships. The stories behind these companies need our attention, for so often the Marxists and carpetbaggers take hold of the narrative and focus on the supposed misdeeds and ill-gotten gains of these men and not the value they provided to their communities. No one can forget the Callaways in the Pine Mountain region. The Callaway family turned to philanthropy after selling their stock in the mills and formed a beautiful private nature reserve and began donating to several causes designed to help the people of West Georgia, including investing heavily in LaGrange College.

Finally, Southern literature, perhaps, has had and will continue to have the greatest impact on how Americans view both the New and Old South. Southerners were certainly conscious of this in the postbellum period. Again, Mencken's slap at the South as the "Sahara of the Bozart" does not quite work. The Agrarians famously took him to task for this claim, and the salutary effect of such a flippant statement helped elevate Faulkner, O'Connor, and others to higher acclaim. College students will still read Faulkner and O'Connor if nothing else from the South. That is a good place to start but by default it accepts Mencken's umbrella condemnation of Southern literature in the period to 1930.

Over a decade *before* Mencken said that about the South and its intellectual worth, several Southern writers and academics produced a multi-volume study of Southern literature titled *Library of Southern Literature*. These types of collections were popular in the late nineteenth and early twentieth century. They were part encyclopedia, part history, and part literature. The editors would select both the best writers and their best works, write nice introductions to the content and then allow the reader to sample why the author was included in the anthology. But the editors of this collection knew something else was at stake. Like the multi-volume Southern history I will discuss in my next talk, the aim of this particular collection was rehabilitation and reunification, of placing the South within the "American nation." The editors were consciously Southern and hoped that their efforts would "enrich" the American experience by providing tales of... home. Edward Alderman, in the introduction to the series, wrote: "The South has been called a sincere and distinctive section of the republic. It is all that and more. Of all our well-defined sections it seems to be the richest in romanticism and idealism, in tragedy and suffering, and in pride of region and love of home. English civilization began on its water courses, and for nearly three hundred years it has lived under an ordered government. It is difficult to imagine how the

Nation could have been fostered into maturity without the influences that came from the South. Under the play of great historic forces this region developed so strong a sense of unity within itself as to issue in a claim of separate nationality, which it was willing to defend in a great war. No other section of our country has ever known in its fullest sense so complete a discipline of war and defeat; nor has any group of men or states ever mastered new conditions and reconquered peace and prosperity with more dignity and self-reliance. Here then would seem to be all the elements for the making of a great literature — experiences of triumph and suffering, achievement and defeat." Alderman was born in North Carolina in 1861 and was serving as the President of the University of Virginia when he penned these lines. He had also been the president of the University of North Carolina and Tulane University. Could anyone image the current President of the University of Virginia, Teresa Sullivan, writing this? Simply uttering the word "Southern" in a public UVA setting would force her to issue a lengthy apology for using such offensive language.

The aging Joel Chandler Harris served as one of the Editors in Chief of the series. Harris, of course, gained fame as both a journalist for Henry Grady's Atlanta *Constitution* and as the author of the *Uncle Remus* stories that delighted children across the United States. Harris was one of the most popular literary figures of postbellum America, but he, and his stories, have been largely forgotten today in part because they use "ethnic" language, the same thing Faulkner used in many of his works, but Harris was viewed as a conservative and Faulkner a liberal, making Harris a fugitive and Faulkner a hero. Of course, this is a misreading of Faulkner but regardless, Harris has been cast aside as an archaic reminder of a South that needs to be buried. This is both unfortunate and historically inaccurate, but what can we expect from a politically correct world?

No one from a Northern institution graced the list of contributors and editors for the *Library of Southern Literature*. Charles Kent, Professor of English at UVA and editor of several good collections of Southern poetry, and C. Alphonso Smith, founder of the Virginia Folklore Society, first Edgar Allen Poe Professor of English at UVA, and author of a fine biography of O. Henry, served as Associate Editors. The list of advisors and executive board members for the series was a "who's who" in Southern intellectual, educational, and political life at the time. The most important classicist of the era, Basil Gildersleeve, lent his name to the project as did Gen. Stephen D. Lee. No less than fifteen presidents or chancellors of Southern Universities were part of the editorial board and several current or ex-governors, judges, congressmen, and ecclesiastical leaders participated as well. No current Southern literary project can match the esteemed—and pro-Southern—members of this group.

The collection not only included men and women of letters, but those who had made an oratory or political impact on the South as well. For example, Volume VI includes speeches by John B. Gordon, Wade Hampton, William Henry Harrison, and Robert Hayne along with works by Harris and William Hamilton Hayne among others. Every other book in the sixteen-volume collection followed the same pattern. By showing that the South was more than just a backwater region with little artistic merit, these Southerners placed the section at the heart of the American experience, and it would not be a stretch to conjoin the literary theme with that of Southern music, perhaps the most enduring aspect of Southern culture and arts. No form of "American" music was born outside of the South, and like music, as Alderman emphasized, to be both good and interesting, literature has to have an attachment to home, to a place and a people, and those people need a story to tell. No section in America has a better story than the South.

In *Ghosts of the Confederacy*, Louisiana State University History Professor Gaines Foster is highly critical of both the motives and the content of the *Library of Southern Literature*. He views it as little more than artful propaganda designed to curry favor with the wave of "Lost Cause" mythology that saturated the South in the postbellum period and to place the South in a better position vis-à-vis the North. Noting that several of the authors held private views that contradicted their public statements in regard to the War and Southern identity and often called "to free history from the stifling sentimentality of the veterans," Foster cannot understand why these professional academics "did little to distance themselves from the commonly accepted interpretations of Confederate history." This statement says more about Foster than it does about the Southern academics of the early postbellum period. Foster is admitting he thinks Southerners made a conscious decision to lie about their past in order to forge a "Lost Cause" myth tied into a "New South Creed." This is why this period of Southern history is critical to our current situation. People like Foster control the narrative. It has not always been so. Perhaps these academics "bought" the history of the period because it was largely *true*. No current establishment academic has dared make that claim. It would be career suicide, but if the academy was seriously dedicated to real scholarship, it would embrace Genovese's call to understand Southerners and Southern society without haphazardly condemning it, and Richard Weaver's insistence that the South has much to teach modern America. But as Clyde Wilson has noted, this would place the burden of the "myth" of the War on the North, not the South, and would take the fire out of the current crusade against Southern symbols. To the political and academic Left, that can never be allowed to happen.

A Crisis of Confidence

PAT CADDELL DIED on February 16, 2019. Several major news outlets ran stories about his influence in both the Jimmy Carter and Donald Trump campaigns. Everyone understood Caddell's role as the voice of the "outsider." A colleague at the College of Charleston, where Caddell served in the Political Science department for the last couple of years, said that Caddell hated everything about modern politics, including the corporate press. Caddell viewed the world as the people versus the establishment. Party didn't matter, only ideas, which is why he could move seamlessly between Democrat and Republican campaigns.

This speaks volumes about the man. Caddell had a Jeffersonian vision for America, one that is largely at odds with mainstream political culture. Where both parties saw potential votes in new social engineering policies and fresh feet from foreign soil, Caddell predicted defeat and the destruction of the American political and social order. He railed against the massive leftward shift in the Democrat Party and never had kind things to say about beltway Republicans. These people sickened him. Caddell advised Carter in 1976 to campaign to the center and then move left once in power, a position that violated every chapter of the Democrat playbook in the last half of the twentieth century. It worked, and it did so in part because Caddell was able to convince Southerners that Carter was as populist as George Wallace without the political baggage that would certainly haunt him in a national campaign. Both were outsiders, but Carter never stood in a schoolhouse door as a publicity stunt. Caddell knew that most Americans secretly liked what Wallace had to say but would not openly support a man who was viewed as the symbol of segregation.

What Caddell understood better than anyone else, even during the 2016 election, is that mainstream America doesn't care for social justice, violent activism, or radical change. They want blue collar jobs, a stable economy, low crime, and a positive future without being hectored by self-righteous hypocrites with a treasury of counterfeit virtue. In other words, they don't like Yankees. Trump may not be from the South, but as a real New Yorker, he was certainly more genuine than the poseurs that masqueraded as candidates from both parties. Americans can tolerate moral failings so long as the candidate seems authentic. Both Carter and Trump have that in common. Caddell groomed them both.

But Caddell is best remembered for being the catalyst in the downfall of the Carter administration. The *New York Times* obituary focused almost exclusively on Caddell's participation in Carter's *Crisis of Confidence* speech. It was Caddell's idea, and while no one would contest that the speech played a role in the ultimate demise of Carter's reelection bid, the narrative has been driven by the very establishment that both Caddell and Carter openly criticized. This very Jeffersonian speech did not have their stamp of approval.

Caddell was able to persuade Carter to move away from a policy speech on energy and instead focus on American malaise. While neither Caddell nor Carter used that term in the speech, Caddell did circulate an internal memo in 1979 titled "Of Crises and Opportunities" where he discussed "a nation deep in crisis…a crisis of confidence marked by a dwindling faith in the future [and] growing real despair of elites and ordinary citizens alike as they struggle to articulate in concepts the malaise which they themselves feel." Caddell blamed every vestige of the establishment for the problems which plagued America but placed most of the emphasis on the "special interest state." Americans, in his opinion, didn't care who was in office because it didn't matter. Washington D.C. ran on its own fuel while the rest of America watched helplessly from outside the beltway.

The establishment hacks in Carter's administration immediately panned it. Walter Mondale threatened to resign as Vice-President if Carter went forward with Caddell's prescriptions. Caddell wanted Carter to get out among the people, to drop in on ordinary Americans and appeal directly to what he considered to be a lingering republicanism in the American spirit. He also advised Carter to avoid the press, which was in his opinion the real enemy of the federal republic. Rosalynn Carter thought his memo was brilliant and advised her husband to fire anyone who seemed to be opposed to this seemingly new direction. You can't take the South from a Southern lady.

Caddell wanted to reorient American values, what were really Jeffersonian values. Money was great, as were markets, but they were shallow representations of Jeffersonian republicanism. Carter agreed. On July 15, 1979, Carter delivered a speech heavily edited by establishment group think but in principle was Caddell's handiwork.

Caddell certainly had a role in perhaps the most Jeffersonian lines from the speech:

> *In a nation that was proud of hard work, strong families, close-knit communities, and our faith in God, too many of us now tend to worship self-indulgence and consumption. Human identity is no longer defined by what one does, but by what one owns. But we've discovered that owning things and consuming things does not satisfy our longing for meaning. We've learned that piling up material goods cannot fill the emptiness of lives which have no confidence or purpose.*

Critics believed that Caddell was too negative, that he was criticizing the American public. This was wrong. Caddell praised American values and American core principles. He was acting as a Roman historian during the days of the early empire urging the Roman elite to move the needle back to what made Rome great. The same could be said for America. This was "Make America Great Again" in 1976 without the red hats and violent social justice critics. Carter urged the American public to "take our greatest resources–America's people, America's values, and America's confidence…and commit ourselves together to a rebirth of the American spirit."

The American public drank deep and joyfully embraced this Jeffersonian vision. Caddell was called a genius by everyone except the establishment goons who sought to muscle their way into Carter's inner circle. What happened next was not Caddell's fault. Carter mismanaged his wife's advice when he attempted to fire everyone who had been disloyal and then bungled the resulting media driven public relations crisis. The Republicans pounced and nominated their own folksy outsider candidate who wagged his finger at Carter and called him soft. Ronald Reagan won in a landslide by using Caddell's blueprint for success. Pat Caddell transformed American politics by infusing a Jeffersonian approach into American political discourse. That was the South Carolinian in him.

What the establishment didn't get then–and what they don't get now–is that the *Crisis of Confidence* speech honestly reflected the American character, and the "silent majority," which may not be a crushing mandate in 2019, still believes in a Southern Jeffersonian order. Promoting it with a Southern accent helps, but most Americans will take a New Yorker with Jeffersonian principles as long as he champions the "rebirth of the American spirit."

GATOR McKLUSKY

EVERYONE WANTED TO be Southern in the 1970s. The rejuvenated interest in Southern music from bands like Lynyrd Skynyrd, Charlie Daniels, and the Allman Brothers (and the unknown Southern influence in the "Motown" sound) was just one component of a larger pro-Southern, working class, populist movement. Southerners had been made consciously Southern again after over a decade of national attention, and the reaction was a positive affirmation of Southern culture and heritage. Hank Williams, Jr. didn't want "little old danish rolls" he wanted "ham and grits," but he also understood that "if you fly in from Boston, you won't have to wait," but "if you fly in from Birmingham, you'll get the last gate." The South could still be the "specimen," the insignificant curiosity in the "American War."

This cultural revival reached its zenith with Jimmy Carter's election in 1976 and his brother Billy's "Redneck Power" brand of comedy. And in film, Burt Reynolds was quickly becoming *the* leading actor of the South with the 1977 release of *Smokey and the Bandit* staring Reynolds, Jerry Reed as "Snowman," and Jackie Gleason as Sheriff Buford T. Justice. Critics never understood why that film was so popular, but Reynolds, who will be celebrating his 82nd birthday on Sunday (Feb 11), knew that films like *Smokey* were part of "a whole series of films made in the South, about the South and for the South."

One historian has disparagingly called these films "hick flicks," and Reynolds stared in several in the decade before *Smokey* became a cult hit. He often teamed with Reed in these good-natured, though sometimes dark, romps through the South. Reynolds also starred in *Deliverance*, which along with *Easy Rider* ranks among the worst portrayals of Southern culture in mid-twentieth century cinema. He corrected that mistake in little known works like *White Lightning, Gator,* and *W.W. and the Dixie Dancekings*, along with the aforementioned *Smokey* trilogy.

Reynolds lived most of his early life in Florida and was a star running back for Florida State University. Reynolds admired Southern culture and the names of the characters in his films (some of which he either produced or directed) reflected an appreciation for all things Southern, particularly the working class South: Gator McKlusky, Bama McCall, Dixie, Leroy, Butterball, Bo, and Cledus. Even his character in *The Longest Yard* is distinctively Southern.

It might be easy to deride these rolls as caricatures of Southerners, but Reynolds never lost the art of faithful comedy and the ability for Southerners to poke fun at themselves with a hint of dark seriousness and pride. Good Southern comedy had always contained a bit of human failing as an essential component of the Southern experience. Southern heroes aren't marble or cast-iron men, and the imperfect, working class hero who sometimes lives on the fringes of (Yankee) law–or even outright rejects it–is part of Southern folklore and tradition. A moonshiner like Gator McKlusky could become a working-class hero like Fireball Roberts or Junior Johnson. Even Lee and Jackson had a humanism that all Americans found moving. This is why Davidson wrote *Lee in the Mountains* and why O'Connor could pen *A Good Man is Hard to Find*.

Film is an important part of Southern culture, and for about twenty years, no one was more recognized as the face of the South in Hollywood than Burt Reynolds. Here's to Gator McKlusky.

THE CONFEDERATE ORIGINS OF MEMORIAL DAY

MANY AMERICANS WILL pause today to honor the men and women who have given their lives in the United States armed forces. What most probably don't know is that this holiday originated in the South after the War for Southern Independence. It was originally called "Decoration Day."

Don't tell the social justice warriors.

The monuments that these modern-day Leninists believe represent "white supremacy" were a byproduct of a movement that began one year after the conclusion of hostilities to remember the over two hundred thousand men who died defending the Southern fight for independence.

It took decades to collect enough pennies to build the monuments that are now being toppled in hours.

Not even the Yankees who faced cannon and rifle fire from these Confederate soldiers were so bold to deny Southerners their memorials. Some, in fact, joined hands at dedication ceremonies across the South. If anyone should have hated Confederate soldiers, it was these men. But they didn't.

Thousands of Union soldiers saluted their Confederate counterparts as they surrendered at Appomattox and wept with them when these Southern patriots gave up their flags. Not one Union soldier burned a Confederate flag or dragged it through the mud when the War was over. The immediate aftermath was magnanimous on both sides.

Reconstruction created tension, but in subsequent decades as the South sought to be once again an integral part of the Union, and as the vigor of youth gave way to the reflection of old age, these grey headed veterans saluted both sides and honored their dead.

If anyone wants to understand why these monuments were erected, simply read the inscriptions. Not one is dedicated to "white supremacy," but all honor the Confederate soldier and many the Southern women who supported the cause. Several are dedicated to the "Principles of 1776" and the "Sovereignty of the States," the same cause Southerners wrote about as they headed off to war in 1861. This is no "Lost Cause" revisionism. That comes from those who disingenuously write that the War began as a moral crusade to end slavery.

The women who held the first "Decoration Day" in Columbus, Georgia in 1866 did so to honor the dozens of Confederate soldiers buried in Linwood Cemetery. This was soon replicated across the South. The Grand Army of the Republic copied the event in 1868, causing another Southern innovation to be coopted by Yankee do-gooders.

American soon honored Confederate dead as part of "Memorial Day" events, including those like President William McKinley who wore the blue.

Southerners eventually decided to hold separate "memorial day" remembrances in April as part of "Confederate Memorial Day." They wanted as a people to reflect on the cost of war. Their newly gained poverty was a daily reminder, but these wives, brothers, sisters, mothers, fathers, cousins, aunts, uncles, sons, and daughters of fallen heroes still burned with the flame of defiance. They put down their swords but did not concede that their men were "traitors."

By the 1870s no one north of the Mason Dixon called them that anymore. They were as American as Lincoln. It was not unfashionable well into the late twentieth century–even for the Left–to honor Confederate soldiers as valiant and courageous men. That list includes every American president from Teddy Roosevelt to Bill Clinton.

Taking down monuments or removing Confederate flags would have been as un-American as rooting for the Soviet Union to win the Cold War.

But as Bernie Sanders demonstrated in 2016, being a Soviet stooge makes you a rock star in modern America. Perhaps that is why adopting the Soviet playbook is so easy for both the uneducated and university indoctrinated masses. Confederate memorials represent a roadblock in their crusade to eliminate Western Civilization and rewrite American history.

When all of the Confederate monuments are gone or "contextualized," where will the Leninists turn next?

If the cultural Marxists want to divest themselves of "Confederate" imagery, then "Memorial Day" would eventually have to go, too.

After all, long after the War for Southern Independence, the Confederate Battle Flag showed up on battle fields from Europe to Asia to the Middle East.

It would be the only "fair" and "equal" thing to do.

What are Symbols For?

IN 1875, REV. MOSES Drury Hoge stood before 40,000 people in Richmond, Virginia, at the foot of the newly dedicated statue of Thomas J. "Stonewall" Jackson and delivered what one historian called the "noblest oration of his later life."

He believed that in the future, the path to that statue would be "trodden" by the feet of travelers from "the banks of the Hudson, the Mississippi, [and] the Sacramento...from the Tiber, the Rhine, [and] the Danube." They would be accompanied by "Honor" and "Freedom," the twin principles by which Jackson lived and died and which these pilgrims would seek to celebrate. Jackson represented the best of American society and his memorial reminded not just America, but the world, of patriotism, heroism, and duty, the highest traits of Western Civilization and of all dead heroes.

But though Hoge was willing to put down the sword and join in common cause with his former foes from the North, he urged the thousands of people in Richmond that day to not "shut our eyes to the fact that this consolidated empire of states is not the Union established by our fathers. No intelligent European student of American institutions is deceived by any such assumption. We gain nothing by deceiving ourselves."

To Hoge, the bronze depiction of Jackson represented more than just a memorial for dead heroes and patriots. It was a symbol of American principles, bequeathed by their patrimony and defended by the blood of thousands of Southerners sleeping in graves across the United States. "And now standing before this statue," he thundered, "and, as in the living presence of the man it represents, cordially endorsing, as I do, the principles of the political school in which he was trained and in defence of which he died...I speak not for myself, but for the South, when I say it is our interest, our duty and determination, to maintain the

Union, and to make every possible contribution to its prosperity and glory, *if all the states which compose it will unite in making it such a Union as our fathers framed, and in enthroning above it, not a Caesar, but the Constitution in its old supremacy* [emphasis added]."

Jackson was defiance. Jackson was America. But Hoge insisted that America could only be maintained if the States stood "on the same level, with such a jealous regard for each other's rights that when the interests or honor of one is assailed, all the rest, feeling the wound, even as the body feels the pain inflicted on one of its members, will kindle with just resentment at the outrage, because an injury done to a part is not only a wrong, but an indignity offered to the whole."

Hoge then boldly added that "if that cannot be, then I trust the day will never dawn when the Southern people will add degradation to defeat, and hypocrisy to subjugation, by professing a love for the Union which denies to one of their states a single right accorded to Massachusetts or New York—to such a Union we will never be heartily loyal while that bronze hand grasps its sword—while yonder river chants the requiem of the sixteen thousand Confederate dead who, with Stuart among them, sleep on the hills of Hollywood."

Southern symbols represent Hoge's spirit and the spirit that animated countless patriots from Runnymede to Appomattox. The progressive Left understands this which is why they need to demonize and destroy these symbols–not of "white supremacy and oppression"–but of defiance to their political, economic, and social agenda. The America the progressive Left loves is not the real America; it's the America that exists within the confines of their own skull, a Utopian dream that will never come to fruition, but one that requires the obliteration of traditional Western Civilization.

The "basket of deplorables" must be marginalized, de-platformed, silenced, and politically eliminated.

The progressive Left, at times, openly admits it. Take for example a statement Brown University History Professor Megan Kate Nelson:

> *I would like to propose that Confederate memorials should neither be retained nor removed: They should be destroyed, and their broken pieces left in situ.*
>
> *On a scheduled day, a city government or university administration would invite citizens to approach a Confederate memorial, take up a cudgel, and swing away. The ruination of the memorial would be a group effort, a way for an entire community to convert a symbol of racism and white supremacy into a symbol of resistance against oppression. Historians could put up a plaque next to the fragments, explaining the memorial's*

history, from its dedication day to the moment of its obliteration. A series of photographs or a YouTube video could record the process of destruction. These textual explanations may be unnecessary, however. Ruins tend to convey their messages eloquently in and of themselves. In this case, the ruins of Confederate memorials in cities across the nation would suggest that while white supremacists have often made claims to power in American history, those who oppose them can, and will, fight back.

People like Professor Nelson seem to be the majority in American society, and as a result, the assault on Confederate symbols will continue for the foreseeable future. This process began in the early 1990s but has only recently embodied the revolutionary zeal of the Jacobin Reign of Terror in republican France. More statues will come down. The toppling of Silent Sam and the removal of symbols, images, and simply the names of Davis, Lee, Jackson and others from public spaces will be, unfortunately, the opening salvo in a much longer cultural war that at its heart will define the American identity for future generations.

Americans must make a choice. Do we want to support the cultural, political, and economic lineage of Washington, Jefferson, Henry, Madison, Monroe, Lee, Davis, and Jackson, the heritage of the Magna Charta and the Jeffersonian spirit of self-determination and federalism, the richness of Southern music, literature, and art, or the Utopian innovations and comprehensive monolithic centralization of Professor Nelson?

The Southern tradition and the Confederate symbols that represent it are like a rose bush. Every tradition has it thorns, but the sweet scent and beauty of its flowers more than outweigh the dangers from its tangled vines. Do we hack down the bush or admire, nurture, and cultivate the roses? As Hoge pointed out and as Europeans understood both during and after the War, the Southern tradition embodied in the efforts of the heroes and patriots of 1776 and 1861, are the American roses, the American contribution to Western Civilization.

Political decentralization cannot feasibly work without a viable and vibrant cultural tradition to undergird its existence. No one will go to the mat for taxes. Both the founding generation who seceded from the British Empire and the Southerners who went to war in 1861 did so to protect the "ancient constitutions" of their ancestors and to defend hearth, home and culture, the traditions–myths in the correct definition of the term–that had been handed down through generations of dedicated, independent, republican patriots.

That is what is being destroyed by the progressive Left. Tens of thousands of people attended Confederate monument dedications; hundreds of thousands of men bled and died fighting for the principles of '76 and '61. We do them no honor by shirking our responsibility to the present and the future. The barbarians have already broken through the gate. Symbols may be destroyed, but as long as the tradition itself continues to exist, the barbarians cannot win.

Why the Southern Tradition is Winning

THE TITLE OF THIS piece may seem odd considering recent events in New Orleans and the mass hysteria over all things Confederate since June 2015. Monuments have come down, flags have been furled, and streets have been renamed.

While these are certainly loses, they are mere skirmishes in a wider cultural war that the Left is losing. They know it, but they don't want you to realize it, and their allies in the mainstream media keep peppering the news cycle with stories trumpeting their "successes." This is done to demoralize the opposition.

But consider the following:

1. Donald Trump won the 2016 presidential election following an election strategy that mirrored Nixon's "Silent Majority" 1972 campaign. Nixon relied heavily on Southern votes that cycle and Trump's political agenda, while not entirely backed by Southern antecedents, contains core components that are recognized elements of the Southern tradition. Not "racism and bigotry" as the Leftist media would claim, but anti-establishment, blue-collar populism.

2. Secession is on the table. Several states, not only in the South, are considering methods to leave the American empire. Nothing is more Southern than the principle of independence, both for the individual and for a political community. The establishment keeps blabbering that secession is illegal–the Supreme Court said so in 1869 (but it really didn't)–and that the War settled the issue, but it couldn't. Coupled with the now robust "Tenth Amendment" and modern "nullification" movements, this renewed interest in all things federalism was not as mainstream just ten years ago. Thank the Internet for that. What is it that "Net Neutrality" is for again? Right.

3. Generation snowflake is now playing defense. Though these delicate flowers have wrestled major concessions from the American academy, much of this is an illusion. Certainly, some college and university administrations have buckled, even recently, but the push back against the illiberal "liberals" has come from both the Right and the Left. The snowflakes may have bitten off more than they can chew. The majority of Americans also don't think the thugish tactics by the left are legal, necessary, or tolerable. And when a leader of the "Take 'Em Down NOLA" group openly admits that he would love to see a statue of George Washington removed in New Orleans because he was a "slave master," it appears the Left has overplayed their hand. Most Americans would draw the line at that demand. We have to remember that Washington is as Southern as Lee. The Left might be able to pick the low hanging fruit–anything Confederate fits that category–but they can't eliminate Washington, Jefferson, Madison, Monroe, the Declaration of Independence the United States Constitution or a host of other Southern–yes Southern–symbols without changing the entire narrative of American history. They have been trying that for years. It hasn't worked and it won't work. Real America is too savvy for that. Remember the Southern tradition is more than a four-year struggle for independence. Even if those symbols are removed, the tradition survives.

4. The Left has been trying for decades to "contextualize"–meaning Yankeefy–Southern history. They have made great strides in doing so, but this war isn't over. Not even close. Many people around the world see the South in a positive light. When the Berlin Wall came down, Confederate flags flew beside the unified German flag. Confederate flags are still seen around the world, and to many people, the flag represents anti-establishment defiance. Northerners also proudly fly the flag. It cannot be eliminated, no matter how hard the Left may try.

The vitriolic outcry against Trump's opinion that the War could have been avoided is indicative of a larger problem for the Left. After decades of controlling the American academy, of dominating the mainstream media, of crafting the "correct" interpretation of history, a large percentage of Americans still don't buy what they are selling. The Left would chalk it up to ignorance, but perhaps real America knows more than the self-appointed gatekeepers of acceptable thought. It seems that journalists, left-wing professors, and their pseudo–historian allies rank with politicians as the least trusted people in the United States. That is a good thing.

SOUTHERN RECONSTRUCTION

A review of *Southern Reconstruction* by Philip Leigh (Westholme, 2017).

CONFRONTING THE ESTABLISHMENT narrative about any historical topic can be a perilous endeavor. There are several that present such large minefields that most historians dare not attempt to cross, among them the "Civil War," Reconstruction, and the Civil Rights movement. Bucking the accepted version of events in any of those fields is a death knell for the professional historian. Fortunately, those rules don't apply to the "amateur" class, and Philip Leigh has proven to be one of the more promising and objective of that group. His recent tome, *Southern Reconstruction*, offers the best summary of the political, economic, and social dynamics of Reconstruction since William A. Dunning's masterful turn of the century study, a work that for political reasons has been castigated by the historical establishment but never entirely refuted.

Leigh takes seriously the impact of Reconstruction on both white and black Southerners. Rather than a narrow "unfinished revolution" as Eric Foner and the modern academy view the topic, Leigh considers the era to be a tragic episode in American history, one that lasted far beyond the recognized though arbitrary end date of 1877. Dunning understood that both political and economic reconstruction continued long after troops were withdrawn from the South. Leigh agrees and points to Republican economic models as the basis for lasting Southern poverty well into the twentieth century.

Leigh paints a picture of a South devastated by the War, physically, socially, economically, and politically. Her people had been fearfully punished and would continue to be punished by Republican policies that gave no thought to the difficult transformations taking place in Dixie. His message is one of understanding, not condemnation, and while Fonerites would be compelled to declare Leigh to be little more than a Southern apologist, he has no sympathy for the systematic racial violence that took place in the "Jim Crow" era. Yet, Leigh also recognizes the role *Northern* voices and *Northern* policies had in stoking the flames, from the political and social origins of Jim Crow laws themselves to the utopian belief that racial readjustment should be financed by Southerners who had no capital to speak of after the War.

Leigh consistently punches holes in the modern "unfinished revolution" narrative and shows real sympathy for the plight of Southerners after four years of hard fighting. For example, those who believe that Southerners were not punished enough by the War, that somehow, they should have been made to pay reparations or have their property confiscated, are shocked into reality. Leigh contends that Southerners *did* pay reparations in the form of Union veteran pensions, many of which were fraudulent and excessive, while at the same time having to come up with pennies to support their own veterans. He additionally points to the tepid interest in confiscatory policies by most of the Northern population, including Abraham Lincoln himself, as the reason massive land redistribution never took place. His position is not a lament for "what could have been," but a practical understanding of what the vast majority of Americans were thinking at the time. Private property was still the cornerstone of American society, and confiscation, no matter the reason, was viewed as an immoral violation of liberty and a punitive police that very few could support. Northern self-righteousness only went so far.

Leigh makes clear that the Gilded Age would not have been possible without the political and economic corruption of Reconstruction. Northern banking and industrial interests fattened their wallets while Southerners, both white and black, faced malnutrition and few economic prospects. Southern governments controlled by "carpetbaggers" and "scalawags" raised taxes and spent lavishly. This is dangerous territory for any modern historian. The contemporary narrative argues that Reconstruction governments were models of fiscal restraint and only spent because of their overarching humanitarian concerns for the wellbeing of freedmen. Leigh calls it being "railroaded" and insists corrupt deals for railroad construction undergirded bloated state budgets. This is an almost sacrilegious assertion but one that Leigh argues well.

One gets the sense in reading Leigh's book that the real tragedy of Reconstruction was a missed opportunity of real reconciliation, not just for the sections, but for Southerners of all races. Southern blacks were used by partisan Republicans as pawns in a larger political game, and the violent reaction of Southern whites was predictable, particularly when in some instances, Southern blacks were prodded to violence themselves by Republican Party zealots. Leigh's chapter on "Racial Adjustment" is one of the finest in the book. He describes the difficulty in emancipation and the problems both white and black Southerners faced in adapting to new social and economic circumstances. White Southerners had no confidence in the ability of Southern blacks to become prosperous citizens, but Leigh believes that the old planter class had enough foresight and compassion to stall some of the more vicious racial violence of the 1890s, even going so far as to suggest that current interpretations of the "Redeemers" lack depth or complexity.

If Leigh's version of *Southern Reconstruction* rather than Foner's dominated our historical consciousness, the violent iconoclasm taking place in Southern towns would not exist, nor would Americans be talking about "contextualizing" statues dedicated to Washington or Jefferson or any member of the founding generation. By insisting that some "unfinished revolution" needs to take place, Foner and his acolytes have created a neo-Marxist vanguard in America determined to destroy any vestige of traditional Western Civilization. Leigh has hope that his narrative could have a calming effect on the current climate. "Just as the hippie and intellectual elites who dominated public opinion during the Vietnam War while they disparage America's soldiers have fallen into obscurity, so also might those portraying Reconstruction as a South-as-evil-twin story might eventually fade in the face of the larger national narrative. If so, countervailing accounts like the one in this book must be told, shared, and expanded."

"Dar's nuttin' lak de ol'-time ways"

MANY PEOPLE ARE familiar with the Slave Narratives from the Federal Writers Project of the 1930s. While some historians reject them for what has been called gross inaccuracies due in large part to the many *positive* memories of the institution (the negative accounts are always used), they have become the standard source for firsthand information on the institution from the people themselves. These accounts are part of the fabric of the Southern history and serve as a window in the lives of antebellum black Americans.

But most people, historians included, fail to consider the importance of antebellum and post-bellum literature in the assessment of black American culture. William Faulkner received great acclaim for his use of dialect in tales about life in Mississippi, but because his stories are fiction, they fail to attract the historical profession as a useful tool in understanding Southern culture, race relations, or Southern life, particularly those that display a complexity, more accurately a positivity, about Southern relationships and the Southern tradition.

Faulkner is the most conspicuous Southern author in his use of dialect, but he was not alone. Antebellum Southern literature is saturated with the true language of both white and black Southerners. Most of it will never be read in American classrooms. After the war, men like Joel Chandler Harris of *Uncle Remus* fame and Thomas Nelson Page were pioneers in the use of dialect, which in turn brought a more complex South into focus. Even into the mid-twentieth century, most Americans had read the tales of *Uncle Remus* and perhaps had at least a cursory understanding of *In Ole Virginia*.

Dialect writing, particularly in black folk tales, is a useful tool in understanding the Southern black community. One writer virtually unknown today but who spent years collecting and publishing black folk tales was Anne Virginia Culbertson. Born in Ohio in 1864, Culbertson traveled around Virginia and North Carolina in the post war years interviewing black Southerners and then re-telling their folk tales. She even learned to perform some of the folk tunes and was in high demand for her work. Most of the stories were decades old and could be traced to the traditions of Southern slaves.

These folk tales are rarely critical of Southern life and instead display a longing for home and hearth similar to that which the Federal Writers Project authors found among former slaves in the 1930s. There is continuity in the story. Race relations were often amicable and informal, and black Southerners loved the South as much as their white neighbors. They could claim a nearly three-hundred-year attachment to the land.

One of Culbertson's works, *Banjo Talks*, is a collection of folk songs Southern blacks sang both before and after the War. None are dreary recollections of Southern life, of the poverty or hardship that the modern reader would expect to find, particularly if current portrayals of all things Southern are to be believed.

One song, titled "With the Spinning Lesson," begins "Dar's nuttin' lak de ol'-time ways, I tell you dem ol' days wuz days!" and shows pride in their work, "'Kase all we had ter eat an' wear Wuz made right yer on dis plantation, Hit sut'n'y jes' beat all creation! We spinned an' dyed an' weabed an' knit. An' tu'ned out gyarmints dat wuz fit Per any pusson in dis nation."

Another, titled "Knockin' De 'Rang-A-Tang" is a song dedicated to a Christmas gathering. "Dough de cabin mighty small, Room fer ev'y comer Dar we darnses one an' all, Lawdy! beats de summer! Lightwood fire blazin' bright Meks de place all warm an' light, Darkies darnse wid all dey might, A happy, singin', laffin' gang, Hit's den we knocks de 'rang-a-tang. We knocks de 'rang-a-tang."

Virtually every story written in the antebellum South, even those by abolitionists like *12 Years A Slave*, told of the special place Christmas had amongst the black Southern community.

Certainly, in many folk songs and slave narratives the prospect of freedom is a welcomed event. A song tilted "'Pen'ence" in *Banjo Talks* expresses joy at the coming of emancipation. The narrator is so overcome with emotion that she declares at the birth of her baby, ""Bress Gawd, dis ain' a slave dat's bawn ter me! I'se gwineter call dis chile, you year me say, 'Mancipation Proclaniation Innepen'ence Day!"

But even with emancipation came a certain social strain, as the generation born after slavery did not seem to respect life and community as much as their elders. In "Jes Lookin' On" an eighty year old former slave shows disgust with the manners of the young folk of his community. "Some er dis wufless young cullud trash Dey calls me "Uncle" an ac's real brash, Jes' laffin' behime my back lak sin, 'Kase I bin a slave an' dey ain' bin. I ru'rr bin bonded my natchel days Dan ter ac' in sech no-kyount, trashy ways. I reckon hit's well we wuz all set free, I s'pose dat's de way folks wuz meant ter be."

Other themes in the book include love, farming, Christianity, and a virtually careless appreciation for life and nature. There was no hint of social angst or physical degradation. Black Southerners, like many of their white counterparts, lived on the land in what we would consider poverty today, but at least according to their folk songs, there was a calm and fluid oneness with the world.

It is easy to accept harsh descriptions of slavery and black Southern life in the nineteenth and early twentieth centuries. They happened. But it is far less agreeable—maybe even palatable for some—to also accept the positive descriptions of black Southern life that came from black Southerners themselves. This is problematic. If we wish to live in a respectful society between black and white Southerners (which, frankly, already exists on a daily basis), then we should be honest with Southern history and show the South and the Southern people in all their complexities. Hasn't that been the stated goal after all? Judging by our simplistic pop culture and "education" system, probably not.

SECTION TWO
SOUTHERN LEADERS

Robert E. Lee vs. Twitter Historians

IN JUNE 2017, *The Atlantic* published a hit-piece on Robert E. Lee titled "The Myth of the Kindly General Lee." The article made the rounds on Leftist echo chamber social media accounts and quickly found favor with the popular Leftist Twitter historians, a collection of "distinguished professors," some without a substantial publication record, who like to trumpet their status as "actual historians" when "amateurs" propose a "lost cause" version of Southern history and the "Civil War." It has since been paraded by these "actual historians" as the conclusive popular article on "the fiction of a person who never existed."

The irony of course is that this piece was written by an amateur, Adam Serwer, who has the same credentials as David Barton, Dinesh D'Souza, Brian Kilmeade, Bill O'Reilly, or Ta-Nehisi Coates, meaning none. That doesn't matter. What matters to the Twitter historian brigade is that Serwer has the "correct" position on Lee. By the way, so do the "conservatives" Barton, D'Souza, Kilmeade, and O'Reilly.

A recent dust-up between Mississippi Senatorial candidate Chris McDaniel and the Twitter historian brigade nicely illustrates the group-think mentality of the "actual historians" in the Twitter brigade. McDaniel stated it was the "truth" that Lee:

> *was the most decorated soldier in the U.S. Army. He was a man of unimpeachable integrity. Lincoln offered him command of the Union Army, but Lee refused only because his loyalty was to Virginia. Lee opposed both secession and slavery. And yet to the historically illiterate left, a man who opposed both slavery and secession has come to symbolize both slavery and secession.*

McDaniel made a mistake in calling Lee "the most decorated soldier in the U.S. Army." That would have been Winfield Scott, the only man other than George Washington to achieve the rank of Lieutenant General in the antebellum period. Scott, however, did call Lee the finest soldier he ever knew, and Lee earned his reputation as "the indefatigable Lee" in the 1840s during the Mexican War, long before the bloody conclave of the 1860s. In other words, Lee was not the most "decorated solider," but he was certainly one of the most respected.

But the rest of his statement contains elements of truth. Regardless, the Twitter brigade pounced on the "amateur" McDaniel in nothing short of an apoplectic rage.

These gate keepers of acceptable thought dissected McDaniel's statement line by line and offered what are now predictable cliches and platitudes: Lee was a white-supremacist and a traitor who explicitly supported slavery by leading the Army of Northern Virginia against the Union.

These "actual historians" knowingly or unknowingly often regurgitate Serwer's *Atlantic* diatribe while advancing a narrative that is saturated with ahistorical and often hypocritical presentism.

Take for example Lee's positions on slavery. Lee could certainly never be confused for an abolitionist. Like most Americans–not just Southerners–of his day, he believed the abolitionists to be dangerous reformers bent on destroying the peace and security of the United States. Abolitionists were run out of town in many Northern States, and the rigid proslavery ideology that most people associate with the South was born in eighteenth-century Massachusetts and Connecticut.

But does that make Lee "proslavery?" There is no evidence that he shared the same positions as Thomas Dew, William Harper, or James Henry Hammond. Lee held the dominant view of race relations in America in the antebellum period. His 1856 letter both condemning slavery as a "moral and political evil" while concurrently insisting that African-Americans were racially inferior and at that point not suited to freedom would not have been shocking or debatable to almost anyone at the time, North or South. Just two years later, Abraham Lincoln made similar statements in the now famous Lincoln-Douglas debates. Virtually all of the founding generation held similar views, as did Leftist heroes like John Muir of Sierra Club fame. Even Harriet Beecher Stowe made racist statements in both the antebellum and postbellum periods.

Why is Lee held to a different standard? Simple. Virtue signaling on the part of the Twitter brigade creates followers and advances careers. You won't become an Ivy League professor by praising Lee or by innocently offering a balanced appraisal of the man. The mob requires obedience to acceptable thought. It is they, not the "Lost Causers," who have become boxed into a "myth."

Lee, of course, became a *de facto* slave owner when his father-in-law, George Washington Parke Custis, died in 1857. Both Serwer and the Twitter brigade consider this period to be the definitive example of Lee's position on race and slavery, and both rely on a misreading and distorted interpretation of Elizabeth Brown Pryor's description of Lee in her Lincoln Prize winning book *Reading the Man* as evidence of Lee's cruelty.

Lee did require Custis's former slaves to work once he became executor of the will, something they had not done in years. He also hired them out to other plantations in an attempt to make Arlington solvent. Custis left the estate in terrible shape, both physically and financially. Serwer and the Twitter brigade cite this as partial evidence of Lee's inhumanity, as an attempt to "break up families." One Twitter brigade historian actually suggested Lee broke up families by selling them off. That never happened. Lee did separate family members in the hiring out process, but he never sold a single slave. Lee was in a difficult situation. In order to keep Arlington and not sell it off, he had to get out of debt. In order to get out of debt, he had to make the estate profitable and doing so required that the Custis slaves be forced to work, either at Arlington or on neighboring plantations, something they did not want to do and openly resisted. This was understandable based on Arlington tradition and Custis's longstanding promises of freedom and his labor practices. But manumission had been made illegal in Virginia, and so to criticize Lee for not immediately freeing Custis's former slaves lacks historical understanding and context. Even Pryor states that "Virginia law made this [immediate emancipation] difficult, but the law had been circumvented before at Arlington." In other words, Lee *possibly* could have broken the law, but it was not easy to do. All of the handwringing, then, concerning Lee's handling of the estate is based on pure speculation on what he could have done differently–and frankly what the courts may have allowed–based on modern conceptions of justice. It's also understandable for Lee to want to save Arlington, his wife's birthright, but the Twitter brigade only seeks to understand one side and condemn the other. That is opinion, not history.

A Virginia court finally forced Lee to sell off portions of Arlington in 1862 in order to meet the final requirements of the Custis estate and to free the slaves. The Southern legal system was complex. Even Pryor describes Lee's actions at this point in fairly sympathetic terms. "Determined to uphold his trust, Lee used his own funds and the sale of land to accomplish all of G.W.P. Custis's exacting requirements. He also tried to help some of the freed men hire their labor, and resisted attempts by the white community in the Pamunkey region to keep them in bondage."

Both Serwer and the Twitter brigade also claim it to be a fact that Lee had at least three slaves whipped, and their wounds washed with brine to inflict pain. Sewer goes so far as to believe that Lee was at the whipping and ordered a more brutal job. This is at minimum debatable and probably a lie. In 1866, a former slave named Wesley Norris gave an interview to the *National Anti-Slavery Standard* where he described the whipping in question. Norris, a cousin, and his sister ran away from Arlington in 1859 and were subsequently recaptured after Lee offered a substantial bounty. According to Norris, Lee ordered them whipped and tortured before hiring them out further South. The story was initially picked up by the abolitionist press in 1859 and then again after Norris gave his interview in 1866. The first articles appeared in the *New York Journal* in June 1859, just a few months before John Brown's raid on Harper's Ferry. Lee publicly refused to answer the charge against him and did not directly comment on it privately, telling his son that the whole business "has left me an unpleasant legacy." If Lee was so vindictive, why would it be "an unpleasant legacy?" Pryor did not include this last statement in the discussion of the event, but even she suggests that these *Journal* articles were "exaggerated."

She certainly believes Norris, however, and asserts that every part of his story can be verified. Not quite. Norris gave the interview to, in Pryor's words, "dispel the notion that Lee was a kind and humane slave owner." She thinks Norris had nothing to gain by the interview. This may be true, but the newspaper that published the story in 1866 absolutely did. Historians–not just "lost cause neo-confederates"–have long questioned the validity of abolitionist accounts of slavery, particularly when "slave interviews" were filtered through abolitionists who could take liberty with the information. They were often purposely sensationalized and written for a sympathetic audience and were by no means non-partisan. The Norris account was published on the one-year anniversary of Lincoln's assassination, certainly as an attempt to draw attention to Lee's character and to validate the "righteous cause myth" of the War. Pryor even contradicts herself by admitting that the whipping itself cannot be validated and that Norris carried no scars from such a violent event. And Lee twice denied it happened later in life. Whom are we to believe? Why would Lee lie in a private letter to his son in 1859 when he had nothing to lose? In either case, it is not a definite "fact" as either Serwer or the Twitter brigade claim that Lee either 1) had the slaves viciously whipped and tortured or 2) that he was there for the event, if it happened at all. To claim either as a fact is to distort the record for purely partisan reasons, something the Twitter brigade consistently chirps against when Lee is described as a "Christian gentleman" but is more than willing to do if it supports their position.

Was Lee a traitor? Next to Lee being a "white supremacist," this is the most common charge leveled against him. Lee opposed nullification and secession his entire career. His father was a firm Federalist, and Lee never showed any hint of dissent from this position during his life. His oath in 1825 after leaving West Point required him to "solemnly swear or affirm (as the case may be) that I will support the constitution of the United States..." and "to bear true allegiance to the United States of America, and to serve them honestly and faithfully, against all their enemies or opposers whatsoever...." Lee did not resign his commission until after Lincoln called for 75,000 troops to put down the "rebellion" and the people of Virginia seceded from the Union. In the mind of most men of the Upper South, Lincoln's quest to use force to crush secession amounted to a violation of the Constitution and made him an "opposer" and enemy of the States, the "them" in Lee's oath. The Twitter brigade claims this constituted a violation of his oath. Lee believed he was defending it by refusing to take up arms against his home, his family, and his State. What could be more noble? One Twitter brigade historian stated that, "One does not oppose secession and then take such a dramatic action to fight for...secession." Lee wrestled with his decision to side with Virginia over the Union, as did many Southerners. To argue otherwise is to show complete ignorance of secession winter and for that matter Lee's painful decision. Even Pryor, whom all the Twitter brigade loves to cite, agrees. "This poignant moment, when a strong, steadfast man paced and prayed in despair, is a scene worthy of Shakespeare precisely because it so palpably exposes the contradiction in his heart." Lee was unequivocally opposed to secession right to the point of making the decision to resign from the army and side with Virginia.

But this Twitter historian goes further. He argues that "Lee wanted to protect Virginia, the South, and its 'institutions...' and by its institutions he means slavery." Except Lee never once defended slavery during the War. What did Lee suggest the men of Virginia were fighting for? This is what he wrote in September 1861:

> *Keep steadily in view of the great principles for which [you] contend and to manifest to the world [your] determination to maintain them.* **The safety of your homes and the lives of all you hold dear depend your courage and exertions. Let each man resolve to be victorious, and that the right of self-government, liberty, and peace shall find him a defender** *[emphasis added].*

Obviously, Lee intended "the right of self-government, liberty, and peace" to mean slavery, slavery, and slavery, and without question "the safety of your homes and the lives of all you hold dear" meant slavery and more slavery. Why? Because obviously every Southerner who had his body blown apart by cannon shot did so because they either wanted to own slaves or did own slaves. The arch neo-Confederate historian James McPherson had this to say about Southern motivation: "The concepts of southern nationalism, liberty, self-government, resistance to tyranny, and other ideological purposes...all have a rather abstract quality. But for many Confederate soldiers these abstractions took a concrete, visceral form: the defense of home and hearth against an invading enemy." Lee would have agreed, but according to the Twitter brigade, there could be no other explanation other than slavery, the historical record notwithstanding.

And what about the postwar Lee? It has become fashionable to attach Lee to the Ku Klux Klan. Both Serwer and the Twitter brigade suggest that Lee supported the Klan and turned a "blind eye" to Klan activities in both Virginia and Washington College, where Lee assumed the role of president after the War. Pryor is often cited to reinforce the argument. But clearly neither Serwer nor the Twitter brigade read everything she wrote on the matter.

The Lexington Freedman's Bureau often complained that local residents harassed African-Americans in the community and charged Lee's students at Washington College with attempting to sexually assault "unwilling colored girls...." One letter–*one letter*–is used as evidence that students at Washington College "formed a chapter of the Ku Klux Klan" to scare "blacks and whites alike with notices depicting skeletons, coffins, and black crape." When did *one letter* become overwhelming evidence of anything?

The fact remains that Lee often took action against racial violence. On one occasion, a former Freedmen's Bureau teacher named E. C. Johnson was bullied after a "skating party" nearly resulted in a melee. What Pryor and the Twitter brigade leave out is that Johnson perpetuated the violence by pulling his pistol on a young boy and threatened to kill him for the simple act of taunting the man. Northern newspapers picked up the story, and *according to the faculty minutes of Washington College, Lee dismissed the students involved.* Just prior to this, Lee dismissed a student who admitted to pistol whipping an African-American during an altercation. When the son of a local judge was shot by an African-American after an altercation, several Washington College students participated in vigilante activities aimed at a lynching. The Freedmen's Bureau contacted Lee to warn him that such activities would be met with a military response. Pryor writes: "Lee had sent out advisories forbidding his students to take part in these activities, and in both instances, Lee promised army and city officials that those participating would be penalized."

That's not what Serwer and the Twitter brigade argue. Serwer: "Lee was as indifferent to crimes of violence toward blacks carried out by his students..." and one Twitter brigade historian: "Lee turned a blind eye towards and did not punish the students involved...[and] never responded to any of the charges or cooperated with the Bureau to investigate." Of course, Pryor contradicts herself just two sentences later by claiming that Lee "at best...gave ambiguous signals..." and suggesting that "The number of accusations against Washington College boys indicates that he either punished the racial harassment more laxly than other misdemeanors, or turned a blind eye to it." Her evidence? *One letter from the same student who suggested that the College had a Klan chapter.* Which source would be more reliable? The Washington College faculty minutes or a letter from a student to a parent based on hearsay? To the Twitter brigade, clearly the latter, but what can anyone expect from such "scholars?"

Our now infamous Twitter brigade scholar concludes that "the "marble man" myth-[is] an image that has no basis in fact and is easily disproven by the historical record. I mean, this stuff isn't secret....[and McDaniel's] assessment of Lee flies in the face of all available historical evidence."

Using this standard, what does "all of the available historical evidence" tell us?

Lee was a *de facto* but never *de jure* slave owner for roughly five years of his life, and for a shade over two years in accordance with the provisions in his father-in-law's will (the slaves should be freed if the estate was solvent or after five years otherwise) managed the Arlington estate in an attempt to make the property solvent in order to save it for his wife and family after years of mismanagement. This included hiring out slaves to other plantations, but he never sold a single slave or legally broke up a family through a sale. Lee did free several slave women and children at his wife's insistence before he took control of the estate, and his wife and daughters taught several of the Lee family slaves to read and write even though Virginia law prohibited it. Mary Custis Lee even entrusted one slave with the keys to the plantation when they were forced to evacuate the property in May 1861. Lee rid himself of the responsibilities in December 1862 partly with his own money, worked to keep these freedmen from bondage after the fact, favored enlisting blacks in the Confederate army in return for emancipation, and called slavery a "moral and political evil." He denied engaging in cruelty three times–once in a private letter in 1859 when he was fully at liberty to speak on the matter—after the abolitionist press attacked his character, and he called executing the Custis will a "miserable legacy." Is that the collective work of a proslavery ideologue?

Lee thought nullification illegal, privately argued against secession, anguished over his decision to leave the army, and was generally a reluctant Confederate who saw it has his honorable duty to side with his family and State. He wrote he wished Virginia would stay in the Union so he would not have to make such a difficult choice. Had that happened, Lee would have certainly stayed in the United States Army and probably would have accepted Winfield Scott's offer to lead Union forces. Is that the work of a "fire-eater" like William L. Yancey or Robert Barnwell Rhett?

Lee held views on race that matched what most Americans believed at the time, including many prominent Republicans like Benjamin Wade and Abraham Lincoln, and while president of Washington College after the War dismissed students who engaged in racial violence. He did not support the Fifteenth Amendment—he was not alone even in the North as New Jersey, Ohio, Oregon, and California all rejected the amendment—but publicly spoke of reconciliation and healing and refused to profit from his fame or have his name attached to cause that might stir sectional tension. One postbellum observer remarked that Lee "was bowed down with a broken heart."

Generations of Americans North and South respected Lee. Like Washington, Lee became the symbol holding the sections together. Northerners like Charles Adams, former Union officer and grandson of John Quincy Adams, admired his honor and integrity, and even into the 1970s, American presidents, both Democrat and Republican, heaped praise on Lee's character. Dwight Eisenhower argued that "a nation of men of Lee's caliber would be unconquerable in spirit and soul. Indeed, to the degree that present-day American youth will strive to emulate his rare qualities . . . we, in our own time of danger in a divided world, will be strengthened and our love of freedom sustained..." while Franklin Roosevelt said at the unveiling of a Robert E. Lee statue in Dallas, Texas (since removed by an "enlightened" city council) that "We recognize Robert E. Lee as one of our greatest American Christians and one of our greatest American gentlemen." Winston Churchill simply said, "Lee was the noblest American who had ever lived."

That's the real Robert E. Lee. "This stuff isn't secret." Perhaps the "amateur" McDaniel is better equipped to discuss Lee than the "actual historians" in the Twitter brigade or at *The Atlantic*. It wouldn't be the first time an "amateur" has outclassed them.

John C. Calhoun: American

OF ALL THE AMERICAN vice-presidents, none is more vilified than John C. Calhoun.

Calhoun is known as the "defender of slavery," the "cast iron man," the "man who started the civil war." His monument in Charleston has been vandalized, his name removed from Calhoun College at Yale, his Alma Mater, and now his home, Clemson University, is debating whether to drop his name from the honors college. Why?

Americans don't understand John C. Calhoun.

It wasn't so long ago that John F. Kennedy called Calhoun one of the greatest Senators in American history. Calhoun's primary adversary in the Senate, Daniel Webster of Massachusetts, labeled Calhoun "A Senator of Rome when Rome survived," while Henry Clay of Kentucky described Calhoun as the brightest star in the House of Representatives in the early 19th century.

Calhoun held almost every prominent position in the general government except the presidency: Secretary of War, Secretary of State, Vice-President, Senator, Representative. Such a man would receive the highest accolades in modern American government. Not so with Calhoun.

He was also the last great American statesman.

As Clyde Wilson contends:

> *A statesman must be something of a prophet—one who has an historical perspective and says what he believes to be true and in the best long-range interest of the people—whether it is popular or not.*

A politician, in contrast, which is all we have now, says and does whatever he thinks will get or keep him in power, and his historical perspective is limited to the next opinion poll or brown bag full of unmarked bills.

Calhoun's mind and his devotion to the American experiment were equal to that of the great men of the Founding generation. He had an advantage over the Founders in that he had forty years of experience near the top of the federal government, and thus a view of how things had worked under the Constitution.

He was the most original political thinker in American history. People from all over the world study Calhoun's *Disquisition on Government* for advice on how to restrain government power. Calhoun never lost sight of the American republican tradition.

For example, Calhoun wrote in that seminal work, "But government, although intended to protect and preserve society, has itself a strong tendency to disorder and abuse of its powers...."

No modern American conservative would argue otherwise, but because of Calhoun's defense of slavery in the 1830s, he is no longer recognized as one of the great leaders of the United States.

This is unfortunate, for Calhoun's position on slavery was hardly original or even unique. New Englanders, as early as 1701, used the exact same language as Calhoun in his now infamous "Positive Good" speech when they defended slavery from abolitionist attacks. But the historical profession ignores this readily available information either by choice or more likely ignorance.

Calhoun presents a problem for modern American society, which is the primary reason he must be marginalized, contextualized, or erased from public memory. In our society of mediocrity, such a deep and perceptive thinker as Calhoun cannot be celebrated. He must be banished lest he makes everyone else look bad. And a man so critical of centralized power is certainly out of step with modern American views.

Take for example what Calhoun had to say about the Congress, the presidency, and the general government.

"The Constitutional power of the President," he said, "never was or could be formidable, unless it was accompanied by a Congress which was prepared to corrupt the Constitution." Congress has been doing that since 1789.

In a statement that would be shocking to modern political pundits, Calhoun suggested that "The Presidential election is no longer a struggle for great principles, but only a great struggle as to who shall have the spoils of office."

And in a stinging indictment of political parties, Calhoun argued that:

> *"The Federal Government is no longer under the control of the people, but of a combination of active politicians, who are banded together under the name of Democrats or Whigs, and whose exclusive object is to obtain the control of the honours and emoluments of the government. They have the control of almost the entire press of the country, and constitute a vast majority of Congress.... With them a regard for principle, or this or that line of policy, is a mere pretext. They are perfectly indifferent to either, and their whole effort is to make up on both sides such issues as they may think for the time to be the most popular, regardless of truth or consequences."*

Replace Republican for Whig and not much has changed. These are words to which all Americans can understand and relate.

Calhoun always insisted he was a Union man so long as the Union continued to protect the liberties of the people of the States. With the current crop of politicians in Washington spending trillions on unnecessary domestic and foreign policy goals, with corruption rampant in all three branches of government, and with federal policy consistently at odds with the life, liberty, and property of modern American citizens, isn't Calhoun more prophetic than ever?

Admitting that, though, would require a level of honesty virtually no one in the modern academy possesses.

Tearing down Calhoun is nothing short of tearing down America.

A Deep Devotion to the Constitution

ACCORDING TO THE MODERN historical establishment, John C. Calhoun is the ultimate American villain. These esteemed historians think lofty assessments from previous decades failed to account for his glaring inconsistencies regarding federal power, his advocacy for American imperialism, or his well-known defense of slavery and racism. Historians may have been critical of Calhoun's advancement of the "positive good" of slavery–Samuel Flagg Bemis famously labeled Calhoun the infamous "Defender of Slavery"–but to the modern social justice warrior turned historian they did not do enough to condemn Calhoun as the fork-tailed godfather of all social evil in the United States. After all, one of the political heroes of the left, John F. Kennedy, had the gall to classify Calhoun as one of the most important Senators in American history. Maybe Kennedy was more honest than we thought. He wasn't afraid to be seen with a Confederate Battle Flag.

Calhoun as the statesman certainly deserves our admiration. His positions on issues such as banking, federalism, republicanism, taxes, trade, and foreign policy offer the modern political class countless examples to emulate, if they would only listen. His "deep devotion to the Constitution" was apparent in virtually every public act, from his time in the Congress to his role as Vice-President, Secretary of State, and Secretary of War. There was no more accomplished public figure than Calhoun during his career, not even the two other members of the "Great Triumvirate," Henry Clay and Daniel Webster. When Calhoun died in 1850, they both regarded him as the most formidable and august member of the United States Senate.

This commitment to the Constitution of the founders also forced him to run afoul of both major political parties. Calhoun was an independent's independent. No better example exists than his penchant for denouncing the inconsistencies of the Democrats during the Andrew Jackson administration. In 1834, Calhoun admonished his fellow Democrats for supporting the illegal acts of King Andrew, and then implored them to "halt in their support of the despotic and slavish doctrines, which we hear daily advanced, before a return of the reviving spirit of liberty shall overwhelm them, with those who are leading them, to their ruin." This was Calhoun the republican, always suspicious of unconstitutional power and willing to forgo his own acclaim to uphold the principles of '76 and '98.

Purists in the Old Republican faction did not trust Calhoun, and early in Congressional career he advanced bills that were constitutionally dubious, including the famous Bonus Bill of 1817. Calhoun, however, maintained that his support for the "national republican" agenda including the Tariff of 1816 was done in the spirit of Union, the true meaning of the "general welfare." Whereas Northern politicians supported "nationalism" when it suited them and sectionalism when it didn't, Calhoun understood that the Union needed to benefit and burden all equally. The War of 1812 sapped the Northern economy, and Calhoun wisely thought that to maintain sectional harmony, the South needed to toss them a bone. As Calhoun later pointed out in his famous speech on the "Compromise of 1850," the South had been continually plundered by the North, so his effort to find sectional harmony speaks volumes about the man. Calhoun always insisted that he was a Union man, but his Union was that of the founding generation, one that respected the political, cultural, and social differences of the sections and states and avoided legislation designed to bring one faction to the fore. Calhoun's infamous "sectionalism" was always a reaction to Northern sectionalism disguised as nationalism.

Calhoun's political philosophy centered on a belief in true separation of powers, not just between the three branches of the general government, but between the four pillars of the American political order: the federal executive, the federal congress, the federal judiciary, and the States. Take away the fourth pillar, and the entire house crumbles. His sagacity in this regard put him in a league of his own politically. To Calhoun, "State's rights" was not an exercise in mere political sophistry or an expedient reaction to Northern attempts to seize the reins of power; he believed in its core principles. He wrote in 1834 that "We may rest assured, that it is only the elevated and commanding position of State['] s rights, that the contest against Executive usurpation can be permanently and successfully maintained....State rights and State remedies the only effectual barrier against usurpation; let them be prostrated, and in the place of an elective Chief Magistrate, we shall speedily have a Military Despot."

He penned these words after placing the blame for executive overreach at the feet of Congress. Calhoun argued that Congress had created the elected monarchy when it broke its constitutional shackles and wrested power from the States. "I hold it then," he wrote," as a fundamental law of the system, that whatever power Congress may take from the States, will endure, not to its advantage, but to that of the Executive." This held true because the executive was uniquely positioned, due to its "patronage" and "influence" to use the breakdown in federalism to seize control of the government and trample the Constitution. "For the cause of all this, we must look to the acts of Congress–to that system of legislation, that drew into the vortex of this Government, the control over the entire industry and wealth of the country–that poured millions into its treasury beyond its legitimate wants, to be wasted in the most profuse & extravagant manner, on objects not authorized by the Constitution." He echoed this position in 1841: "The Constitutional power of the President never was or could be formidable, unless it was accompanied by a Congress which was prepared to corrupt the Constitution."

Every president since has used Congressional waste to his advantage. Money fosters both loyalty and corruption, what Alexander Hamilton called the most beneficial component of the British constitution, a component he wanted to foist on the American political system. The office seeker and rent seeker sells his soul to the general government and in the process becomes the paid bulldog of the general authority, the American version of the "courtier" who owes his life to his federal overlord. He is thus an unquestioned sycophant of federal power. Calhoun saw this long before anyone blew the whistle on the "imperial presidency" and its seductive allure of patronage and power.

Calhoun contended that his political positions flowed in a direct line from the Founders. "I have done nothing," he wrote in 1824, "in which I have not been supported by the examples of the political fathers of the Republican [s]chool. My acts are all covered by the acts of Jefferson, Madison, and Monroe." Calhoun thought that the federal balance between the States and the general government "is the only portion [of the Constitution] that is novel and peculiar." Like Jefferson, Calhoun argued that the distribution of power allowed for the reconciliation of freedom and safety for the American States, "But it is not only in the abstract, that I admire the distribution of power between the general government and the States. I approve of the actual distribution of the two powers, which is made by our Constitution."

The cogency in his philosophy is remarkable. The Calhoun in this 1824 letter mirrored the Calhoun on his deathbed in 1850. Calhoun predictably defended federalism and "state rights" during the nullification "crisis" of the 1830s, but his thoughts on the issue did not dissipate once that conflict cooled. He wrote in

1844, "But I wish all of my friends to understand, that my adherence to the great conservative doctrine of State interposition, and confidence in its efficiency when properly called into action was never stronger than at present. I entertain no doubt that the salvation of our Union and the permanency of our free institutions depend on it....As much as I value our Union and our glorious *Federal* system, in the same degree do I value State interposition, as the only means by which they can be preserved." Notice that Calhoun called nullification or State interposition "the great conservative doctrine." This would be considered political heresy several years ago, but Calhoun was correct. Nullification was *the* political tradition of the founding generation, from the Stamp Act Crisis through the early nineteenth century. It was a commitment to local self-government and federalism that set apart the American colonists from their brethren in Parliament. The Empire could regulate foreign trade and organize a defense of the colonies, but the colonists themselves had full legislative authority in all other matters. That tradition carried forward into the federal republic, from Jefferson's declaration by the "free and independent states" of North America to the Articles of Confederation and the "more perfect union" established by the Constitution for the United States. Calhoun held the American political tradition to be that of Jefferson, not Hamilton.

Calhoun extended both his suspicion of executive power and his admiration for the founding generation to American foreign policy. Calhoun was hawkish on war with Great Britain in 1812, but only because he saw no other means to resist what had become oppressive violations of American honor. The British provided hostile Indian tribes with guns, impressed American sailors, and thumbed their nose at treaty restrictions on their continued presence on the frontier. Calhoun saw no other choice but armed conflict. But he did not rush headlong into war. In 1811, Calhoun cautioned that "War, in this country, ought never to be resorted to but when it is clearly justifiable and necessary; so much so, as not to require the aid of logic to convince our reason nor the ardor of eloquence to inflame our passions." In the same speech before the House of Representatives, he warned the United States to avoid "A bullying menacing system" for "in expense it is almost as considerable as war–it excites contempt abroad, an destroys confidence here."

He adhered to this position well into the 1840s, even during the War with Mexico in 1846. In an 1841 speech in the Senate, Calhoun opined that "our true policy, in connection with foreign relations, is neither to do nor to suffer wrong, not only because the principle is right of itself, but because it is, in its application to us, wise and politic, as well as right." He succinctly declared that "Peace is pre-eminently our policy. Our road to greatness lies not over the ruins of others, but in the quiet and peaceful development of our immeasurably great internal resources...." This was no neoconservative "national greatness" imperial sophistry.

"War," Calhoun said, "so from accelerating, can but retard our march to greatness." Just five years later, Calhoun worried that the War with Mexico would create a "precedent...pregnant with evil," namely the ability of the president "to bring about a state of things, in which Congress shall be forced, without deliberation, or reflection, to declare war, however, opposed to its conviction of justice or expediency. In a word, it divest Congress virtually of the war making power, & transfers it to the President, and even to the commanders on the frontier." That Calhoun was prophetic in this regard is an understatement. Virtually every war from 1861 to the modern age has been imposed upon the American public in this manner. We need to look no farther in the past than George Quincy (W) Bush or Lyndon Johnson for examples of Calhoun's prophecy, but the laundry list of executive war making abuse includes virtually every president from Abraham Lincoln to the present. Only a few avoided the siren song of imperial and military glory for the United States.

We cannot grasp Calhoun's felicity to principle without understanding his sense of duty. That, perhaps more than anything else, is Calhoun's lesson for future generations. Compare what Calhoun wrote in 1811 to a letter he jotted to his daughter in 1848 just two years before his death. 1811: "All know, that in the short time I have been in publick service, I have ever stood obstinate against all local, party, or factious interest. That, I often advocated unpopular questions, from a belief of their utility....I love just renown; but, to me undeserved popularity has no charms." 1848: "Far higher motives [than success] impel me; a sense of duty; to do our best for our country, & leave the rest to Providence....Indeed, I regard this life very much as a struggle ag[ai]nst evil, & that to him, who acts on proper principle, the *reward is in the struggle, more than in victory itself*....So strong is my faith in this belief...that no appreciation of my efforts, either by the present, or after times, is necessary to sustain me in struggling to do my duty in resisting wrong, especially where our country is concerned...." Nothing had changed in thirty years.

This classical republicanism, a sense of duty, sustained the founding generation in their darkest days in the struggle for independence just as it sustained Calhoun in his solitary defense of federalism during the difficult decades of the 1830s and 1840s. As he wrote to the New England scholar Orestes Brownson in 1841, "... it is ever better to be defeated in a good cause, than not to make the effort to maintain it...." Such is the case with the South, and such is the case with Calhoun's reputation. If Kennedy could see the value in Calhoun's life and political thought, there should be a glimmer of hope that modern America could come to its senses and return Calhoun to a place of respect.

Calhoun the Marxist?

NEO-CONSERVATIVES CAN'T seem to make up their mind about the Confederacy. They all agree that the Confederacy represented everything evil about early America (which places them squarely in league with their intellectual brothers on the Left) but why they hate it presents the real conundrum.

It borders on schizophrenia.

Neo-conservative historian Victor Davis Hanson, for example, often rails against the Confederacy when issues involving "state's rights" and secession come up. He opposes "sanctuary cities" as a vestige of the "New Confederates", and blasts California secession as a rekindling of the Old South on the West Coast.

On the other hand, neo-conservative journalist John Daniel Davidson thinks that the Old South, the Confederacy, and John C. Calhoun wrote the blueprints for the modern bureaucratic, centralized state.

So, which one is it? Is the Confederacy behind unwanted decentralization or unwanted centralization?

To these "intellectuals" it is just unwanted.

But more than that, the South represents a convenient straw man to push over whenever their Lincolnian dream of a centralized proposition nation is threatened. To the Straussian, Jaffaite, neo-conservatives, everything bad originated in the South—except one line from the Declaration of Independence, "that all men are created equal."

Hanson doesn't like the South and doesn't like secession. The Confederacy exemplifies the most visible threat to the New England and Lincolnian myth of American history, and thus it must be denounced whenever possible. Topple monuments and symbols, deride "neo-confederate" ideas, and champion the unitary state so long as "your guy" is in power. This grab-bag of tools to erase the Confederate "stain" on American history would find handymen at *Mother Jones* or the *Daily Kos*.

Davidson's argument masquerades as a serious challenge to the "Lost Cause myth" but is nothing more than a regurgitation of several easily discredited neo-conservative fallacies and one characterization of Calhoun as the "Marx of the Master Class."

Davidson insists that the "now so familiar" narrative of the South as a decentralized "rural backwater" is woefully wrong. To prove it, he cites a *USA Today* piece by Lincolnite scholar Allen Guelzo claiming that the Confederacy "centralized political authority in ways that made a hash of states' rights, nationalized industries in ways historians have compared to 'state socialism,' and imposed the first compulsory national draft in American history."

Part of this is true, but Guelzo leaves out important element of the story. Several Southern states openly resisted attempts by the Confederate government to trample civil liberties and centralize power, so much so that "states' rights" were often *blamed* for the defeat of the Confederacy. The Confederate federal court system was never implemented, leaving the state courts in complete control of the legal mechanisms in the South. State courts routinely defied Confederate law, even going so far as to issue writs of *habeas corpus* after it was suspended by the central government. The Confederacy had at most three or four "major" industrial centers and thus had to maximize output to have any shot at keeping pace with the Northern industrial machine. This did involve government control of vital industries—in clear violation of the Confederate Constitution—but classifying this as "state socialism" is stretching the truth.

It's also clear that Davidson has never read Calhoun and relies upon the Jaffaite interpretation of the man to buttress his arguments. Calhoun was called the "Marx of the Master Class" by Richard Hofstadter in 1948. This was not meant as a critique. Hofstadter thought Calhoun was a thoughtful person, indeed the last American statesman philosopher, who had a sharp mind and penetrating intellect. Harry Jaffa distorted this label by insisted that, like Marx, Calhoun favored "scientific" political thought. Davidson calls it "the junk pseudoscience of racial inequality and Darwinism." Calhoun did not believe that all men were equal—he never mentioned race in the *Disquisition on Government*—but neither did any other conservative from time immemorial to the 1970s. Is that "junk pseudoscience" and "Darwinism?" If so, then Russell Kirk and other giants of American post World War II conservative thought should be held in contempt. They, too, reflected positively on Calhoun's contributions to American constitutionalism and political philosophy.

Davidson claims that Calhoun's concurrent majority was intended to "circumvent the forms and restrictions of the Constitution so the government can do things they think need to be done." More insidiously to Davidson and Jaffa, Calhoun distorted "the Founders' and Abraham Lincoln's understanding of the Constitution." This statement would be laughable if it wasn't so sadly stupid.

Calhoun wrote in the *Disquisition* that written Constitutions, while laudable and better than any other restraint on government, could not keep numerical majorities from crushing minorities because they often lacked an enforcement mechanism to keep government power at bay. Whereas Jaffa and Davidson think Calhoun's "negative" would lead to anarchy, Calhoun expressly rejected this in several passages by arguing that "anarchy" would be the result from unlimited government power. In other words, Calhoun thought the negative would *prevent* anarchy. Simply put, the Tenth Amendment to the Constitution needed teeth. The "concurrent majority" provided those teeth and would allow "liberty" to flourish, even if that meant secession.

He also insisted that the concurrent majority would lead to greater political suffrage, not less, as homogenous communities would be more peaceful and open to larger numbers of people with ballot access. Calhoun was not anti-democratic. He was anti-irresponsible universal suffrage, as were all conservatives of his age, and he opposed alien peoples having control over foreign political communities. Massachusetts certainly did not want South Carolina dictating terms about suffrage or representation. Why should South Carolina accept the opposite?

To reach the conclusion that Calhoun would somehow recognize his views on government in the modern bureaucratic state is lunacy. Calhoun was concerned with political minorities and the dangers of mob rule, but again, until the 1970s so was every other conservative. As he pointed out in the *Disquisition*, the result of a majoritarian system would be the constant scrambling for the spoils of power by two factions and the destruction of the written constitution. Each side would retreat to the shield of the constitution when it was out of power but would ignore it while wielding the reins. Has he not been proved correct?

Calhoun was a "progressive" in that he held a positive view of human society, but he was not a progressive in the modern political usage of the term. Davidson is so far out in left field with that argument he might as well join the CPUSA. They would at least be receptive to his interpretation of Calhoun and the South.

The neo-conservatives like Hanson and Davidson are as much a threat to traditional America as the Left. By continually disparaging the South and its traditions they are unknowingly destroying the very fabric of conservative American society they supposedly wish to defend. More important, they are undermining the bedrock of Western Civilization, and as several American intellectuals noted well into the twentieth century, the South produced the only truly unique and highly cultivated civilization in American history.

That said, decentralization and Calhoun's argument for some type of negative on the general government are fast becoming popular positions in American society. They are *the* ideas of the twenty-first century. The Founding generation insisted on a limited federal republic to protect the separate interests of a heterogeneous people. That is the key to understanding American government. Calhoun knew it better than most.

Robert E. Lee: American Hero

SEVERAL YEARS AGO, leftist blowhard Richard Cohen at the *Washington Post* wrote that Robert E. Lee "deserves no honor — no college, no highway, no high school. In the awful war (620,000 dead) that began 150 years ago this month, he fought on the wrong side for the wrong cause. It's time for Virginia and the South to honor the ones who were right." He echoed a piece in the *New York Times* by the equally abrasive "establishment" historian Elizabeth Brown Pryor that portrayed Lee as an abject traitor to his family, a man who was not torn by his decision to side with Virginia and who with equal vigor embraced secession and supported slavery.

A contemporary Internet search for "Robert E. Lee traitor" brings up several articles that lambaste Lee for turning his back on his "country" and violating his military oath. This would not have been the case less than fifty years ago, but Lee has been reduced to a non-American, an insignificant other of American history who had a foot fetish and propagated a "myth" of Southern righteousness. After all, as Cohen wrote, "he offered himself and his sword to the cause of slavery.... Such a man cannot be admired."

Would either say the same thing about Washington or Jefferson, men whom Virginia Royal Governor Dunmore believed were fighting *for* slavery in 1775? Dunmore "freed the slaves" through a carefully calculated "emancipation proclamation" in the early stages of the American War for Independence. The Continental Congress—replete with non-racist, morally sound and benevolent Yankees—urged Virginia to resist the move. After all, the new American Union was a slaveholding federal republic, and both Washington and Jefferson, along with thousands of other patriots North and South, were either slaveholders or

91

profited from the institution. Did Washington then offer "his sword to the cause of slavery?" No sane historian would advance that position, but these are the bizarre charges leveled against Lee.

Lee represented the best of American society in 1861. He was, like Washington, the quintessential American.

Lee's views on government embodied the Jeffersonian model of the early federal republic. This may seem odd. Both his father and most of his kin were ardent Federalists who despised the Jeffersonian Republicans. "Light-Horse" Harry Lee was almost killed by a partisan mob during the War of 1812, and Washington, the model for the Lee household, believed in the necessity of a stronger central government after the States secured their independence from Great Britain in 1783.

But the degree of separation between Washington and Jefferson was slight. Both men considered the English tradition of armed opposition to tyranny born at Runnymede in 1215 to be the guiding principle of self-government. Both were reared in a masculine society dedicated to a rigorous physical, spiritual, and intellectual training of its sons but softened by refinement of manners. Both were agrarians with large estates that rivaled their European counterparts. Jefferson certainly favored a central government with less power than Washington wielded during his second term, but neither man would have raised a hand against Virginia in 1861. Both had descendants who fought for the Confederate cause.

That was still Lee's Virginia on the eve of war in 1861. Lee was no traitor, and no one among the founding generation would have considered him so. Secession was the American tradition, secured and codified by the Treaty of Paris in 1783 and openly discussed and advanced by both Northern and Southern Founders as early as 1794, a mere five years after the general government under the Constitution was formed. Jefferson called Virginia his "country." Lee believed the same. His vision of America clashed with Abraham Lincoln's, particularly in regard to political power, but that does not make it any less American.

Lee's America, in fact, dominated all levels of society for the first eighty years of American history. An irrefutable case could be made that Lee's America *was* the embodiment of the American tradition, born with the first settlers in Jamestown in 1607 and advanced through several generations of independent people. They blazed trails, built farms and businesses, subdued the frontier, secured political liberty, and jealously defended the rights of Englishmen. Was Lee any different?

Not even the worst of the Lee detractors can impale his character. Pryor tried in her *Reading the Man*, but her accusations fell flat. The charge that he was fighting for slavery also creates the false dichotomy that the North was fighting against it. Even Lincoln did not make that case for most of the War, particularly when it began, but that myth, the "treasury of counterfeit virtue," still exists. Lincoln's America is more of a myth than the supposed "Lost Cause" which Cohen scribbled should "get lost."

Americans who honor Lee as one of the truly great people America has produced recognize, perhaps unconsciously, that Jefferson's America still has currency.

Perhaps it is fitting that Lee's birthday falls on the day before another political revolution is set to take place. Donald Trump is certainly no Lee, Washington, or Jefferson, but the people that supported him, the same type of people who formed the backbone of Jefferson's America, the rock-ribbed "forgotten men" of American society, wait in anticipation for the same type of message the South sent to the general government in 1861. They said no and exercised their right of self-determination.

Lee had the courage of his convictions and selflessly sacrificed his own peace and prosperity for the cause of independence, a government "of the people, by the people, and for the people." Lee should not be remembered solely as a Southern icon, but like Washington and Jefferson, as an *American* hero.

Things As They Are

William S. Belko, *Philip Pendleton Barbour in Jacksonian America: An Old Republican in King Andrew's Court* (The University of Alabama Press, 2016).

SOMETIMES A PROFESSIONAL historian gets it right. William Belko has produced a quality tome that both expands and enhances our understanding of American history. While most academics write about the same subjects and regurgitate fashionable theories with "new" evidence—particularly if such "evidence" supports a cultural Marxist version of the American past—Belko bucks that trend in spades. He not only saves the "obscure" Barbour from the dustbin of history, Belko provides a deeper perspective on Southern society and the political battles of the early nineteenth century. As Belko writes, "Barbour's political career undeniably demonstrates that subjects of an economic nature, rather than the efficacy and spread of slavery, dominated, determined, and shaped the great political battles and partisan attachments during the formative years of Jacksonian America." Refreshing.

Belko's assessment of Barbour's life and career is more than a political biography. He details the social and cultural environment of Barbour's Frascati plantation and explains what shaped his political views. Barbour was born and bred to be an Old Republican. His father, Thomas Barbour, opposed ratification of the Constitution and stood for election to the Virginia Ratifying Convention in 1788 from Orange County. He was defeated by James Madison. But more than that, Philip Barbour was a Virginian first and foremost, a student of the classics who admired both Greek and Roman history and the English political tradition. He was no simple minded provincial reactionary narrowly focused on race and slavery, for that matter nor were any of the Old Republicans regardless of what most mainstream historians believe. He was both a gifted speaker and a real student of history who had one of the finest libraries in the South. Belko argues that "Barbour became a quintessential Old Republican precisely because of his social surroundings in a county replete with intense Revolutionary Whig and Jeffersonian Republican predilections." These "Whig and Jeffersonian Republican predilections" included the "Spirit of '98," the writings of John Taylor of Caroline, and the speeches of Richard Bland and Patrick Henry.

Belko portrays Barbour as a consistent statesman who never deviated from his Old Republican roots. His speeches against protective tariffs, federally funded internal improvements, and central banking displayed cogency from year to year, and Belko attests led the way in developing the constitutional attack against Henry Clay's American System and John Marshall's Supreme Court. Barbour warned that the fusion of "economic and judicial nationalism...threatened American liberty." The imaginative construction of men like Clay and Marshall would form "a breach...in the Constitution, by which, not only these powers may be let in, but a flood of others, strong enough to break down all the barriers erected to preserve the residuary rights of the States and the People." Barbour was as prescient as he was principled.

Barbour was also consciously Southern. Belko relays several stories that prove cultural differences between the North and South extended beyond preferred methods of labor. For example, in 1829 Barbour told several fellow Virginians at supper "about the odd names which the New England people give to their children." This amused him, particularly when the "Congress role was called" for their names were "as wild and uncouth as intoxication or insanity would dictate." Barbour called the prominent Massachusetts politician Daniel Webster "a cold uninteresting speaker" who "*felt* nothing" because "he was always cold blooded." Contrast that with the glowing praise often heaped on Webster after his performance in the Webster-Hayne debates and it becomes clear that not everyone believed Webster to be the greatest or most persuasive speaker of his day. Barbour did not count on much from New England, once saying that he, "never saw or expected to see anything like eloquence form any man north of the Potomac."

Belko heroically contradicts the prevailing interpretation of state's rights and slavery. By using Barbour's statements during the Missouri debate as the litmus test for the "indirect defense of slavery" argument advanced by such prominent historians as William Freehling, William Cooper and others, Belko contends that "Barbour consistently and genuinely railed against unwarranted and dangerous centralizing tendencies coming from an ever-increasing loose construction of the Constitution, whether he was attacking the protective tariff, federally sponsored internal improvements, Marshall court decisions, or the blatant disregard of the rights and equality of a sovereign state upon its admission into the Union."

Translation: the defense of slavery was not the root of Southern support for state's rights in the early antebellum period. As Barbour continually emphasized, Congressional meddling over slavery was not an enumerated power and therefore outside of the scope of legislative business. The institution was solely a state issue (one that Belko believes Barbour "wished to escape"), just like any other "municipal" function of government in the Union. Belko ultimately argues that "Barbour's sincere fear," one that "proved weightier than the attack on the institution of slavery itself," was "that continued Northern discussion of slavery was the real ploy, that constant reference to this subject by Northern congressmen simply veiled a desire to enlarge the powers of the federal government by an enlarged construction of the Constitution." By agreeing that Barbour's position was "weightier than the attack on the institution of slavery itself," Belko opens the door to a more textured reading of American political history.

Belko's portrait rests on several fundamental impressions about Barbour's life and career. First, Barbour was a conservative who wished to, as he said in an 1830 speech, "look at things as they are." Belko colorfully described it as a warning against "the siren's song enticing people to visions…of splendid development and glorious and magnificent edifices, which charmed and captivated the people." Too often Americans have refused to call an orange an orange, even in the antebellum period. Our perspective is often distorted by what we wish to see not what we actually see, thus the imaginative construction of the Hamiltonian nationalists and bogeyman approach to American government. Create an evil or a crisis where one does not exist and exploit it to gain political power. That was not how Barbour chose to govern.

Second, Barbour's conservatism was predicated by his commitment to the old Virginia order and the necessity of "permanence," meaning land as opposed to personal property. Agrarianism ran through Barbour's bones, and like Taylor of Caroline, Barbour "preferred a rich people and a poor government, rather than a poor people with a rich government." Protecting real property from hordes of tax collectors and scheming bureaucrats offered the only tangible method of controlling government spending and unconstitutional usurpation of power. The central authority had to be starved for revenue or it would naturally spiral beyond its enumerated boundaries.

Third, Barbour was a Unionist of the Old Republican stripe. He opposed nullification as impractical but favored secession as a last resort. If conflict arose between the central government and the states as political rivals, then no "common umpire" existed and the sovereign people of the sovereign states had the right and duty to seek redress through independence. In that regard, Barbour thought the only way to maintain the Union was to limit the power of the general government to those areas which were strictly enumerated. Agitation only occurred when one faction of states sought to control another. This is why Barbour believed in the "Virginia doctrine," meaning real federalism as outlined by the Constitution with a clear delineation between state and federal power. To Barbour, nationalism, not state's rights, was the fly in the ointment that would lead to disunion. He made this clear throughout his entire political career, even in his brief time on the bench of the United States Supreme Court. Barbour, in fact, lamented that what had been labeled the "Virginia doctrine" was at one time recognized North and South as "American doctrines."

This is the key to understanding American history. Southern "sectionalism" has only been labeled as such by partisans of a uniquely nationalist stripe, one clouded by a version of history inconsistent with "things as they are." Southerners, particularly Old Republicans like Barbour, insisted on maintaining the Union as designed by the founding generation and ratified by the Constitution. Even when Southerners like Madison, James Monroe, and John C. Calhoun—perhaps even Henry Clay—advanced a nationalist political and economic agenda, they did so in the spirit of true equity and unity of the states. Northern dedication to "nationalism" on the other hand was always a thinly disguised brand of Yankee imperialism aimed at lining their pockets with Southern tax revenue. When New Englanders could not control the spoils, they resorted to bellowing about secession. Northern "nationalism" was in reality petty Northern sectionalism. The dominant Northern political class never advocated one policy that would not unequally benefit their section and burden the South. The same cannot be said for Southerners.

Belko has done a remarkable job in bringing an Old Republican like Barbour to the forefront of American political history and in portraying Southern conservative thought as more than a myopic defense of race and slavery. Alas, few academics will read it and even fewer will be persuaded, but that is the nature of the modern academy. There is no gold at the end of that rainbow, particularly when rehashing the tired "slave power" thesis of the 1840s and 50s results in Ivy League positions, book awards, and "atta boys" from the academic "elite."

The Vanishing Republic of Our Fathers

THE NEW SOUTH is one of the more misunderstood periods in American history. The contemporary narrative generally describes the period and its leaders as dense political hacks riding the coattails of Northern business elites. They were "wannabe" statesmen whose political ideology was singularly tied to race. This perspective is clouded by present conditions and our own short-sighted infatuation with racial politics. Historians often miss the complexity and deep-rooted origins of Southern political thought in this period, of its Jeffersonian origins and ties to the old republicans of the founding generation. There was more to these men than the plight and status of Southern blacks.

No one better exemplifies this than Oscar W. Underwood of Alabama. He was one of the dominant political figures of his day, a man of the Deep South who had a real shot at the presidency in 1912 before a pseudo-Southerner, Woodrow Wilson, grabbed the nomination. Underwood was a throwback to the Democrat Party of Grover Cleveland and by default the politics of the early republic. He served his State in the United States House of Representatives and the United States Senate for over twenty years and led an effort to denounce the Ku Klux Klan and eliminate it from the Democrat Party in the 1920s. His opposition to the Klan led him to decline running for re-election in 1926. His opponent, future Supreme Court Justice Hugo Black, not only had Klan support, he was a Klan member.

After Underwood retired, he authored *Drifting Sands of Party Politics* in 1928, a partly autobiographical sketch of his time in Congress. Underwood railed against what he saw as unnecessary expansion of the general government, particularly in foreign policy and in executive power. He was also no fan of legislating "morality," a key component of the social gospel arm of the progressive movement. In each case, Underwood relied on a substantially old republican approach to the powers of the general government.

In 1927 Underwood penned an opinion piece for the *New York Times* that offered a summary of his political philosophy. Titled "The Vanishing Republic of Our Fathers," Underwood's op-ed cautioned the American public that American imperialism and executive overreach were destroying the Constitution. This piece could have been written in 2016.

He began by recounting his early years in government as a Cleveland Democrat:

> So far as our people at home were concerned they possessed real States' rights. The affairs of government that most nearly entered into the homes of American citizenship were controlled and dominated by the force and impact of the State Governments and not by national control. It is true that in some places the border line had been crossed, but except in the realm of taxation and in the violation of revenue laws the citizen hardly realized that the Federal Government affected his life or his business affairs in time of peace.

Underwood contended the turning point was the Spanish American War of 1898. As in our day, foreign policy and war had a dramatic effect on the powers of the central government. This was truly a Jeffersonian position, one born in the notion that the United States should avoid what Jefferson called entangling alliances and foster peace with all nations. War always strengthened the powers of the executive branch and by default those of the central authority. This strain of thought dominated American foreign policy until the late nineteenth century. It was only then that the United States was conquered by Spain, as the famed libertarian sociologist William Graham Sumner sarcastically wrote.

Underwood said it just as well: "The door of the Republic we had inherited from our fathers was closed and the gateway to international ambitions and centralized government at Washington had been opened. It was just the beginning."

He of course ignored the effect Lincoln's war on the South had on the powers of the executive branch, but nevertheless, Underwood understood that the general government was past the point of no return, and congress was as much to blame as the president.

"When the Constitution of the United States was written," Underwood wrote, "at least a majority of those who adopted it were jealous of strong executive control and endeavored to place the great power of the government under the control of the Congress of the United States....It was then expected that we would have a government of law, made and controlled by the representatives of the people and not a government controlled and regulated by commissions to whom the Congress had delegated the great powers originally vested in it by the Constitution."

Underwood then rattled off several constitutionally dubious boards and commissions–including the Federal Reserve–that undermined the original intent of the Constitution and the separation of powers. He concluded that this "concentration of all these powers in Washington, placed in the hands of men appointed by the head of the nation, has destroyed the simple government of law that was contemplated in the beginning and has brought us to a complicated bureaucracy that every day is becoming more and more oppressive to the vast majority of American people."

He wrote he was often asked what had changed in the general government between 1895 and 1927. His response was troubling:

> *The new Government to which we have fallen heir is not content alone with surrendering the powers delegated to the representatives of the people to commissions holding them under longer terms of office, but we have progressed in the line of interference with American independence and American rights to the extent that the Government has attempted to exercise the taxing power delegated to it to raise revenue for the purpose of regulating the affairs of human life.*

The best and most prescient portion of the piece, however, was its conclusion, one that featured both a quote from Jefferson and a firm understanding of real federalism:

Nation-Wide Scope

> *It may be said that we cannot regulate the business affairs of the nation except by Federal control, that the regulation must be uniform and nationwide. I do not concur in this sentiment. There are good local laws in Maine that require the householder to clean the snow off his front sidewalk in the Winter months. Such a law would be both foolish and oppressive in Alabama, where the sun always cleans the snow from the sidewalk a few hours after it falls. So it is with business. What may be sensible regulation in one State may be unnecessary or oppressive in another.*

Regarding local self-government we cannot repeat too often what Thomas Jefferson so well said in the young days of the Republic:

"Our country is too large to have all its affairs directed by a single Government. Public servants at such a distance, and from under the eye of their constituents, must, from the circumstance of distance, be unable to administer and over-look all the details necessary for the good government of the citizens and the same circumstances, by rendering detection impossible to their constituents, will invite the public servants to corruption, plunder and waste....What an augmentation of the field for jobbing, speculating, plundering, office building and office hunting would be produced by an assumption of all the State parent into the hands of the general Government."

These words are prophetic. They are as true today as they were the day they were first uttered more than a hundred years ago.

Many important events have come and gone in the kaleidoscope of time within the last three decades—victories in war and peace, great advancement in science, learning and art—but I doubt whether there has been any happening in the era beginning with the advent of the material control and centralization of power—just as the war with Spain was begun and which seems to still be with us—that has so adversely affected the lives, happiness and liberties of the American people as the surrender by the Congress of a government of law and the inauguration of a bureaucratic government in its place.

From here where do we go? No man can predict. Has the era spent its force and will the pendulum swing back, or shall we go on until we have a republic only in name that promulgates its rules and regulations to please the fancy and desire of the chosen few who are to constitute the governing class for the future?

Clearly, the pendulum never swung back. The political class is now above the law–see Hillary Clinton–and the wisdom of Jefferson has been replaced with nationalism of Hamilton. Underwood was fighting a losing battle in 1927, but at least he was aware of the catastrophic transformations taking place in government in the early twentieth century. If he recoiled at a billion dollar Congress, imagine what he would say about the four trillion dollar variety with layers of bureaucracy, unelected "tsars," regulatory agencies, taxation, and sycophantic government sponsored and supported industries?

Underwood was a dinosaur in his own time, a relic of an age when statesmen led and understood the principles of American government, and when the South had a prominent role in the direction of public policy. Perhaps if Underwood wrote this piece today, he would cite these lines from Jefferson:

He has erected a multitude of New Offices, and sent hither swarms of Officers to harass our people, and eat out their substance....In every stage of these Oppressions We have Petitioned for Redress in the most humble terms: Our repeated Petitions have been answered only by repeated injury. A Prince whose character is thus marked by every act which may define a Tyrant, is unfit to be the ruler of a free people....

To quote Underwood, "From here where do we go?"

What If We Listened to the Southern Founders?

MEL BRADFORD'S OUTSTANDING tome *A Better Guide Than Reason* lifted that phrase from a speech John Dickinson made during the Philadelphia Convention in 1787. Dickinson worried that the delegates to what we now call the "Constitutional Convention" were insistent on crafting a document that would reinvent the government of the United States, something James Madison proposed with his now famous "Virginia Plan." Dickinson cautioned against this course of action. He thought any new constitution should not be the best document the delegates to the Convention could imagine but should instead be the best document that the States would accept, meaning one that relied on the customary and familiar traditions of the American experience. These were the time-tested maxims of government, society, and law.

This August 1787 speech, more than Alexander Hamilton's troubling exposition in June 1787 on the potential beauty of a soft monarchy, set the tone for the rest of the Convention. Other members of the founding generation echoed Dickinson, both during the Convention and in the State ratification debates, but Dickinson said it best.

Unfortunately, no one continues to listen to either Dickinson, or more importantly, the other "friends of the Constitution" who insisted on adhering to the document as it was ratified in 1788. That Constitution, not the one the so called "anti-federalists" warned against, is the one we should follow today.

Certainly, men like George Mason and Patrick Henry have been proven correct in their description of what would happen should the States ratify the Constitution, but this is no badge of honor. They were publicly informed throughout the months during the ratification process that their fears were unfounded, that the government under the Constitution would never abuse its authority, and that the people of the States had nothing to fear from this "more perfect Union." This would be true if we listened to these now forgotten "friends of the Constitution," many of whom were prominent Southerners. It is certainly more fun to hold up Mason or Henry and say, "See, they told you so," but it is more productive to read the statements of the proponents of the document when engaging in debates about the meaning and nature of the Constitution.

Don't be Joseph Story. It was Story, after all, who famously told us that the Constitution means what the *opponents like Henry* said it would mean. If anyone had believed that in 1788, the Constitution would never have been ratified.

So, who were these Southern "friends of the Constitution?" In addition to the well-known Madison, two later served on the United States Supreme Court, James Iredell and John Rutledge, and one helped found the University of North Carolina, William Richardson Davie. Even John Marshall argued that the Constitution did not have the judiciary powers he assumed as Chief Justice less than twenty years later.

To these "friends of the Constitution," the powers of the central government were limited by the language of the document and the mere process of writing them down. As Madison, among others, insisted, every power which is not granted is reserved to the States and to the people. Iredell would take that one step further. Any unconstitutional act would be void.

Rutledge said during the Philadelphia Convention that a potential federal veto over State law would and ought to "damn" the Constitution, but that is exactly what has happened in the modern era. The "national" cultural war we face today is a direct result of unmitigated nationalism and the usurpation of power by the general government at the expense of the States. Without the express promise of federalism–meaning complete State control over their internal affairs and "internal police"–the States would never have ratified the document. That is the dirty little secret.

In reality, the United States Constitution is a flawed document. It does not provide an enforcement mechanism for the Tenth Amendment, and its ambiguous language leaves the door open to "innovative" interpretation. The debates over ratification, however, underscore the importance of "State powers" to the founding generation, both North and South. They were the building blocks of the federal republic both before and after ratification. The various State constitutions, the Articles of Confederation, and the Confederate Constitution of 1861 are all part of this story and conclusively show that the "Free and Independent States" of 1776 never relinquished their sovereignty. Certainly no one believed that the States became mere corporate entities of the general government in 1788, particularly in the South.

But most Americans, even Southerners (many of whom are decedents of men who bled for the founding principle of self-determination both in 1776 and 1861), don't know this history. Americans on both the Left and the Right know the system is broken. They just don't know how to fix it. The blueprint has been there all along. It's federalism, small is beautiful, think locally, act locally, self-determination, and independence. It's the unbroken chain of the Anglo-American constitutional tradition as outlined by the "friends of the Constitution" in 1788, including the Magna Charta of 1215 and the 1688 English Bill of Rights.

"Reviving the (singular) American republic" should never be our goal but insisting on the "federal republic" of the founding generation in an increasingly volatile political and cultural climate could restore some semblance of sanity in the American political process. Education is the key, and the process must begin now. Not doing so will result in the France of 1793 rather than the America of 1788. That is outcome everyone should avoid.

Two Lees

A REVIEW OF *ROBERT E. LEE at War: Hope Arises from Despair* (Legion of Honor Publishing, 2017) by Scott Bowden and *The Myth of the Lost Cause: Why the South Fought the Civil War and Why the North Won* (Regnery History, 2015) by Edward H. Bonekemper III.

Did Robert E. Lee lose the War for the South? If you believe Edward Bonekemper, then yes. His first published book, *How Robert E. Lee Lost the Civil War* leaves little doubt about his position on the conflict. Bonekemper is the latest in a growing chorus of social justice conservatives who blame the South for all that ails the United States, and Lee, more importantly the "myth" of Lee, is at the center of the "Lost Cause" narrative they find so problematic.

Bonekemper hasn't found a Southern position he can't criticize, nor a "myth" he supposedly can't debunk, including that of Lee's reputation as the greatest of all Southern military leaders during the War. He first creates a straw man–the godly Lee crafted by Douglas Southall Freeman–and then precedes to punch holes in his logical fallacy. Freeman certainly admired Lee, as much as he admired George Washington, and his four-volume biography still stands as the best and most thorough treatment of the man. Southerners, particularly those from outside the Old Dominion, often bristled at some of the hagiography surrounding Lee in the twentieth century, but no one considered him to be anything less than the embodiment of the Southern tradition. It seems that this fact, more than anything else, taints Bonekemper's opinion of Lee. To a social justice conservative like Bonekemper, Lee represents a deviation from Abraham Lincoln's "proposition nation," an actual myth that forms the backbone of their disparagement of the South. This is what passes for "conservative" today. In one particularly laughable passage from *The Myth of the Lost Cause*, Bonekemper appeals to J.F.C. Fuller for an "objective" assessment of Lee. Fuller was a fascist British military theorist who dabbled in occultism and outright rejected Christianity. He admired Adolf Hitler and thought the German political model superior to that of Great Britain.

Fuller advocated the use of mechanization in the modern military and believed offense to be the key to victory. He is also considered to be the father of the German *blitzkrieg*. Fuller thought Lee focused too intently on Virginia and did not develop a broad strategy capable of winning the War. Funny. Lee was the commander of the Army of Northern Virginia and never held a position in the Confederate government, nor was he tasked with overall strategy. His job was to win the War in the East, not the West. Bonekemper, like the fascist Fuller, can't seem to figure this out. The West wasn't Lee's problem. Had Jefferson Davis relinquished control over broad Confederate military strategy to Lee, perhaps the War would have gone differently. As it stands, Lee can only be blamed for his actions in the East, and while Lee is not above criticism, Bonekemper places the entire loss of the War on Lee's shoulders.

In contrast, Scott Bowden has produced a aesthetically beautiful tome on Lee's military mind and his actions in 1862. Unlike the attorney Bonekemper, Bowden has written several critically acclaimed works on military history–both European and American. This book is designed to visually engage the reader as well as provide a detailed analysis of Lee's operations in Virginia in 1862. It could be enjoyed by both the well-read student of the War and the novice looking for a greater understanding of General Lee rather than citizen Lee. Bowden carefully traces Lee's actions through the Peninsular Campaign and weaves his character into the narrative so effortlessly that the reader can almost visualize the smoke of battle. You also won't be bombarded with a social justice conservative assault on the South or Lee's character. Men like Bonekemper would suggest this is simply the continuation of the "Lee myth" made famous by Freeman and others, but Bowden shows that Lee, while not infallible, well understood the cost of battle and the technology of the day.

It might be fitting for social justice conservatives to elevate Union heroes above men like Lee, for Lee would not be recognizable in today's "conservative" movement. Ulysses S. Grant fits the warmongering of the social justice sect, and while he may be popular today, no one in the 1860s admired Grant the way they admired Lee. This was true well into the twentieth century. That, more than anything, is what makes Lee special. His character, his rearing, his Christian gentlemanly code, is sorely lacking in modern society. Lee still has much to teach America, even social justice conservatives like Bonekemper.

The State of Virginia is currently undertaking an effort to purge Lee and other Confederate leaders from public view, including removing his statue from the United States Capitol. This might be fitting. No one as grand as Lee, even if it is just his likeness, should be surrounded by such reptiles in Washington. More importantly, the Virginia the bred men like Lee ceased to exist long ago. That is the real tragedy of the Old Dominion.

THE MAN WHO MADE THE SUPREME COURT

A review of *John Marshall: The Man Who Made the Supreme Court* (Basic Books, 2018) by Richard Brookhiser

JOHN MARSHALL PRESENTS a curious problem for Southern history. How can a man, born and bred in the same State, who breathed the same air and shared the same blood with Thomas Jefferson, have been such an ardent nationalist? The same question could be asked of Washington, and to a lesser extent, Henry Clay and Abraham Lincoln. The answer in Marshall's case is perhaps best explained by his opposition to Jefferson's Republican faction. Marshall feared both a French-inspired revolution on American soil and the fragmentation of the Union, and to Marshall "nationalism" provided the only tangible remedy for Jacobin terrorism and Jeffersonian democracy. The center had to hold in order to maintain the legacy of the American War for Independence.

Yet, none of those men were original thinkers. That is to say, they were not Alexander Hamilton. Clay and his political acolyte Lincoln rarely had a novel thought and were little more than political opportunists intent on salvaging their own careers. The "Union" meant whatever was best for Clay and Lincoln. Washington was the "indispensable man," the glue that held the federal republic together through his persona and reputation, if not his impeccable cavalier rearing, but he was not interested in the finer points of government or in political and economic philosophy.

Marshall does not compare to any of them. He was a political partisan but more of a statesman than either Clay or Lincoln. He styled himself a Washington Federalist without Washington's refinement and copied Hamilton nearly (if not literally) verbatim in his major decisions. But the Constitution and the American legal system–if not American history–would not be the same without him.

Richard Brookhiser argues in his newest tome that John Marshall "made the Supreme Court." This might be an understatement. Marshall, more than any other man, is responsible for the way most Americans think about "checks and balances" and "separation of powers." Marshall almost single-handily saved the independence of the Supreme Court and made it at times the superior branch of government. As Brookhiser tells it, Marshall "brought order" to the chaos of the early American experience. But at what cost? The Brett Kavanaugh circus would not have been possible without Marshall, nor would our "one size fits all" general government be the focal point for every political question in America. That is Marshall's ultimate legacy.

Brookhiser's account shows Marshall to be a fairly consistent defender of "popular government," meaning Marshall placed the power of the general government at the feet of an amalgamous "American people," what could more accurately be labeled the "one people theory" of the American founding. Marshall, Brookhiser contends, was a "populist." He points out that Marshall could be inconsistent, even contradictory, but Brookhiser believes that Marshall was ultimately right in his attempt to arrest the factionalization of the American polity. Marshall feared demagoguery and the petty, narrow political agendas of State actors. To Brookhiser, this was the correct conservative approach, and he is often laudatory of Marshall's devotion to American nationalism. Unfortunately, Brookhiser highlights the wrong inconsistencies, namely the fabrication and codification of the "one people theory" and his duplicitous statements during the Virginia ratifying convention of 1788.

Historians, Brookhiser included, often label Jefferson's reading of the Constitution as the "compact theory" of government. The term "compact theory" has become almost a pejorative in American political discourse. It is the burr under the saddle of good government and the antithesis of original intent, but this belies the historical record. The "one people theory" made famous by Marshall's *McCullough v. Maryland* decision had very little support during the eighteenth century and was expressly rejected by the "friends of the Constitution" during the ratification process. Marshall himself insisted on the sovereignty of the States in the Virginia ratifying convention. "It is not rational to suppose that a sovereign power should be dragged before a court," he said. He also suggested that the federal court system would not have the authority to invalidate a State law, even if to Marshall judicial review was the logical and proper purpose of that branch.

Marshall, of course, would do the opposite as chief justice. He knocked down State laws he found repugnant, narrowly interpreted the Eleventh Amendment, which was ratified after Georgia was "dragged before" the Supreme Court, and used the "supremacy clause" to centralize power in the way opponents of the Constitution feared in 1788. Marshall shredded, not buttressed, original intent. That is not how Brookhiser describes it.

Perhaps it is ironic that a Southerner was more responsible for codifying the principles that undermined the federal republic than anyone north of the Mason-Dixon. Hamilton wrote the blueprint, but without Marshall, Hamilton's nationalist dream would have died in the early nineteenth century through congressional action. There is a reason Jefferson worried about the lasting influence of the federal bench.

That said, as Brookhiser illustrates, Marshall's nationalism was not Daniel Webster's. The two were allies, even conspirators, at pivotal points in the rush toward national supremacy, but in contrast to the Senator from Massachusetts, Marshall defended American nationalism as a disinterested political philosopher. Whereas Webster saw nationalism as a way to advance the political and economic interests of New England, Marshall was truly interested in the lasting benefits of the American union, as were all Southern nationalists in the early federal republic. Their design failed, not because of Southern sectionalism, but because of Yankee sectionalism disguised as nationalism. Brookhiser agrees with Joesph Story who eulogized Marshall as "a Federalist of the good old school of which Washington was the acknowledged head." That brand of federalism and that federalist faction died with Washington in 1799. Marshall clung to a ghost. His rulings allowed a cancerous type of nationalism to metastasize in the American polity, one that would eventually kill the original federal republic and the Constitution as ratified in 1788.

Brookhiser has done an admirable job in condensing Marshall's thirty years as chief justice into a readable, popular narrative. His portrait rightly places Marshall at the center of every major legal debate of the early nineteenth century, and without question proves that Marshall defined how modern Americans view the powers of the judicial branch. That is not a unique position, but Brookhiser summarizes it better than most.

Reconsidering Richard B. Russell

THERE WAS A TIME both before and after the War when the South dominated the United States Congress. In the antebellum period, James Madison, John C. Calhoun, John Randolph of Roanoke, and Henry Clay placed their mark on congressional debates, and several other Southerners ranked among the best statesmen of the era. But most Americans, even those in the South, don't realize that by the mid-twentieth century, Southerners controlled every major committee in the Senate and played a substantial role in the legislative proceedings of both houses of Congress. This process began during the Wilson administration and continued virtually unabated until the 1970s. The "Southern Bloc" mentored promising young Southern congressmen by grooming them for power. Southerners held the formal procedures of Congress in high regard and considered being a United States Senator a position of honor and respect.

Much of the legislation these men advocated contained an obvious Jeffersonian influence. From farm bills to anti-trust harpoons against big banks and big corporations, Southerners used the mechanisms the North created in the aftermath of the War to strike back at Yankee finance capitalists. Their robust populism was undergirded by a regional cultural and political tradition based on land, family, Christianity, and decentralization, of home rule and suspicion of Northern political economy and Yankee meddling.

Every issue could be viewed through this lens, even foreign policy, where Southerners often cautioned against rushing headlong into foreign wars. That was the Jeffersonian approach to the world.

No senator personified these traits better than Richard B. Russell of Georgia. He was the "senator's senator," and other than the president the most powerful man in Washington. For nearly four decades Russell dominated the Senate. To the left, Russell's legacy was his determined effort to block civil rights legislation, but this was only part–and perhaps a much smaller part than often portrayed–of his influence on the legislative record. In fact, Russell could not single-handedly block any civil rights legislation from reaching the Senate floor, nor did the "Southern Bloc" regularly have the sufficient votes to stymie any legislative effort, including civil rights. They needed Republican help. That is the dirty little secret today. Republicans, not Democrats, often held up civil rights legislation in committee. The "Southern Bloc" had a better record in proposing and crafting legislation and in using the procedural rules to slow things down, take apart executive overreach, or expose government abuse than outright obstruction.

Undoubtedly, if it wasn't for the race issue, Americans would better appreciate Russell and his commitment to sound American government. Calls to rename the United States Senate building or the federal courthouse in Atlanta would be non-existent, but this is the world the Left created. No matter how committed or brilliant a statesman, the stain of "white supremacy" invalidates every good deed, but only if you are Southern. Northerners with the same views get a free pass. See St. Abraham.

Russell's position on American foreign policy would be a refreshing departure from the modern establishment effort to bomb the world to submission. His efforts to keep Douglas MacArthur out of the spotlight in 1951 probably avoided the beginning of World War III, and as recently released tapes of phone conversations between Lyndon Johnson and Russell in 1964 show, Russell also warned Johnson about getting more involved in Vietnam. Southerners eventually became the leading voices for non-escalation in Southeast Asia.

Russell needs more scholarly attention, as do many of the members of the twentieth-century Southern congressional leadership. Placing race as the central focus of their political careers often distorts the Jeffersonian contributions these men made to American government and society. For some, like Theodore Bilbo of Mississippi, this was certainly the case, but for others who are as maligned–if not more so–than antebellum Southern statesmen, a better effort could be made to understand rather than condemn their role in shaping the American century. That would be the real "historical" approach to take.

THE LAST REPUBLICAN PRESIDENT

JIMMY CARTER MAY have been the last Jeffersonian to be president. A recent article in the *Washington Post* labeled him the "Un-Celebrity President." In either case, Carter reflects a people and a place. He is the most authentic man elected president since Calvin Coolidge, and like Coolidge a true Christian gentleman.

At the very minimum, Carter represented the Founders' vision for a republican executive. He walked to his inaugural, refused to have "Hail to the Chief" played while he boarded Air Force One or Marine One, carried his own luggage, and when soundly defeated by Ronald Reagan went home to Plains, Georgia to the same two bedroom rancher he built in 1961. He's never left.

It used to be standard practice for a president to go home and forget public affairs. George Washington had been almost dragged from Mt. Vernon to assume office and gladly resumed the life of a planter when he stepped down in 1797. John Adams snubbed Jefferson in 1801 by taking what amounted to a public bus back to Massachusetts, but he never again left his home State and stayed away from the public eye. Jefferson resumed his very busy life at Monticello in 1809, happy to leave behind the nasty business of politics. James Madison spent his last years editing his papers and correspondence and was briefly involved in Virginia politics, but he only offered policy positions when asked in private letters. James Monroe went home and was never heard from again. That was the Founders' executive, the republican who puts down the plow and enters office out of duty but who quietly goes home and resumes a private life once their time in Washington is over.

Carter, of course, was the consummate outsider and probably the last agrarian who will ever hold that office. Other than Thomas Jefferson's *Notes on the State of Virginia,* his *An Hour Before Daylight* is the only agrarian treatise written by a president. Carter admired Harry Truman, perhaps the most middle-class man

119

to ever hold the office. Both men reflected positively on Southern heroes, their Southern homes, and their Confederate ancestors. But unlike Truman, Carter was never a political thug who would sink to purchasing votes for power. He was probably too nice for Washington. That should be a badge of honor. Truman would kneecap his opponent and then lie about it. Carter refused to get in the gutter.

Certainly, Carter had his problems as president, but most of this involved perception not policy. Carter can be credited with beginning the deregulation of the Ronald Reagan era and with installing Paul Volcker as Federal Reserve chairman, a move that helped end the destructive inflation of the 1970s. He also pushed for American energy independence long before it was trendy. Carter's record on taxation and foreign policy are mixed at best, and no one would credit him with doing anything to end the Cold War, but he was as interested in negotiation and diplomacy as Reagan but without a willing partner in Moscow. Carter's insistence that people put on a sweater when it was cold and turn down the thermostat rubbed the consumerist American culture the wrong way, but that was the Southern man in him. "Environmentalism" was in fact just a Northern distortion of Southern agrarian. Carter could eloquently discuss Civil Rights and race because unlike most men who lived at Pennsylvania Ave., he had been around African-Americans his entire life. He was a reconciliationist in Washington, something most ideologues could not and cannot understand.

Family remained important to Jimmy Carter and his brother Billy shared the public eye, perhaps often stealing the show. Billy drove a tow truck, smoked and drank a lot of beer, and waxed philosophic about life at his gas station. He was even less of a politician than Jimmy and that's saying something. Billy was as unfiltered as the cigarettes he smoked. Jimmy Carter dedicated an entire chapter to the Carter lineage in his *An Hour Before Daylight*. Southerners would understand. It's not what you do but where you're from and who was your grandaddy.

Carter smiled and made poor public speeches. It was Carter who first "felt your pain." Bill Clinton just made it more famous. When Reagan gave the opening remarks at the ribbon cutting for Carter's Presidential Library, it seemed as if the clouds parted and the heaven's opened. Carter strode to the podium when Reagan finished and humbly remarked, "That's why you won in November 1980, and I lost."

It's fitting that Carter never profited from his time as president. His books don't sell much. He scribbles, paints, and makes furniture, teaches a bi-monthly Sunday school class, works with charity and humanitarian organizations, and walks around town with Rosalynn. They have been married for seventy-two years, and she is as Southern as Jimmy. Their house is unremarkable, and his "museum" is nothing more than the former Plains public school. He flies coach and the American taxpayer spends less on Carter's retirement than any other living president. Carter is just another citizen of his hometown, just as Jefferson became just another citizen of Charlottesville.

People often remark that no one cares what Jimmy Carter thinks when he is asked to comment on current events. He is castigated by those on the "right," and generally ignored by those on the "left." His loser image in his most enduring legacy. Perhaps that's fitting. After all, the South has been tarred with the "loser" moniker since 1865. Carter as a man is too good for the swamp, just as the Southern people are too good for the rest of America. Carter may not have always been right in D.C., but he was always Southern, and that more than anything else is why the rest of America couldn't and still can't understand him and why the South still deserves him.

WASHINGTON VS. LINCOLN

ABRAHAM LINCOLN AND George Washington stare silently at one another across the reflecting pool on the National Mall in Washington D.C., their paths inextricably linked by the historians who consider both to be the greatest presidents in American history.

One is a monument, a testament to the man and his influence on American history, the other a memorial to the Lincoln legacy, a persistent reminder of the new United States.

Washington was at one time the symbol of America. Even twenty years after his death, Americans painted their mantles black in mourning for the indispensable man, and many American families hung portraits of both George and Martha Washington in their homes.

Lincoln became a messianic figure, the martyr in a cause to forge a new nation based on the proposition that all men are created equal in an indissoluble union.

"Honest" Abe supplanted Honest George as the quintessential American, and thus two American symbols had been born. One represented the original American order, the other a new America; one conservative and rational, the other revolutionary; one built on the refined ancient constitutions and customs of Western Civilization, the other in a rough-hewn world of log cabins, dirty jokes, foul language, and shifting political sands.

While the monuments of each man may serve as pseudo sentinels guarding the United States Capitol building, America and its legacy cannot be both Washington's and Lincoln's. It may seem that both men had much in common, but they, and the symbolic America they represent, are in fact incompatible.

Washington represented the cavalier elite of early American society. He was reared as a gentleman. He was refined, an excellent conversationalist who knew how to dance and flirt properly with women. His father and grandfathers had acquired large Virginia estates, and though they were considered to be middling plantation owners, Washington eventually befriended members of the Fairfax family, the wealthiest landowners in Virginia.

Lincoln was born to a shiftless farmer who lost most of his landholdings due to poor claims, and who preferred to pull up stakes rather than plant roots in one area. Lincoln grew up in the wilderness around rough men and women. He never had any social graces and clumsily interacted with the opposite sex. Lincoln was never reputed to be a fine dancer.

Both men were physically imposing and stood near 6'4". Reportedly, Lincoln wrestled and split logs, but he never learned how to defend himself in individual combat. Albert Taylor Bledsoe had to teach him how to use a broadsword when Lincoln was challenged to a duel, and his career as a soldier lasted only a few months during the Black Hawk War. Lincoln did not see any action.

Washington hunted and soldiered. He was the best athlete in Virginia, a master horseman, and a real war hero who saved his men from annihilation in 1755 at the Battle of Monongahela, led the American States to their independence in 1783, and was called out of retirement in 1798 to lead American forces against the French in a war that never materialized.

Washington avoided political life by resigning from every political post after the American War for Independence. He could have been president for life, an elected king, but instead chose to retire to Mount Vernon to be a planter and spend time with his family. Washington never campaigned for an office. He was important because of who he was as a man, because of his character. Washington was the greatest man in America before he became president.

Lincoln became a lawyer, represented big business against the little man, consistently sought office, and molded his public statements to gain maximum political effect. Lincoln was important because he was elected to office. He would be forgotten to history if not for the general government in Washington D.C.

Washington faced a "rebellion" on the frontier, and while he eventually agreed to send troops into Western Pennsylvania (at the insistence of Alexander Hamilton), he spent nearly two years exhausting all other means to reach a settlement on the issue. Washington tolerated dissent. He looked the other way when John Jay was burned in effigy and the press excoriated him for supporting the awful Jay's Treaty with Great Britain in 1794. Even the Whiskey Rebels were treated with kid gloves. The press and elections both remained free.

Lincoln faced an open crisis as president and marched hundreds of thousands of troops into the Southern States to put down a "rebellion" when other options were available. He could have chosen peace but chose war and never negotiated or sought compromise with those who opposed his administration. He rounded up dissenters, shut down newspapers, and barred free elections.

Washington's Union tolerated differences between the Northern and Southern States, and even Washington himself appealed to their common interests in maintaining a common bond.

Lincoln's Union forced the will of one section on the other, and his Republican Party openly admitted theirs was a crusade to "forge a new Union" and remake America.

Washington held the Union together through his statesmanship. Lincoln held it together by the bayonet. Washington accepted self-determination. Lincoln waged a war against it.

Lincoln was described as a "gorilla," "a first rate second rate man," "an ordinary Western man," a "fool," "weak," and a man of inferior character.

Washington was "First in war, first in peace, and first in the hearts of his countrymen," the "Father of His Country."

Lincoln inherited a federal republic and created a myth of national supremacy. Washington never pretended to be anything but the president of a federal republic.

The chasm between Washington and Lincoln is larger than the reflecting pool or one spot in a historical presidential ranking.

Lincoln has become America and America is worse for it.

Reconsidering William Henry Harrison

WHO WAS THE GREATEST president in American history? Ask this question to a group of people who are cynical of the imperial presidency and at least one person will answer William Henry Harrison, the man who died one month after taking office.

Who could be better than a president who impacted the office in such a minimal way and who had little time to destroy the Constitution?

This response is designed to draw a few laughs, but is there some actual merit to the idea that Harrison was a great president?

He didn't do much while in office, but perhaps that was his intent from the beginning. After all, Harrison was from old Virginian stock and was born before the American War for Independence began. He was sixty-eight when he took the oath of office in 1841.

His father, Benjamin Harrison V, signed the Declaration of Independence, and Harrisons held prominent positions in Virginia society for generations. William Henry Harrison eventually made his way to the frontier as an Indian fighter and military governor and became a national hero during the War of 1812, but it was Virginia, not Indiana, that determined his political outlook.

Harrison made one political speech as president, his Inaugural Address, the longest in history at over 8,000 words. Much of it was dedicated to emphasizing the strictly limited role of the executive branch in American government and to extolling the benefits of a real union, one not burdened by excessive partisanship or sectionalism.

Harrison believed that the presidency should be limited to one term in order to curb the potential for executive abuse. He warned against the drift toward executive government and promised to arrest that progression while in office. More importantly, Harrison chastised those who considered the president to be "legislator in chief."

I can not conceive that by a fair construction any or either of its provisions would be found to constitute the President a part of the legislative power.... In the language of the Constitution, "all the legislative powers" which it grants "are vested in the Congress of the United States." It would be a solecism in language to say that any portion of these is not included in the whole.

As for the veto, Harrison argued it should only be used in three circumstances: to protect the Constitution from misconstruction, to protect the people from "hasty" or unwise legislation, and to protect political minorities from "combinations." In other words, Harrison could find no evidence that the veto should be used as a legislative hammer to bend the Congress to the will of the executive. This would be news to men like Franklin Roosevelt who used the veto power more than anyone else to push his legislative agenda through Congress.

Harrison also warned against the cultural imperialism that seemed to be festering in 1830s New England. "Experience," he said, "has abundantly taught us that the agitation by citizens of one part of the Union of a subject not confided to the General Government, but exclusively under the guardianship of the local authorities, is productive of no other consequences than bitterness, alienation, discord, and injury to the very cause which is intended to be advanced." He predicted that excessive meddling by one State in the internal affairs of another would result in "the certain harbingers of disunion, violence, and civil war, and the ultimate destruction of our free institutions." John C. Calhoun would say the same thing less than a decade later.

New England sectionalism disguised as "nationalism" proved to be the sharpest thorn in the American political order, and to Harrison, "The spirit of liberty is the sovereign balm for every injury which our institutions may receive." Only in this way could "the weaker feeling of the mistaken enthusiast... be corrected, the Utopian dreams of the scheming politician dissipated, and the complicated intrigues of the demagogue rendered harmless."

Democracy provided cover for American demagogues. This American civic religion, an attachment to "popular" rule, was "the old trick of those who would usurp the government of their country. In the name of democracy they speak, warning the people against the influence of wealth and the danger of aristocracy." Like Washington, Harrison argued that factions, the party spirit, would always "result in a dangerous accession to the executive power introduced and established amidst unusual professions of devotion to democracy." American kings would be made by American democracy. In this, Harrison has been proven prophetic.

Harrison referred to Jefferson four times in his Inaugural Address, and Madison once. He never mentioned Hamilton or Washington, though his speech reflected much of what Washington wrote in his 1796 Farewell Address. This is telling. Members of the Whig Party are often described as the heirs of Hamilton not Jefferson, but neither Harrison nor John Tyler, who assumed office after Harrison died in 1841, could be classified as Hamiltonians. They were men of Virginia dedicated to a Virginian view of government, Whigs in the truest sense of the term. They opposed unconstitutional executive power and like Jefferson favored the strict limitations of real American federalism on the central authority. They believed in a union that benefited and burdened all equally. Harrison reaffirmed this position when he insisted:

> It is union that we want, not of a party for the sake of that party, but a union of the whole country for the sake of the whole country, for the defense of its interests and its honor against foreign aggression, for the defense of those principles for which our ancestors so gloriously contended.

Not many American presidents articulated a better definition of union or showed the same type of dedication to executive restraint. Harrison's Inaugural Address should be classified as one of the great political speeches in American history. His spirit of moderation and peace won't register with the American monarchists who typically rank American presidents. Harrison should not simply be a punch line for the "best president in American history" because he died in office. No. If other presidents can be classified as a "great" president because of a few idealistic speeches, Harrison's refreshing understanding of American federalism and the Constitution should place him among the top ten in American history. This won't happen, but here's to Tippecanoe!

SECTION THREE
SECESSION

Taylor and Jefferson on Secession

ONE OF THE MOST enduring myths of American history centers on the "compact theory" of the Constitution. According to the standard interpretation, Thomas Jefferson and his fellow Republicans invented the "theory" to challenge Federalist control of the general government in the 1790s.

This implies that Jefferson and the other Republicans acted in bad faith by playing fast and loose with the history of the Constitution in a partisan hatchet job design to gain power. Simply put, they lied.

History does not support this position.

Jefferson certainly enjoyed political roughhousing, and he could be petty, but he was always a committed federalist—not Federalist—who understood the original intent of the Constitution better than most.

This led him to view the Union as it was established in 1776, a general government for commerce and defense where all other issues were left to the States. Both the framers of the Constitution and the men who ratified it sold the document on this very promise. The States would not be abolished and would have virtually the same powers they enjoyed under the Articles of Confederation. The Constitution, then, was a compact "between the States so ratifying the same" as Article VII clearly stated. This was a fact, not a theory.

The founding generation believed that real federalism and the compact fact of the Constitution would minimize conflict between discordant sections.

The Union may have worked well if the general government adhered to the terms of the agreement, but by the 1790s, it was clear that the Federalists, particularly those in New England, desired a "national" government in order to control the political spoils. There was just one problem. The Constitution did not create a "national" government. That prospect was explicitly rejected at both the

Philadelphia Convention and in the State ratifying conventions. Why? Because no one thought it would be beneficial for one section to control the fortunes of another. Why should Massachusetts be governed by Virginia and vice versa?

Jefferson knew it as did John Taylor of Caroline, the leading political thinker of his day. Neither man considered Federalist rule to be advantageous for the Union or the South, particularly Virginia, Jefferson's "country."

In June 1798, Taylor wrote a friend that he believed the Union was on the verge of dissolution, a "scission" as Taylor called it. Jefferson was shown the letter and he quickly scribbled a reply. This is perhaps one of his most important letters for it was written just five months before he penned the Kentucky Resolutions in reaction to the Alien and Sedition Acts.

Jefferson agreed that Virginia was under the yoke of Massachusetts, and

> *that they ride us very hard, cruelly insulting our feelings as well as exhausting our strength and substance. their natural friends, the three other Eastern states, join them from a sort of family pride, and they have the art to divide certain other parts of the Union, so as to make use of them to govern the whole.*

This led in Jefferson's mind to an unnatural political problem in America, for he thought that,

> *the body of our countrymen is substantially republican through every part of the union. it was the irresistable influence & popularity of Genl. Washington played off by the cunning of Hamilton which turned the government over to antirepublican hands, or turned the republican members chosen by the people into anti-republicans. he delivered it over to his successor in this state, and very untoward events since, improved with great artifice, have produced on the public mind the impression we see.*

Jefferson claimed this would soon be rectified by the voting public. They would only suffer so long under the heel of these petty tyrants, and he insisted that a "scission" of the Union would do little to arrest the problems of political division, what Jefferson considered to be a natural occurrence in a "deliberating" society. If New England were removed from the Union, Jefferson argued that a division between Virginia and Pennsylvania would soon rise and that would be met by another round of division until the entire Union would be torn asunder for even the Southern States would feel the sting of partisanship and division. He therefore concluded that:

I had rather keep our New-England associates for that purpose, than to see our bickerings transferred to others. they are circumscribed within such narrow limits, & their population so full, that their numbers will ever be the minority, and they are marked, like the Jews, with such a peculiarity of character, as to constitute from that circumstance the natural division of our parties. a little patience and we shall see the reign of witches pass over, their spells dissolve, and the people recovering their true sight, restore their government to it's true principles.

Taylor did not share Jefferson's rosy prognostication of a future in which New England would be checked by simply voting better. His letter in response serves as a powerful rebuttal to the idea that the "compact theory" arose as a product pure political partisanship. To Taylor, the real divisions between New England and the rest of the United States gave him pause as to the future prospects, and more importantly the benefits, of the Union.

Taylor considered the partisanship of New England to be a byproduct of both geography and "interest," and unlike Jefferson he did not think that party divisions were natural occurrences. He cited Connecticut as an example of a fairly unanimous electorate and thought that the rigid—almost religious—belief in "checks and balances" failed to fully arrest the sword of despotism in the United States. In other words, the Constitution was doomed from the beginning.

Taylor told Jefferson "that the perfection, and not the scission of the union, was the object of the letter you refer to...." This spirit of Union mirrored what John C. Calhoun said about secession and Union. Calhoun always insisted he favored the Union, but only if it could maintain liberty. Taylor declared the same sentiment, for in his mind, liberty had to be the direct end of government and if the Union failed to protect liberty, then it was a worthless bond of oppression.

The question became how to fix it. He proposed four changes aimed at reducing the influence of "artful" corruption in American politics: expanded suffrage, annual elections, annual tax laws—meaning that all taxes had to be passed annually—and an improved mode of checking bad legislation. His proposals sounded much like New England criticisms of the Constitution in 1788 (Massachusetts bristled at a lack of annual elections) or Virginia's headlong rush to universal suffrage in the 1820s, but regardless, Taylor was attempting to right what he considered to be structural deficiencies in the document.

Most important, however, was his belief that the only entities powerful enough to check the center were the States. In Taylor's view, the "right" of the States to "expound the constitution" made them the natural repositories of liberty. But if that didn't work, Taylor suggested, *"the people in state conventions, are incontrovertibly the contracting parties,* and possessing the impinging rights, may proceed by orderly steps to attain the object [emphasis added]." That sounds like the "compact fact" of the Constitution.

Of course, the retarding agent in all of this was unchecked taxation from the center, a problem that Taylor considered to be the heart of the nationalist takeover of the general government:

> *Taxes are the subsistence of party. As the miasma of marshes contaminate the human body, those of taxes corrupt and putrify the body politic. Taxation transfers wealth from a mass to a selection. It destroys the political Equality, which alone can save liberty; and yet no constitution, whilst devising checks upon power, has devised checks sufficiently strong upon the means which create it. Government, endowed with a right to transfer, bestow, and monopolise wealth in perpetuity is in fact, unlimited. It soon becomes a feudal lord over a nation in villenage.*

Taylor's conclusion should give anyone pause. While written in 1798, it makes the modern effort to suppress civil liberties that much more nefarious, for Taylor predicted our current state of affairs:

But since government is getting [sic] into the habit of peeping into private letters, and is manufacturing a law, which may even make it criminal to pray to God for better times, I shall be careful not to repeat so dangerous a liberty.—I hope it may not be criminal to add a supplication [sic] for an individual—not—for I will be cautious—as a republican, but as a man.

All told, Jefferson's advice to vote better has been steamrolled by Taylor's more reasoned arguments in favor of real federalism and liberty. This makes the agrarian Taylor, the true embodiment of "Jeffersonian" republicans, the real prophet without honor. If only we had listened.

Conventions: The Voice of the People

WITH THE RECENT interest in the 10th Amendment and the idea of nullification, the question of how to pull it off is often asked. The Constitution contains no explicit language detailing how a nullification effort would or should work. The 10th Amendment has no enforcement mechanism. The founding generation openly discussed *what* would be considered unconstitutional federal legislation but not *how* to oppose such legislation. Some members of that generation mentioned the federal courts; Patrick Henry, for example, said during the Virginia Ratifying Convention that he hoped the federal court system would be used as a backstop for an out of control general government. Not everyone was convinced.

But this presentation is not focused on the compact fact of the Constitution, varying interpretations of the document, or the ratifying debates. It is concerned with one lost component of nullification and the nature in which the Constitution was conceived and ratified, that is the purely American model of a convention.

As other speakers have noted or will note, nullification is a broad term and can be applied in various ways. I was perusing Edmund Morgan's *Stamp Act Crisis*, published in 1953 the other morning and noticed a chapter entitled: Nullification. This is a lost story of the period leading to the American War for Independence. The Suffolk Resolves clearly advocated a position of nullification in regard to external taxation, and the judicial model of Virginia allowed local courts to essentially nullify decisions they did not believe to be constitutional that cascaded from the courts in Richmond. Nullification, then, was born in the American constitutional crisis that became independence in 1776. During the Stamp Act crisis, many colonies simply refused to issue the stamps, while the assembly of Rhode Island passed a law protecting judges who refused to comply with provisions of the law.

The historian Jack Greene has in my mind conclusively proven that the American War for Independence was nothing more than a conflict over the nature of central power and the relationship between the Parliament in London and the colonial legislatures in North America. Morgan also nicely outlined this by expanding on the political ideology of Francis Bernard, Royal Governor of Massachusetts in the period leading to the infamous Stamp Act of 1765.

Bernard believed that power was far too decentralized in the colonies and pushed for tighter Parliamentary control of local government—as did most British officials, including the great William Pitt. He also conceded that unless the colonists were represented in Parliament, they should have some control over local matters. This in fact was the custom and precedent that had been established by the years of Salutary Neglect. American colonists would often concede that Parliament had power to regulate international trade and provide for the common defense of the colonies but all other issues, meaning internal trade, monetary policy, and taxing, would be left to the local assemblies. Bernard also understood that the people of Rhode Island and Massachusetts were different and could not be lumped together in any reasonable way culturally, but nevertheless, he thought that consolidation was the only way to improve factional, divisive, and inefficient government in the North American colonies.

This should sound familiar. I provide this brief narrative to illustrate the nullification was not fabricated out of thin air in 1798 by Jefferson and Madison but had been the preferred method of resistance to unconstitutional acts *before* the establishment of the United States central government. In fact, the federal model adopted by the founding generation was intended to mirror that which the colonists lived under in the nearly two hundred years of English then British colonial rule. The general government would be responsible for the common defense and general welfare of the Union, meaning the establishment of a free trade zone in North America and the regulation of international trade, while the States would handle all other issues. This is how the Constitution was sold to the States during ratification in 1787 and 1788. The evidence is clearly all on our side.

But what about conventions? The colonies sent delegates to several "congresses" during the prelude to the American War for Independence. The Albany Congress of 1754, the Stamp Act Congress of 1765 and the Continental Congress of 1775 are all examples of such gatherings. They were not called "conventions" but they had the same legal status. These "congresses" were not legally authorized by the British Crown and had no *de jure* legislative authority, but they had the legitimacy of the people of the colonies. The delegates to each congress were "ambassadors" of their colonies—that is what John Adams called them—and were given instructions on how to proceed from their respective legislatures. The delegates to the Stamp Act Congress were chosen by the colonial legislatures themselves and were not directly elected by the people of each colony. That makes them different from a convention but their extra-legal status and charge to deal with one issue directly gave the meeting an added air of authority and legitimacy. This was an issue too large to deal with in the regular political channels and thus required a special meeting to asses a response to the crisis. In other words, it was officially "extra-legal" but carried the weight of a legal body due to its status conferred by the legal assembly.

I want to quickly discuss this term "legitimacy." This is an important concept in government. How do we define legitimacy and who has it are two of the most important philosophical debates in modern society? In the American model, the people confer legitimacy. This is most often accomplished through traditional annual, biannual, or quadrennial elections, but it can also be manifested through the popular convention of elected delegates, the true "voice of the people." Should such an election and convention occur, the results of such a convention are considered the legally legitimate and thus supersede all other legislation on the matter within the confines of that State.

Nullification was unnecessary during the time the Articles of Confederation served as the official governing document for the United States. The Congress did not pass "laws" but "resolutions" and the States could simply refuse to comply with these "resolutions." This happened less often than the modern historical profession would have you believe, and as Patrick Henry pointed out, the Union did well in its war against Great Britain and generally complied with requests for money and troops. Several States had efficient governments that thoroughly protected the civil liberties of its constituents. Virginia is a nice example. Its "anti-democratic" structure nevertheless allowed for greater personal liberty than States with much more thoroughly democratic institutions, such as South Carolina. But that is a topic for another conference.

With the ratification of the Constitution in 1788, nullification would again become a popular mode for resistance to unconstitutional federal edicts. Oliver Ellsworth of Connecticut informed his ratifying convention that States could not be coerced in their "political capacity," meaning that according to the proponents of the Constitution, the States had sovereign immunity and ultimately final say in any constitutional question. That was the purpose of the 10th Amendment, for the majority of the ratifying conventions did not trust the promises of men who had been well known nationalists in the period leading to ratification and thus wanted to ensure that the way the Constitution was sold and ratified would be the accepted interpretation of the document when put into effect.

But the way this new Constitution was written and ratified is the most important part of the story for my purposes today. The Constitution was hammered out by 55 delegates from 12 States in a convention that met in Philadelphia in 1787. These delegates were chosen by the State legislatures and as per the Articles of Confederation were operating outside of the legal authority of the United States government. The Annapolis Convention of 1786, which was attended by delegates from five States, including Hamilton, Madison, Tench Coxe, John Dickinson, and St. George Tucker, was elected in the same manner but did not have a quorum to conduct business. But had delegates from enough States shown up, it would have had the same legal weight as the Philadelphia Convention of 1787. The Philadelphia Convention proposed a new Constitution, but it was a worthless scrap of parchment until 9 States through conventions ratified it. Not much has changed. The political class and the general government still consider it to be a worthless scrap of parchment.

The Philadelphia Convention spawned the 13 ratifying conventions that eventually gave the Constitution its life and validity as Madison put it. These conventions were elected by the people at large in districts for the sole purpose of debating the merits of the new constitution. They could accept or reject the document and thus it proves that the people of the States, not the "one American people," had full control over the destiny of the United States central government. As John Taylor once wrote believing that a Constitution by or for the "American people" is like believing in a Utopia for Utopians.

The historian Pauline Maier wrote the most detailed discussion of the ratification process. Her work, entitled *Ratification: The People Debate the Constitution* has several problems, not the least of which is her complete disregard for the importance the founding generation placed on the maintenance of State powers and by default real federalism, but she did highlight how the ratifying conventions and subsequent ratifying debates were the fullest expression of popular legitimacy in American history to that point. These conventions had more power than the State legislatures. That was by design. If these conventions rejected the Constitution, as North Carolina did in its first ratifying convention, it would not legally bound to the new central authority. Rhode Island did not call a convention until 1790 and thus remained a virtual independent republic until it rejoined the Union following its ratification convention. The framers in Philadelphia knew that the Articles of Confederation required unanimous consent of the 13 States to alter the document. Article VII of the Constitution only required nine States in convention to make it valid. Conventions served as a popular extra-legal method to skirt the requirements of the existing governing document for the United States. This set an important precedent. These ratifying conventions in essence nullified the Articles of Confederation without the consent of the State legislatures and erected a new central authority in clear violation of the current governing document for the United States.

In other words, these conventions had legitimacy. All conventions do. This is also why the Constitution allows for a convention method for altering the Constitution. A convention of the States could render the Constitution a dead letter, scrap it, or change it. It could abolish the executive branch or the judicial branch (hosanna in the highest) or alter the powers of any branch of government. This convention could also abolish the Constitution.

Moving forward in American history, we see that conventions were the preferred method to address difficult political questions in all the States. Conventions were called to amend or write new State constitutions. They were also used in relation to the principle of nullification.

This is unfortunately the lost history of nullification. The first instance of the convention method in relation to nullification took place in 1814 in Hartford Connecticut. There, delegates from five states, MA, CT, RI, VT, NH, met to discuss action against the "unconstitutional" acts of the central government. They were elected by the state legislatures and carried "extra-legal" weight. Proceedings were secret and there are few records, but in addition to nullification and amendments, these delegates also debated the possibility of New England secession (if only that had happened—we should be all over this and continuously advocating it today—why should we leave?—they are the abnormality). Daniel Webster had insisted in 1812 that it was the duty of the States to stand between the people and unconstitutional acts of the general government. The proposed amendments to the Constitution clearly show the sectional conflict was more than a debate over the merits and humanity of slavery. For example, they wanted rotating executives with singular terms, the removal of the three-fifths compromise, and a 2/3 majority for admitting new states to the Union. This was the voice of the New England people in 1814-15.

Fast forward almost twenty years to South Carolina. In 1832, the State legislature called for a convention to address the tariff controversy. In this case, the delegates were elected by the people of the State in districts and these delegates were charged with deciding the method of resistance to what was perceived to be an unconstitutional federal law. South Carolina issued an Ordinance of Nullification on 24 November 1832 which expressly stated the move was made by "the people of the States of South Carolina" in convention assembled. When the general government finally reduced the tariff but passed an unconstitutional force bill, the convention reconvened, rescinded its ordinance of nullification in regard to the tariff but then issued another ordinance that nullified the force bill. They then adjourned. Nullification had the desired effect. The tariff was reduced, and no bloodshed came of the event, though it was predicted.

Daniel Webster of course switched sides in the debate and ended up becoming an American nationalist because it now suited NE to do so, but this does diminish the role of the convention in the nullification process.

It also must be emphasized that it was the convention process that led to the secession of the Southern states in 1860-61. These conventions were elected by the people of each Southern State and voted for secession in numbers larger than that which supported the Am. War for Independence in 1775/1776. A convention was also called to meet in Washington D.C. in 1861 with the express objective of coming up with peace proposals that would be acceptable to all states and sections. 21 States were represented at this "convention" and it had extra legal authority to make proposals to the States. There is nothing in the Constitution that authorized this meeting, but at any time the people of the States can use the convention method to make recommendations at the very least.

This brings us to the current push for nullification efforts across the United States. How could the convention be used to further the call for greater restrictions on federal overreach? There are only seven states that do not have language in their respective constitutions authorizing conventions: AZ, AR, IN, MS, NJ, TX, VT. Some states have specific language in place that details about elections and parameters of the conventions while others have brief, vague language. But this does not matter. As history has shown, any state legislature can call a convention for any reason and charge it with a singular or multiple objective. Whether these delegates are chosen by the people at large or by the State legislature is up to the State, but typically those that have been led by the people at large are better representative of the voice of the people than those chosen by the state legislature.

Unfortunately, this history has been lost and the apathy that saturates the American polity would make calling a convention difficult. We are fighting a long war that requires tremendous education efforts, both for the people at large, and our representatives in government. Most people don't even understand how a convention would work or the important history they played in the formation of the American Union and of efforts to beat back unconstitutional government. We think we are hamstrung by phony rules that do not apply to the convention process, the voice of the people. But this should not deter us. If we truly believe in a government of the people, by the people, and for the people, then conventions are the only mechanism available that can truly be called the voice of the people. They are not a Utopian fallacy but a practical and workable extra-legal method to deal with major political questions. The Union was created by convention; it can be amended or destroyed by a convention; and it can also be sheared of its unconstitutional acts by convention.

Perhaps that is why no one in the political class talks about conventions any longer. They have often feared the "voice of the people." Even our modern political conventions are rigged. Just ask Bernie Sanders. That alone should be enough to prod people in a different direction. We have history on our side and real examples of change. It is now up to us to make this method known.

Is Secession Treason?

A REVIEW OF *With Malice Toward Some: Treason and Loyalty in the Civil War Era* by William A. Blair (University of North Carolina Press, 2014) and *Secession on Trial: The Treason Prosecution of Jefferson Davis* by Cynthia Nicoletti (Cambridge University Press, 2017).

Was the act of secession in 1860-61 treason? This is one of the more important and lasting questions of the War. If so, then the lenient treatment of Confederate officers, political figures, and even the soldiers themselves following the War was a great gesture of magnanimity by a conquering foe never seen in the annals of Western Civilization. If not, then the entire War was an illegal and unconstitutional invasion of a foreign government with the express objective of maintaining a political community by force, an act that represented the antithesis of the American belief in self-government regardless of Abraham Lincoln's professed admiration for government "of the people, by the people, and for the people."

Until recently, the modern academy has not given the topic much scholarly attention. Post war discussions of secession and treason were best addressed in what is now classified as "Lost Cause Mythology." Historians regularly cast aside works by Albert Taylor Bledsoe, Jefferson Davis, and Alexander H. Stephens as examples of special pleading written by sore losers determined on refocusing the narrative away from slavery. Most mainstream historical literature considered it a foregone conclusion that the War was a "righteous cause" to forge a new union, as many of the Radical Republicans professed during Reconstruction. The South had been defeated, its leaders were on the "wrong side of history," and secession, while not necessarily classified as "treason," was forever buried as an illegal and inexpedient over-reaction to a Lincolnian bogeyman.

But as historians William Blair and Cynthia Nicoletti illustrate, during the War and its immediate aftermath, these questions were far from settled. And in 2018, with the charge of treason being leveled against anything Confederate in popular culture, finding a historical understanding of the subject has become a pressing need.

Did Northerners consider Confederate citizens to be traitors? Blair argues that during the War the answer was a resounding yes, though his confidence waivers when discussing the sentiment of Northern Democrats, many of whom regarded the War as an unconstitutional invasion of a separate government and the bastardization of American principles. Blair documents both the strategy and tactics by the Lincoln administration and the Northern public at large to combat "treason" in the North and occupied South. He concludes that Lincoln violated the Constitution, though he considers the offenses minor and necessary to preserve order, argues that the United States military went too far on several occasions regarding treatment of Southern civilians, and does not understand why troops were deployed to Northern polling places during the War. The abuse of civil liberties was palpable.

But by 1868, Blair suggests that the "traitor coin" turned up heads. Northerners discarded their acrimony for reconciliation, though in the early twentieth century some began dusting off what can properly be labeled the "righteous cause myth," my words not Blair's. Union veterans and their descendants bristled at the universal acceptance of Confederate leaders and soldiers as "American" heroes. Were they not sill traitors? Most of the American public didn't seem to think so, and with good reason. They weren't, at least regarding a legal understanding of treason. It seemed Bledsoe, Davis, and Stephens had won the legal argument and perhaps even the "hearts and minds" of the American public. Even Republicans Teddy Roosevelt, William H. Taft, Warren Harding, and Calvin Coolidge buried the Party's longstanding tradition of anti-Confederate sentiment and embraced the former Confederacy as part of the American tradition.

Nicoletti's treatment of the potential Jefferson Davis treason trial underscores Blair's position on postbellum Northern sentiment. Nicoletti has written the first comprehensive study on Davis's incarceration, the details of his impending trial including fine profiles of the legal teams both for the defense and the prosecution, and Northern public reaction to the issue. Some of her arguments buttress long held assumptions concerning why the trial was never held—most importantly the prosecution was unsure if they could secure a conviction—while others favor the modern establishment agreement on secession and the War that followed, i.e. it was all about slavery and "white supremacy," and that the Supreme Court finally "settled" the issue in the 1869 decision of *Texas v. White*. It didn't. This is unfortunate because she missed an outstanding opportunity to reshape both the public perception of secession and the historical "consensus" on postbellum American thought.

Nicoletti, in fact, explains why she feared writing this book and why she went out of her way to "show" she despised the South and the "Lost Cause:" she wants a job and tenure. That speaks volumes about the historical profession. Historical inquiry, even on sensitive and "controversial" topics should produce accolades, not resentment or punishment, but the gatekeepers of acceptable opinion do not reward independent thinkers who tackle topics that may point to conclusions they wish to avoid. The Davis case showcased some of the best elements of Northern society, and Northern reaction to his release and the resulting silence on the treason question is one of the more fascinating episodes of American history. How could a section that just waged four years of bloody war against another people cheer when the leader of that effort was released from prison? And how could men who denounced the Confederacy pool money to free one of its most conspicuous symbols? Simple. The majority of the Northern people considered Davis to be an American, the Confederacy to be American, and the Confederate cause to be worthy of respect. The same cannot be said for modern American society, which is why studying Northern opposition to "Mr. Lincoln's War" and the postbellum response to secession are more interesting in many ways than the War itself, both North and South.

Blair argues that for most Northerners "treason" was always a political rather than legal question, a pejorative used to rally support for the men in blue and demonize those in butternut. The fact that Davis never faced trail in open court is a validation of that position, for once the issue moved from the realm of political to legal, it became unclear if Americans, both North and South, could hang a man for a "crime" that the founding generation committed in 1776. That would be un-American and nearly everyone in America in 1867 could understand that, even if a few "righteous cause" mythologists grumbled about the result and modern Monday morning quarterbacks assert that they would have hung every Southern "traitor" from the highest tree and fearfully punished the Southern people.

What these armchair generals don't realize is that the South was fearfully punished, and by blustering about retribution, they expose how truly un-American the United States has become. But one should expect no better with a modern education establishment that embraces "righteous cause mythology." Magnanimity and reconciliation are now deemed to be detrimental to the American experience while victimization, reprisal, and "justice" dominate public opinion. If the trial were held in 2018, Davis would not make it to the courtroom.

Progressive Neo-Confederates

GREETINGS FELLOW NEO-CONFEDERATES. You have been right all along. How do I know this? Hillary Clinton said so, and if the smartest woman in the world said it, then it has to be true. Of course, she did not directly call herself a "neo-Confederate," but the progressives have rediscovered federalism and by default have vindicated every evil "neo-Confederate" in America.

Clinton sent a series of tweets defending the ability of the States to protect their citizens from evil right-wing policies:

> A reality of a Supreme Court with a right-wing majority is that the states are a new important front in protecting civil rights—especially the rights of the most vulnerable among us. Winning back state legislatures is also important in this last election before the 2020 Census. State legislatures redraw congressional districts every 10 years based on those numbers, and Democratic legislative majorities can shut down gerrymandering that disenfranchises voters. State legislature races are also a great way to make an impact as an activist. The budgets and walk lists are smaller than those of congressional races, so you can move the needle with a few volunteer hours or donations.

I thought States only destroyed civil rights? Seems Clinton is undermining the entire narrative of the Left, but it wasn't so long ago when progressives used "think locally, act locally" to infiltrate and then dominate both major American political parties. It started at the bottom.

City zoning ordinances, direct democracy measures (recall, referendum, and initiative), prohibition, universal suffrage, universal healthcare, and a host of other "reform" policies originated in the States and found their greatest success there. And minorities in America are still better represented at the State and local level than in DC.

So are those who oppose the Cultural Marxists. States have been more effective than the central government in beating back the headlong rush into Leftist insanity. They have only been undermined by the Supreme Court.

With everyone jawing about a return to civility in American politics, we all should be reminded that American politics have never been civil. The solution was always federalism, the ability of the States to control their own "internal police." The Constitution would not have been ratified had any "friend" of the document promised otherwise.

The real threat to civility in America has always been nationalism. We don't need to listen to people in other States with other agendas tell us what to do. We simply need to live and let live, sweep around our own backdoor and stop thinking that every issue, no matter how small, is a "national" crisis.

Hillary Clinton and the progressives are at least rhetorically figuring this out. Their commitment would only be as lasting as their time out of power, but maybe the few clear-headed sycophants among them might listen. One can hope.

The Extreme Northern Position

IF YOU LISTEN to the modern historical profession, Southern secession in 1861 represented "treason." David Blight, Professor History at Yale University, has made this belief the part of the core of his attack on Confederate symbols. If we should not take them down because they represent "white supremacy," then they should be removed because Southerners were "traitors."

Traitors to whom or what?

Certainly, this was an open question in 1860 and 1861. Secession–political, economic, social–had been advanced by various groups since the founding. The very act of independence in 1776 was an act of secession. Secession had been an American principle and an American tale for generations.

It was not until the War that secession became synonymous with treason and even that was the extreme Northern position. Most Americans thought otherwise. How do we know this? Clearly the vast majority of the South believed that secession was legal and justified. The several State secession conventions elected to leave the Union by crushing majorities. Nearly seventy-five percent of the Southern white male population fought for independence (secession) and their enthusiasm was only trumped by Southern women who would shame the men into joining the cause.

As for the North, the Lincoln administration faced constant opposition from the opening shots of the War, and he received only fifty-five percent of the NORTHERN popular vote in 1864. His opponent, George McClellan, ran on a moderate peace platform and probably would have opened negotiation had he won the election. If you add the large minority vote in the North to the crushing support for secession in the South, the majority of American believed the Confederate States not only had *de facto* but also *de jure* independence from

1861-1865. In other words, secession happened, and it was not treason. The Southern States were independent and no longer bound by the language of the United States Constitution.

There were Northerners after the War who rushed to prosecute Southerners for treason. Only one, Henry Wirz, had his neck stretched, but that was not for treason. Every Confederate leader avoided being convicted of the charge, including Jefferson Davis. Thousands were charged with treason and faced trial in kangaroo courts as the Union army occupied the South. Union partisans in East Tennessee were particularly aggressive, but again, even where these Republican led courts found men guilty of treason, the verdicts were quickly overturned in higher courts.

Post-bellum secession took various forms until the modern era, from advocacy for regionalism, to the creation of semi-autonomous communities like the Tuskegee model advanced by Booker T. Washington. These were acts designed to embrace the American concepts of legitimacy, consent of the governed, and self-determination and were opposed to monolithic nationalism. It wasn't until the early 1990s that political secession was back on the table due in large part to the increasingly unresponsive and oppressive national centralized structure entrenched by twentieth century progressives.

The one Supreme Court decision that somewhat addressed the issue of secession, *Texas v. White* in 1869, never classified the act of secession as treason. This makes the modern insistence that secession equated treason somewhat bizarre. It exemplifies the lack of understanding the establishment historical profession has for the original Constitution and exposes the "noble dream" of objectivity. These historians, like Blight, are biased toward the extreme Northern position of the immediate post-bellum America, a position that most Americans rejected. The modern historical politically motivated objection to secession is not to facts but to interpretation.

The fact remains that the charge of "treason" has never been comprehensively accepted by the American public, even to this day. See General Kelly's statements to Laura Ingraham. The case for Confederate monuments and symbols thus becomes more pressing. Should antebellum Southerners be cast as treasonous villains in a larger Northern righteous cause mythological drama, the American principles of self-determination and consent of the governed quickly fade into oblivion. You aren't free if you can't leave. The founding generation North and South believed this, as did most Americans until 1861.

Confederate monuments and symbols represent the American political soul, not of "white supremacy," but of what William B. Travis called "the American character" in his letter from the Alamo in 1836 or what Thomas Jefferson labeled a "right" and a "duty" in the Declaration, namely to "alter or to abolish" government that does not protect life, liberty, or the pursuit of happiness. We can argue whether secession was justified in 1861–a minority of Southerners did just that (many were large slaveholders)–or if secession is a preferred course of action today, but we should never call it "treason." That is un-American.

If You Can't Blame the Confederacy, Secede!

AMERICAN POLITICAL THEATER has become the most entertaining show in town. Trump refuses to shake hands and Pelosi rips up his script.

This is red meat for the duly indoctrinated in the mainstream political parties, but in case you thought that Trump's impeachment and subsequent acquittal would calm the waters and draw the final curtain on a five-month Greek comedy, the woke lunatics and their Girondist media allies have decided the show must go on.

And who can we blame? Why the Confederacy, of course, the fly in the ointment of good American government. If it wasn't for those dastardly traitors of 1861 and their political progeny, America would be a glorious City Upon a Hill.

CNN's John Harwood seems to think something nefarious is afoot from below the Mason Dixon.

While he clearly doesn't know basic American geography or history, he certainly knows that the Confederacy is behind whatever problems ail America. How could these modern Confederates be so blind to the necessity of John Bolton's important testimony, the same John Bolton whom leftists consistently called an untrustworthy warmonger until he had some dirt on Trump? They held the right opinion of Bolton before the show required a plot twist making the enemy of their enemy their friend. Except every viewer knew the end of the story before it showed up on the small screen. These people telegraph their punches like a drunk itching for a bar fight.

But Harwood's geographic determinism thinly veils his real motivation: these Republicans who voted against his wishes are racist just like their ancestor traitors to the United States. And people wonder why Southerners still cling to the War, God, and guns.

The left won't let them forget, except if they want to pack up or demolish a few hundred statues and remove the Confederate flag from every public space in the South.

"Hey deplorable, the War is over, except when we say it isn't over."

Of course, we all know that an independent South would be a vastly different country than the United States. The late Bill Cawthon did a splendid job explaining how several years ago.

And some leftists get it. The failed impeachment process has brought these woke secessionists out of the closet.

I'm all for it. "Jesusland" would be a pretty nice place to live and would be freed from the burden of being constantly overruled by some Yankee self-righteous do-gooder. It does, however, makes you wonder if these progressives realize that Trump is a byproduct of the U.S. of Canada? Maybe all these loving people north of the border are just bombastic jerks after all. Nah. That would make them Yankees, and Yankees are supposed to be the good guys.

Several hundred thousand dead Southerners would tell a different story, but what do they know? They were the ones who had the backbone to let the North go in peace in 1861 if they just sent the bluecoats back over the Mason Dixon. They tried "Jesusland" but were blown to pieces by Lincoln's cannons. If they had their way, "kim" would already be living in a separate country.

And while the founding generation worried about the prospect of secession, very few would have wanted to go to war to prevent it. Patriots don't kill other patriots, especially those who understood that self-determination is the bedrock of the American political tradition.

So, who are the real traitors to America again?

Red States for California Secession

CALIFORNIA ATTORNEY GENERAL Xavier Becerra has given the green light for CalExit proponents to begin collecting signatures for a California secession ballot initiative in the 2018 general election.

This is good news. California is the logical place to begin having a conversation about secession, and every red state American should be actively supporting the proposal.

As California goes, so goes Oregon and Washington, and in the not so distant future perhaps Massachusetts, Connecticut, Maine, Vermont, and New Hampshire. Maybe Hawaii might finally get the chance to regain its independence.

One can dream.

What would this mean for red state America?

Imagine a world without Senators Pocahontas, Crazy Bernie, Diane Feinstein, or Kamala Harris?

Add to that list Maxine Waters, Nancy Pelosi, and even Susan Collins and the Congress becomes a much more hospitable place.

Imagine all the red state people living in peace with no Deep North or West Coast hell.

It's easy if you try.

Would the Congress be perfect? No. There would still be a host of neocons taking up space. They can be more problematic than the Democrats in regard to foreign policy, but certainly issues such as immigration, the welfare state, taxes, fiscal restraint, healthcare, abortion and a host of other hot button topics would take a decided turn in the direction of real federalism. The Senate would be split 51-31 and the House 220-126. Those are not super majorities but close.

The left would be reduced to an insignificant other in red state politics. In fact, you could envision a mass exodus of American pinkos pulling up stakes and moving to the grand west coast socialist utopia or its cousin in the Deep North.

Red state America would look a lot more like real America. Chuck Thompson quipped the North would be better off without the red states. I think it's the other way around. Heck, many Southerners might even like the United States flag again. It would be free from the stain of Yankee invasion.

The irony, of course, is that only the North could pull this off in modern America. Their "treasury of counterfeit virtue" allows them the ability to say good riddance to the hayseeds in fly over country. Always being on the "right side of history" gets you bonus points in the world of emotivist politics.

And it was the North not the South that agitated for secession first. Oliver Ellsworth and Rufus King told John Taylor of Caroline they wanted out in 1794. Taylor was shocked, but perhaps he should have asked how Virginia could help. It would have solved nearly eighty years of unnecessary conflict and kept New England from bloviating about secession in 1801, 1804, 1815, and 1848. They just never had the stones to pull it off. As usual, the South acted while New England debated.

The key word, though, is "unnecessary."

Wouldn't it be better to leave one another alone rather than trying to bully each other into submission?

We were supposed to learn that lesson in primary school (that's what it used to be called before Red Republican Carl Schurz gave us "kindergarten" and the Yankees "elementary school") or from our mothers and grandmothers. Maybe the anti-secessionists never got the memo.

Either way, decentralization is the more humane and polite thing to do. If we can't see eye to eye, a peaceful divorce is preferable to a hostile marriage.

Family court is full of these stories. Every American gets it on a personal level, so why can't it be expanded on a larger scale?

The answer is that Americans have been taught that secession is illegal and the "Civil War" solved the issue. Even the CalExit folks believe that it would require a constitutional amendment to secede.

Tell that to the founding generation, Ellsworth and King among them, who thought secession was not only moral but entirely legal and possible. Just read the Declaration of Independence.

Some suggest this would weaken security or destroy the American financial sector and ruin the economy.

News flash, the American economy is already in the tank. Federal bankruptcy is not too far in the distant future.

As for security, wouldn't it be possible for these new confederacies to work out a mutual protection pact if any were invaded by a foreign power? Red state Americans have spilled a lot of blood in wars throughout United States history, most of which did not concern their immediate wellbeing.

So red state America, here is our opportunity to rid real America from the cancer to the west and north.

The California attorney general has gotten the ball rolling. Red state America should not only push it along, it should become the most vocal CalExit cheerleaders.

Give me an S E C E S S I O N. What's that spell? Secession!

Maybe Howard Dean could finish off the cheer with a yell.

After all, Dean could become president of some northern confederation.

It could keep him. We'll keep our guns and Bibles.

And we'll wave at one another, peacefully, across the border.

LET THE BEAR FLAG GO

A LARGE PORTION of California wants to secede.

That's a good thing.

American conservatives should not only applaud the move, they should be doing everything possible to help them find the door.

Image a world without Nancy Pelosi, Maxine Waters, Diane Feinstein, or Kamala Harris; where Democrats would not start the presidential election cycle with nearly one quarter of the Electoral College votes needed to win the election; where the United States Court of Appeals for the Ninth Circuit would disappear; where every radical Leftist group could set up shop and get out of real America; where every illegal immigrant could find a home in the sanctuary State.

And that is only the beginning.

Real America could finally get its culture back without the perversions of Hollywood.

They can keep the Grammys, the Golden Globes, and the Emmys.

A divorce of incompatible things is preferable to an abusive marriage.

Adios!

Unfortunately, many mainstream American conservatives have a strange—almost pathological—aversion to the idea.

Victor Davis Hanson is one of these conservatives.

His argument against California secession goes something like this:

A. Some Californians who don't like Donald Trump want to secede.

B. Thirteen Southern States who didn't like Abraham Lincoln seceded and formed the Confederate States.

C. I think the Confederacy was bad.

D. California secession is bad.

This argument would have failed Logic 101.

Hanson has frequently bellowed that "state's rights" is an "old Confederate idea" as if it were created out of thin air in 1860 and 1861.

That isn't true.

The entire political history of the United States was built on "secession and nullification."

And it was more often the North than the South that pursued it.

When the British passed the infamous Stamp Act in 1765, several colonies *nullified* the law by simply refusing to enforce it, most famously Rhode Island which passed legislation protecting judges who let people go after violating the law.

The Suffolk Resolves of 1774 urged the people of Massachusetts to resist sending any tax revenue to the British. In other words, they were attempting to nullify the Coercive Acts.

The Declaration of Independence is a secession document. The "thirteen united States of America" seceded from the British Empire and became "Free and Independent States" like the "State of Great Britain."

The Constitution for the United States—the same Union of sovereign States that existed under the Articles of Confederation—allowed the States to secede from the Articles by acceding to the new governing document. This was expressly prohibited by the Articles.

Two members of the Philadelphia Convention which drafted the Constitution in 1787, Rufus King of Massachusetts and Oliver Ellsworth of Connecticut, told Senator John Taylor of Caroline, Virginia in 1794 that they wanted the North to secede.

Northerners again threatened secession during the contested presidential election of 1800 and again in 1803 after President Jefferson acquired Louisiana. Their leader was the former Secretary of State Timothy Pickering of Massachusetts.

The Hartford Convention of 1815 urged Northern states to nullify laws in support of the War of 1812 (several had already done so in fact but not by legislation) and insisted that if nothing changed, they would have to resort to secession. Daniel Webster, the same man who called nullification disunion in 1830, believed in it enough in 1812 that he made several speeches in support of the idea around his home district.

Several Northern States passed personal liberty laws during the 1840s and 1850s that effectively nullified the Fugitive Slave Act within their borders.

Abolitionist leader William Lloyd Garrison thundered in 1848 that the only way to rid America of the "slave power" was secession...of the North.

I'm sure all of these Yankees would have found a comfortable home in the "Old Confederacy" as Hanson calls it.

Certainly, Southerners advanced the idea more forcefully. Two Southerners, Jefferson and Madison, codified the principles of nullification in the Virginia and Kentucky Resolutions of 1798 while the people of South Carolina were ready to go to war to prevent King Andrew from collecting the tariff in 1832. And of course the South had the huevos to pull of secession in 1860-61 while for years the North just blew hot air.

That merely proves that a large portion of the American public for nearly eighty years in every State considered both nullification and secession to be as American as the cause of independence in 1776.

We call this self-determination.

Secession does not have to end in war. That is another fallacy of logic parroted by many conservatives today.

No one sent in the tanks when fourteen members of the Soviet Union seceded in 1992. Americans even cheered the development. Are we worse than the Commies?

A better question would be was Lincoln worse than Gorbachev?

There are many good people in California who would not want to be part of the socialist Bear Flag Republic. Real America would welcome them with open arms, perhaps even by coming up with some dough to relocate them here.

I'm sure there would be thousands of vacant properties after all of the pinkos, hippies, and social justice warriors head west.

While they're at it, maybe they could rope in the other blue States. A rekindling of the secession spirit in New England would go a long way to making America great again.

That may be too much to ask. For now, we should be content, and encouraging, to let the Hollywood elite go.

We'd all be better for it.

"Rational" People Now Want Secession

ACCORDING TO REPRESENTATIVE ZOE LOFGREN of California, secession is now being advocated by "rational people, not the fringe."

This is an insult to all rational people.

Rational people for generations have supported secession, including every scholar at the Abbeville Institute. But now that idiot Leftists in California, Oregon, and Washington are for it, somehow secession has become "rational."

I think George Washington, Thomas Jefferson, James Madison, Patrick Henry, James Monroe, John Rutledge, Francis Marion, Nathaniel Macon, John Taylor, John Tyler et. al. were "rational people" who favored secession. So did a host of Yankees from that great generation of men.

Robert E. Lee, Jefferson Davis, and "Stonewall" Jackson were also "rational people," more so than the "esteemed" representative from California.

How about Sam Houston and David Crockett? They seemed to be "rational."

Would she consider Yankees like Lysander Spooner, William Lloyd Garrison, Daniel Webster, and Thomas Pickering to be "rational people?" Secession worked for them, too.

Alas, this is the world in which we live, the world the Yankees made.

Once professor at UCLA grumbled that secession can't happen because a constitutional mechanism doesn't exist. He earned his degree from an "outstanding" research institution (Yale) and now is the director of The Center for American Politics and Public Policy. You see, this professor believes the issue was "settled by the Civil War." Since when has any legal issue been "settled" by war? A bully can bloody their opponent, but that never solves the issue, particularly one over legal interpretation. And the evidence is all on the side of secession.

Perhaps this is the best anyone who believes in decentralization can hope for. Once the Yankees figure out it is good idea, then we can all sit around the campfire, hold hands, sing a few songs, wish them well, and send them on their way. As Lincoln made a miraculous political discovery that the Union was "indissoluble," perhaps these modern day Lincolnians can arrive at a new discovery, that secession is, after all, legal.

That would be rational. It's something we've been saying for years. Welcome to the party. We won't fight to keep you around.

#CalExit

DONALD TRUMP WON and California wants to secede.

Mises Institute President Jeff Deist tweeted during the election: "look for the Dems to discover the virtues of secession, nullification, and states rights."

It didn't take long for leftists to realize the value of secession. Within hours of Trump's stunning victory (a victory yours truly predicted as early as February this year), social media was set ablaze by Californians wanting out. Celebrity blogger Perez Hilton posted, "we must secede!"

He was quickly egged on, with many wanting Oregon and Washington to join California in a Pacific union.

Why not? Such a confederation would have substantial economic muscle and would be able to pursue their crazy socialist and hedonistic utopia without interference from us Southern lowlifes.

Heck, we provided the blueprint, though one would hope that secession in the 21st century would be a peaceful process. Southerners wouldn't fight to keep you in.

In reality, the South should have never led the way. The Deep North should have had the honor of leaving first. They just never had the guts, though they threatened from 1794 through the 1840s.

And secession is legal. The UK *Metro* said it quite nicely when reporting the development: "there is no specific ban on state secession in the US Constitution. In fact, there's nothing on secession in there at all."

California even has a secessionist past. The short lived "Bear Flag Republic" attempted to break free of both Mexican and American grasp in 1848 at the conclusion of the Mexican War.

As America transitions to the Trump administration, it would be wise to remember that the left needs secession, too. We cannot forget our disaffected brothers and sisters who simply want to govern themselves. Tears could be turned to cheers.

Crazy as these Californians may be, who are we in the South to say you can't go your own way? I'm sure Fleetwood Mac would give them the right to use the song in their campaign.

California would be free from the stigma Southern secessionists endure. They can't be labeled racists, homophobes, Christian bigots, or hayseeds. I could think of some other terms, but unlike them, I'll play nice.

Call the convention and get the ball rolling. Give the Abbeville Institute a call if you need advice on the history and possibility of secession.

We'll show you the door. Don't let it hit you on the way out.

Ya'll don't come back now, ya' hear?

DECENTRALIZATION FOR HUMANITY'S SAKE

THE ROMAN HISTORIAN Titus Livius once called Rome "the greatest nation in the world." He wrote those words in a time of moral and political decline, and Livy was hoping by outlining the greatness of the once proud republic, the Roman people would arrest the decline and embrace the principles that had made Rome great. Livy argued that without understanding their history, the Roman people would neither be able to "endure our vices nor face the remedies needed to cure them." But Livy failed to recognize the catastrophic effect empire and expansion had on the Roman spirit. For example, by expanding north and attempting to assimilate the Germanic peoples and the Celts into Roman culture, Rome sealed its own demise. The Germans and Celts never fully embraced Rome, and those who did retained some element of their own political and cultural heritage. Romans were outnumbered by Germanic peoples in their own army, and the disintegration of the Empire seemed inevitable as the fringes of the Empire came under constant assault from groups unwilling to assimilate. There was never a Roman "nation" outside of Rome. The men, money, and material needed to build and then hold the Empire were wasted, while the vices and decadence of the ruling class in Rome wrecked the republic. The human cost of the Roman Empire was incalculable.

On a human scale, decentralization made more sense for those under the yoke of Roman domination. Constant wars against foreign peoples, heavy taxes, and alien government was for many an unfair trade for Roman laws, "stability," and "protection." Certainly, many people in Europe prospered under Roman control and the "Pax Romana," but the internal tensions and cultural sacrifices were too large of a burden for the Empire to contain. It was only a matter of time before people realized that they were better off under local control.

Studying the rise and decline of empires has long been instructive for Americans, and for decades, historians, philosophers, economists, diplomats, statesmen, and others have warned against the American Empire. Yet, rarely did those who railed against expansion focus on the human cost of the empire and the political and social marginalization that naturally follows an impersonal government. Like Rome, a demographic map from the 2000 United States Census (see below) emphasizes that an American "nation" does not exist, and it is only through the power and propaganda of the "United State" that decentralization has failed to materialize. Obviously, sections still exist and the human cost of the American empire within the 50 States appears to be significant on several levels.

First, the United States should be at minimum broken into the several cultural sections clearly defined by the map. The Northeast, or Deep North, has a cultural identity vastly different than the South. The West, most importantly the Southwest, has a cultural mix inconsistent with the rest of the United States. Richard Henry Lee, among others, recognized this in 1787 when he wrote in the *Letters From the Federal Farmer to the Republican* that, "free elective government cannot be extended over large territories [and] one government and general legislation alone, never can extend equal benefits to all parts of the United States: Different laws, customs, and opinions exist in the different states, which by a uniform system of laws would be unreasonably invaded. The United States contain about a million of square miles, and in half a century will, probably, contain ten millions of people; and from the center to the extremes is about 800 miles." The United States now covers almost 4 million square miles and around three-hundred million people. If Lee was correct in 1787, and he was, then he would surely be correct today.

Second, one of the longstanding critiques of large governments is the impersonal and ultimately tyrannical nature of powerful centralized authority. The French philosopher Baron de Montesquieu in his *The Spirit of Laws* opined that a large republic was unmanageable unless consolidated in a federal or confederated system. British philosopher David Hume, in *Idea of a Perfect Commonwealth,* argued that decentralization was the only way to ensure the greatest level of liberty. Of course, the founding generation was well aware of the arguments for decentralization set forth by the classical Greeks and those of both Enlightenment philosophers. Lee, in the same *Letters From the Federal Farmer*, followed a similar line of thinking we he suggested that the people of the States should have a means of defense against the central government. He said, "I believe the position is undeniable, that the federal government will be principally in the hands of the natural aristocracy, and the state governments principally in the hands of the democracy, the representatives in the body of the people. These representatives in Great-Britain hold the purse, and have a negative upon all laws. We must yield to circumstances, and depart something from this plan, and strike out a new medium, so as to give efficacy to the whole system, supply the wants of union, and leave the several states, or the people assembled in the state legislatures, the means of defense." In other words, Lee was arguing for the States to have a limited negative power over the central government—a "defense"—to protect the cultural, economic, and social interests of their separate communities, an action called nullification or state interposition today. It was the most democratic thing to do.

Third, most opponents of decentralization, secession, or nullification argue that minorities would be unjustly impacted should States begin to reassert their sovereignty through nullification or secession. This is dead wrong. As John C. Calhoun emphasized, nullification was used to *protect* minority interests from the tyranny of the majority. Secession followed the same pattern. Regardless, American minorities today believe that they have the greatest power in the central government, and that State and local communities, particularly in the South, would infringe on minority rights. But this position belies reality.

Data from two Southern States, Mississippi and Alabama, clearly indicates that black Americans are better represented at the State level than in the central government. There are currently two black members of the United States Senate, and blacks only comprise approximately nine percent of the United States House of Representatives. In total, blacks account for around thirteen percent of the American population, so they are vastly underrepresented in Washington D.C. Conversely, blacks hold thirty percent of the seats in the lower house of the Mississippi legislature and twenty-five percent of the seats in the upper house. In Alabama, blacks comprise twenty-three percent of both the lower and upper house. Blacks account for thirty-seven percent of the total population in Mississippi and twenty-six percent of the total population in Alabama, making representation in both States more equitable than in Washington D.C. If counties could have a negative veto over State law, minorities would have an even greater political and social impact in their own community. This would comport to Hume's ideal republic and to the nature of minority Cantons in the Swiss federation.

As Kirkpatrick Sale and Don Livingston have repeatedly emphasized, decentralization has once again entered the public discourse. Unfortunately, it is often portrayed as simply reactionary when it is, in fact, the American tradition. Selling it in an era of economic and social collapse has become easier, but the rhetorical roadblocks of racism and treason still exist. See any social media comments after someone simply presents the option. Thus, decentralization still is a hard sell, but it can be done by emphasizing that the prospect of more local control offers greater political and economic liberty and stronger protection for cultural, religious, and racial minorities. It is the future of America and the future of a free world.

The Winds of Change

THIS ISN'T 1990. The Winds of Change have stopped blowing. When the Soviets present a more docile response to self-determination than a "western democracy," the situation is bad. How painful is it to pine for the days of passive Soviet resistance to secession?

Images and videos of the jack-booted thugs bulldozing their way through crowds of peaceful voters (including firemen and unarmed police officers) in Catalonia are a distressing reminder that the heavy hand of the state is still alive and well when it comes to self-determination.

Spain went full Lincoln, quickly. At least the people of the Southern States held conventions and voted before being bludgeoned and shot.

This was probably to be expected. Donald Trump offered his encouragement for a unified Spanish government before the referendum was held, clearing a way for Spain to avoid condemnation, at least from one major ally. The court of public opinion has not been so kind.

Even before the election was held, the *New York Times* tepidly supported the referendum, as did an opinion piece at Townhall.com. Both pointed out the cultural distinctiveness of the Catalonian people. That was the real issue at hand. Can a unique people thumb their nose at what they consider to be illegitimate authority?

Obviously, Spain and the United States said no but the people said yes.

And perhaps this is indicative of more to come around the globe. There are already several secession efforts underway in the United States, and with the newly inflamed cultural war burning in the American mind, this might be the right time to talk about a divorce of incompatible things.

There are now at least two Americas and nothing is going to change that any time soon.

"Blue America" favors a "libertine" society under-girded by the "social justice" identity triplets of race, class, and gender. Mob violence and property destruction are used in conjunction with "peaceful" forms of "resistance" like anthem protests, federal court orders, gender studies, sensitivity training, and character assassination to bully people into capitulating to their desired goal, namely a society that lacks traditional western civilization. In other words, they will use any means necessary to achieve their goal to "erase bigotry," including state machinery like the courts and favorable legislation. Of course, this can work against them, too, as the results of the 2016 election made clear.

"Red America" wonders what happened. "That ain't my America," they say while pulling the lever for someone, anyone, who will talk tough and stand against this neo-Marxist nonsense. They aren't necessarily opposed to a strong central government because it can work in their favor, and they are weary from years of being made to feel guilty for traditions they admire and support. But "Red Americans" need to understand their love affair with the state can be dangerous. They are barely a majority, if at all, and once the other side is in power the repercussions will be severe.

Catalonia should be a wake-up call for both sides. Young people are already more receptive to secession than any other group in America, and their aversion to violence and a general acceptance of "divorce" could lead to more peace, rather than less. It will require Americans to rethink the Union and to re-evaluate their admiration for both President Lincoln and the mega-state he forged through blood and iron. We don't need a repeat of 1861 nor even Catalonia of 2017. East Germany of 1989 would be preferable.

You can go your own way never sounded better. Maybe shacking up in 1788 wasn't the right thing to do.

SECTION FOUR
PC LUNACY

The 1619 Project

A slightly different version of this essay was originally published in the February, 2020 issue of *Chronicles: A Magazine of American Culture.*

SEVERAL YEARS AGO, I purchased a used copy of Robert Fogel and Stanley Engerman's *Time on the Cross*, one of the five most important books on American slavery. The previous owner inserted a series of newspaper clippings of book reviews and essays written around the time the book was published in 1974. This material also included his thoughts on the subject, including a description of a Liberty Fund conference on slavery in the late 1990s. He expressed shock at the sensitive nature of the topic and was dismayed by the relative lack of civility from the panel even thirty years after the height of the Civil Rights movement. To this man, time should have allowed for greater nuance and dispassionate conversation. He failed to realize that American slavery has always been a subject of imagination and popular perception wrapped around political power. This is still the case in 2020.

The ongoing 1619 Project in the *New York Times Magazine* highlights the undeniable fact that American slavery is still a potent political issue in the twenty-first century. As the editor of the magazine Jake Silverstein wrote, "We [the project's creators] are journalists, trained to look at current events and situations and ask the question: Why is this the way it is? In the case of persistent racism and inequality that plague this country, the answer to that question led us inexorably into the past...." While no historian would question this type of motivation—indeed, many fell in love with the past because of their interest in current events—beginning with a premise and then working backward to "prove it" destroys the very nature of historical inquiry. In this case, both Silverstein and Nikole Hannah-Jones, the project's creator, operate under the assumption that slavery is still inexplicably linked to ongoing issues of race in America. In short, without slavery, American racism would not exist., and more importantly, to the contributors of the project, "white privilege" was established and sustained by a permanent victim class in American society comprised primarily of black Americans.

The goal of the project has clearly been political not historical or "educational." Modern colleges and universities teach the "truths" of the project on a regular basis. Entire departments have been founded to perpetuate race and gender studies, and these professors regularly teach American history survey courses to a supposedly unindoctrinated American public. This raises several questions. First, is the 1619 Project a novel approach to the subject of race and slavery in America, particularly in the popular imagination? Second, did slavery create American racism? Third, how unique was American slavery? And fourth, did black Americans make America a "democracy" as Hannah-Jones suggested in the opening essay to the project, and if so, is the 1619 Project little more than a thinly veiled political polemic?

Silverstein argued that, "The project was intended to address the marginalization of African-American history in the telling of our national story and examine the legacy of slavery in contemporary American life." This would imply that American pop culture has been devoid of material dedicated to race and slavery. Indeed, it assumes that Americans are unfamiliar with the issue and that there has been a veritable conspiracy to keep black American history off the pages of American history textbooks and out of the popular imagination. The 1619 Project echoes the recently developed *Teaching Hard History* by the Southern Poverty Law Center, a report designed to give educators the necessary tools to provide "an intervention in the ways that we teach and learn about the history of American slavery." Both the 1619 Project and the Southern Poverty Law Center ignore the pervasive role of slavery in popular imagination dating to the nineteenth century.

American secondary schools regularly assign Harriet Beecher Stowe's *Uncle Tom's Cabin* as the definitive treatment of American slavery. The book sold 300,000 copies in 1852 and nearly 1.5 million copies around the world by the end of the 1850s, making it the bestselling fictional work of the period. It has remained in print since 1862. There have been dozens of film and theatrical adaptations of the book, and it has inspired several artistic representations, among them a sculpture in Brussels, Belgium by Louis Samain. No work had a more dramatic and lasting effect on the perception of slavery in America than *Uncle Tom's Cabin*, particularly in the North and in Europe. To date, the book has been translated into seventy languages and was named the second most influential story in the world by 108 literary critics at the BBC in 2018.

Solomon Northrup's *12 Years a Slave*, published one year after *Uncle Tom's Cabin* and dedicated to Stowe, was made into a major motion picture in 2013 and landed an Emmy and Golden Globe for best picture and earned almost $200 million worldwide. Other dramatic representations of slavery have been financial successes at the box office and on the small screen, the most conspicuous example being Alex Haley's *Roots* which won nine Emmy awards, a Golden Globe and Peabody award and was the second most watched television finale in American history. Steven Spielberg's *Amistad*, Quentin Tarantino's violent *Django Unchained*, and a 2019 theatrical biography of Harriet Tubman round out recent representations on the big screen. These films are in line with the 1619 Project and SPLC versions of American slavery and race, and the runaway Broadway hip-hop hit musical *Hamilton* is an "American story" centering on race and diversity and aimed at challenging the "great white male" version of the American founding.

A study conducted between 2004 and 2005 by education professors Sam Wineburg and Chauncey Monte-Sano asked both high school students and adults to choose the top ten most heroic Americans. They could not select a president or the wife of a president, and the survey did not provide possible answers. Both the high school students and the adults selected Martin Luther King, Jr., Rosa Parks, and Harriet Tubman as the top three choices, and all white classrooms in heartland states like Indiana were more likely to list King and Parks than more diverse schools in other parts of the country. Wineburg and Monte-Sano praised the findings as the result of decades of "diversity" education.

Conversely, very few Americans have heard of William Gilmore Simms or the nearly one hundred "anti-Tom" books published in the 1850s (mostly by women including a Northern friend of Stowe's) intended to refute the *Uncle Tom* version of the South. Boston minister Nehemiah Adams's *A South-Side View of Slavery*, published in 1854, does not appear on any required reading lists on American slavery. After reading *Uncle Tom's Cabin*, Adams traveled to the South to validate Stowe's description of Southern society. He ended up writing a work that William Lloyd Garrison called "as vile a work as ever written" because he simply described what he witnessed during his travels. It wasn't what Garrison wanted to hear or what he imagined the South was like. Adams argued that many of the abolitionist claims against Southern society were grossly exaggerated or outright fabrications. These books have been marginalized or forgotten in American society, criticized for being overtly reactionary or partisan, and ignored by popular media. Simms, perhaps the most important Southern writer of his generation, was blacklisted in Northern literary circles. That continues to this day.

The evidence indicates that the 1619 Project and the SPLC overstate their case regarding the "marginalization of African-American history in the telling of our national story." With the success of several books, films, and television shows focusing on the legacy and history of slavery in America, no one could accurately claim that black American experience is underrepresented in pop culture. American students at all levels are being exposed to a 1619 Project story on race and slavery on a regular basis either through popular media or "diversity" centered curricula or academic departments.

But did slavery cause American racism? Alexis de Tocqueville remarked in his *Democracy in America* that, "Race prejudice seems stronger in those states that have abolished slavery than in those where it still exists, and nowhere is it more intolerant than in those states where slavery was never known." De Tocqueville blamed this on slavery, for "Memories of slavery disgrace the race, and race perpetuates memories of slavery." So even in the New England, a region de Tocqueville incorrectly believed had been little touched by the institution, the mere fact that Africans had been made slaves determined they would be forever treated as slaves even with legal freedom. This may be a case of putting the cart before the horse.

Race relations in colonial America were complex, particularly in the South. The historian Eugene Genovese remarked in his seminal *Roll, Jordan, Roll* that, "Wherever racial subordination exists, racism exists; therefore, southern slave society and its racist ideology had much in common with other systems and societies. But southern slave society was not merely one more manifestation of some abstraction called racist society. Its history was essentially determined by particular relationships of class power in racial form." In other words, to Genovese, racism as an "abstraction" had little to do with Southern society. It was reinforced by slavery but not created by the institution. As he later wrote, "The racial distinction between master and slave heightened the tension in an unjust social order..." but it did not create it. Genovese also argued in his *Mind of the Master Class* that historically, "Neither slavery nor serfdom was racially determined. From ancient times Europeans had recruited slaves without regard to race, and white overwhelmingly predominated among the millions of slaved held in Europe." This was certainly the case in early colonial British North America where the earliest slaves were Europeans. The Africans who arrived in 1619 entered an already existing slaveholding society, though one that would change over time.

By the sixteenth century, both Europeans and Muslims equated slavery with Africa. This was not the result of European kidnapping raids into the African interior as Hannah-Jones suggests in the 1619 Project. Europeans did not have the military muscle to pull it off. The historian John Thornton wrote in his *Africa and Africans in the Making of the Atlantic World*, "Africans played a more active role in developing the commerce, and they did so on their own initiative." These slaves would be "purchased more often than captured" for there were no "dramatic European conquests in Africa." Africans set the terms, the prices, and the supply. If anything, the identification of slavery with Africa was created by Africans who lived in a "deep-seated legal and institutional" slaveholding culture, as Thornton claimed. Europeans may have demanded the labor, but Africans drove the institution.

Certainly, Northern and Southern Americans lived in a racially stratified society, one that was based on their understanding of history and theology, not the existence of slavery. Classical texts reinforced (and refuted) the primacy and viability of slave societies. Genovese maintained that, "Southerners, defending slavery as a historically recurring and justifiable feature of well-ordered societies from ancient times to the present, recognized that they were defending racial as well as class stratification." Southerners defended racial slavery as the "foundation for the southern way of life," but Genovese believed "race relations did not count for everything."

Notions of race had been developed by Greek and Roman philosophers and historians and had filtered through successive generations to American thinkers. Northern theologians dominated American proslavery literature from the early 18th century forward and argued that Africans were an inferior and barbaric race in need of civilization and Christianity. The Biblical defense of slavery became a common theme, both North and South. The historian Larry Tise in his history of proslavery thought contended that, "The adoption of a proslavery ideology by the South in the 1830s marked, not a departure from the rest of the nation either ideologically or psychically, but rather a full adoption of what may have been ate the time America's strongest sociopolitical and cultural philosophy and tradition." Even the abolitionist Massachusetts Senator Charles Sumner thought that African-Americans would eventually become a contented laboring class because they were incapable of anything else. Racist statements were commonplace among some of the most ardent anti-slavery advocates in the United States. As Fogel and Engermann wrote in *Time on the Cross*, "It is one of the bitterest ironies of history that the antislavery critics who worked so hard to break these chains [of slavery] probably did as much as any other group, perhaps more, to fasten the spikes that have kept blacks in the agony of racial discrimination during their century of freedom." C. Vann Woodward noted in his *Strange Career of Jim Crow* that the idea of racial segregation was born in the North, and the term dated to at least 1850s Connecticut and its efforts to segregate rail cars. African slavery reinforced but did not create American racism.

In fact, in many cases African slavery *refuted* the notion of black inferiority. Distinguished historian Clarence Ver Steeg noted that slaves were used as front-line troops during the Yamasee War in 1715 and that "blacks were entrusted with responsibilities for defense that almost equaled those of whites." Fogel and Engermann found that slave labor was *more efficient* than white labor, both North and South, and that because of economic necessity, slaves and freedmen alike were often entrusted with highly skilled tasks and trained to accomplish those tasks. Horace King, for example, was born a slave in South Carolina and in time became one of the most prominent engineers and bridge builders in the entire South. Richard Wade discovered that slaves at the Tredegar Iron Works in Richmond, Virginia "did the skilled work such as puddling, heating, and rolling as well as the usual common tasks" and in the process produced a high quality product that successfully competed with Northern manufacturers. These slaves were required to work ten-hour shifts but were *paid overtime* (62 slaves received bonuses in 1860) if they exceeded those hours. To our accustomed eight-hour workday sensibilities this sounds brutal but consider that free white women in the free wage Massachusetts Lowell textile mills in the 1850s were required to work eighty-hour work weeks with no overtime pay. Fogel and Engermann argued that the economic exploitation of slaves has been exaggerated, writing that "Over the course of his lifetime, the typical slave field hand received about 90 percent of the income he produced." Genovese found that Southern "Paternalism's insistence upon mutual obligations—duties, responsibilities, and ultimately even rights—implicitly recognized the slaves' humanity."

This humanity was manifested in the way slaves lived and worked in the South. Genovese reported that trials for slaves accused of even capital crimes were commonplace throughout the South and were conducted with scrupulous attention to duty and to the law. Convictions for rape and murder were frequently overturned in appellate courts. Lower class white Southerners and black slaves generally shared the same diet. Slaves reared and nursed Southern white children, cooked their food, and easily mingled in Southern society. The African population in North America increased due to natural birthrate, a situation that was unheard of in the rest of the slaveholding Atlantic world.

Genovese and Fogel and Engermann generally concluded that living conditions among slaves were comparable or *better* than those of other laboring classes in the nineteenth century. Indeed, Genovese wrote that, "Were anyone perverse enough to bother, he might easily find that the living conditions of a large minority or even a majority of the world's population during the twentieth century might not compare in comfort with those of the slaves of Mississippi a century earlier." Even W.E.B. DuBois would have agreed with this conclusion, though he well understood, as did everyone in antebellum America including slaveholding Southerners, that power and the potential for abuse was the real issue in American slavery. But even here, Genovese and Fogel and Engermann determined that cruelty to slaves had virtually disappeared by the late antebellum period due in large part to *internal reform* rather than pressure from Northern abolitionist attacks. Genovese said, "The white South, almost with one voice in the late antebellum period, denounced cruelty to slaves and denied that much of it occurred. Here and there, yes, one could find it; to a significant and noteworthy extent, no. Northers who knew the South well often agreed." Slavery in North America was unique not because it was more brutal and oppressive than slavery in comparative history, but because it was far less harsh than slave systems even in the Western Hemisphere during the same time period. This is not to excuse the institution but to give it historical perspective.

One of the most egregious claims from the 1619 Project is that black Americans "made" America a democracy. Hannah-Jones wrote that because black Americans fully embraced Jefferson's statement that "all men are created equal," they formed the backbone of the American democratic experience. This is an understandable though politically charged assertion. Lincoln's historical invention of the "proposition nation" at Gettysburg in 1864 opened the door for this type of revisionism. But "democracy" was alive and well in eighteenth century America, so much so that the founding generation sought to curtail the "evils of democracy" when they drafted and ratified the Constitution in 1787 and 1788. We must not confuse "democracy" with egalitarianism or universal suffrage, and this is precisely what Hannah-Jones does. By making the case that black Americans have been the true "democrats" in American history, she intends to link various minority groups together in a socio-cultural radical political campaign aimed at destabilizing the foundations of Western Civilization. For most of American history, slavery was a political issue masquerading as a social crusade. Hannah-Jones is still drinking from that well, or perhaps she has ingested too many "sun people" lectures from Leonard Jeffries. Either way, her essay is political, not historical.

This, of course, ignores the complicated history of black America and Africa in general, from black slaveowners (some of which were regarded as the most brutal tyrants in their regions) to the anti-egalitarian social order in various African civilizations. As Thornton wrote, "African societies surely did possess inequalities and exploitation...." Even the leftist historian Arthur Schlesinger, Jr., maintained in his 1991 *Disuniting of America*, nearly thirty years before Hannah-Jones and the other authors scribbled the 1619 Project, that, "In this regard [the condemnation of the West] the Afrocentrists are especially absurd. The West needs no lectures on the superior virtue of those "sun people" who sustained slavery until Western imperialism abolished it (and sustain it to this day in Mauritania and the Sudan), who keep women in subjection, marry several at once, and mutilate their genitals, who carry out racial persecutions not only against Indians and other Asians but against fellow Africans from the wrong tribes, who show themselves either incapable of operating a democracy or ideologically hostile to the democratic idea, and who in their tyrannies and massacres, their Idi Amins and Boukassas, have stamped with utmost brutality on human rights."

The 1619 Project is nothing more than whimsical romanticism buttressed by popular imagination—and refuted by the historical record. Silverstein suggested the "facts" of the project are not in dispute, only the interpretation. This is clearly not the case.

Is "White Supremacy" an Exclusively "Southern" Ideology?

"WE ABHOR THE DOCTRINE of the "Types of Mankind;" first, because it is at war with scripture, which teaches us that the whole human race is descended from a common parentage; and, secondly, because it encourages and incites brutal masters to treat negroes, not as weak, ignorant and dependent brethren, but as wicked beasts, without the pale of humanity. The Southerner is the negro's friend, his only friend." George Fitzhugh, 1854

On April 23 (judging by the pictures) five idiots—probably all FBI informants—showed up at Stone Mountain, GA to hold a "white supremacist" event. All waved what appeared to be newly purchased Confederate Battle Flags. These knuckleheads were met by a mob of violent "protestor" knuckleheads— probably all on a Marxist organization's payroll—who started throwing rocks at police and igniting fires. Eventually, the riot squad was called in, arrests were made, and order was restored, but not before pictures of the "white supremacist" kooks waving Confederate Battle Flags were plastered all over the Internet.

The message was clear: The Confederate Battle Flag is a symbol of hate and white power.

In other words, that flag represents exclusively *Southern* traits.

But is either position correct?

If you listen to the mainstream media or historical profession you would think so. Many almost go to hysterics to "prove" that the root of Southern society was "hatred" for black Americans. The Confederacy was simply an extension of that fact. The common narrative is that the South has had a three-century long monopoly on racism in the United States. The North, on the other hand, was the happy land of free thinking, benevolent, egalitarian, civic minded statesman fighting for equal rights and social justice.

There is one problem with this particular story. It is based on a romantic, Utopian vision of Northern society and culture, the true "lost cause myth" in American history. Both that North and that Northerner were almost as rare as a Unicorn in both antebellum and post-bellum America.

Were antebellum Southerners racist? Absolutely, but no more so than antebellum Northerners. Were post-bellum Southerners racist? Again, absolutely but no more so than post-bellum Northerners. Did antebellum Southerners consider blacks to be an inferior, "child-like" race? Yes, but so did antebellum Northerners. Racism as we understand it today was an *American* trait for *most* of *American* history.

"White supremacy" was in fact a popular idea in the North both before and after the War, perhaps even more popular there than in the South.

The proof is readily available.

Several historians in the 1960s—most conspicuously Leon Litwack in *North of Slavery* and Eugene Berwanger in *The Frontier Against Slavery*—sought to outline the hypocrisy of Northern attacks on the South during the Civil Rights era. These were not pro-Southern ideologues but dedicated academics who wanted to describe the complex history of race relations in America. That story has been lost in current mainstream history or explained away by revisionists in an attempt to salvage the good name of their Northern heroes. Abraham Lincoln, for example, may have been a racist in his youth, even up to the time he was elected President in 1860, but he changed during the four years of war. And even if he didn't, Lincoln and the Republicans should be given a pass because they advocated the end of slavery. You see, it is far easier to demonize the South than to accept guilt in the comprehensive *American* legacy of racism and slavery. One act of political and military expediency, which is how Lincoln classified the Emancipation Proclamation, makes up for years of vitriolic racist language.

As for examples of Northern "white supremacy," there are far too many to list, but here are several.

David Wilmot, the Pennsylvania Democrat who introduced the Wilmot Proviso in 1846—a rider to a defense bill that would have excluded slavery in any territory acquired by the United States in the War with Mexico—wrote this about the Proviso: It was "the cause and the rights of [the] white freeman [and] I would preserve to free white labor a fair country, a rich inheritance, where the sons of toil, of my own race and own color, can live without the disgrace which association with negro slavery brings upon free labor." He later wrote privately, "By God, sir, men born and nursed of white women are not going to be ruled by men who were brought up on the milk of some damn Negro wench!"

The radical abolitionist Benjamin Wade of Ohio, famous for advocating the execution of Southern secessionists, the confiscation of Southern lands, the arming of former slaves, and as co-sponsor of the Wade-Davis Bill of 1864, said this when he arrived for the first time in Washington D.C. in 1851: "On the whole, this is a mean God forsaken Nigger rid[d]en place. The Niggers are certainly the most intelligent part of the population but the Nigger smell I cannot bear, yet it is in on and about every thing you see." He then complained that the food was "cooked by Niggers, until I can smell & taste the Nigger." Several years after the War, Wade said that he was "sick and tired of niggers."

Jacob Brinkerhoff, an Ohio Democrat, said in 1846 that, "I have selfishness enough greatly to prefer the welfare of my own race to that of any other and vindictiveness enough to wish...to keep [in] the South the burden which they themselves created," of course meaning black slavery and a large population of black Americans.

A Wisconsin resident, fearful of extending voting rights to black Americans, thought that giving suffrage to blacks would give them permission to "marry our sisters and daughters, and smutty wenches to [marry] our brothers and sons."

William Sawyer at the Ohio convention for revision of the state constitution in 1850 said, "the United States were designed by God in Heaven to be governed and inhabited by the Anglo-Saxon race and by them alone....[Blacks were] very little removed from the condition of dumb beasts—they wallowed in the mire like hogs and there was nothing of civilization in their aboriginal conditions."

William H. Seward of New York, Lincoln's Secretary of State, said blacks were a "foreign and feeble element, like the Indian, incapable of assimilation [and] unwisely and unnecessarily transplanted to our fields."

John Fairfield of Maine avoided dinners with Congressional colleagues in Washington D.C. because he did not like "black odoriferous niggers" around.

An Ohio Republican pleaded with Democrats to stop "shouting Sambo at us. We have no Sambo in our platform...We object to Sambo. We don't want him about. We insist that he shall not be forced upon us." The Republican Party, he claimed, was created for the benefit of the white race alone.

James Harlan, a United States Senator from Iowa, asked in 1860, "Shall the Territories be Africanized?" to which he answered that he favored territorial extension only for the white race.

Lyman Trumbull of Illinois said in 1859 that, "We the Republican party, are the white man's party. We are for the free white man, and for making white labor acceptable and honorable, which it can never be when negro slave labor is brought into competition with it."

The Iowa Republican Party used "WE ARE FOR LAND FOR THE LANDLESS, NOT NIGGERS FOR THE NIGGERLESS" as their campaign slogan in 1860.

A Kansan writing to the *New York Tribune* in 1855 summarized the sentiment of most Northern Republicans and Democrats:

> *First, then be not deceived in the character of the anti-Slavery feeling. Many who are known as Free-State men are not anti-Slavery in our Northern acceptation of the word. They are more properly negro haters, who vote Free-State to keep negroes out, free or slave; one half of them would go for Slavery if negroes were to be allowed here at all. The inherent sinfulness of Slavery is not one thought by them. One-third of the Free-State party is made up of men who act from convictions of conscious—the remaining two thirds are Free-State men from conviction that the profits of Freedom, derivable in the shape of customers would be greater than if slavery existed.*

While many Union soldiers eventually accepted abolition as a war aim, a large percentage bristled at Lincoln's Emancipation Proclamation in 1863. One Ohio private declared, "we did not enlist to fight for the negro and I can tell you that *we never shall*...sacrafise [our] lives for the liberty of a miserable black race of beings....Abolitionism is traitorism in its darkest collar."

A Union lieutenant colonel from New York wrote, "I did not come out to fight for the nigger or abolition of Slavery. [Lincoln] ought to be lashed up to 4 big fat niggers & left to wander about with them the bal[ance] of his life." Another New York soldier wrote, "I'm no nigger worshipper."

During the War, a Pennsylvania newspaper suggested, "The producing classes, the mechanic, laborer, etc., had better cut the throats of their children at once than hand them to 'impartial freedom,' degradation and amalgamation with negroes."

A New York newspaper reported that, "Filthy black niggers, greasy, sweaty, and disgusting, now jostle white people and even ladies everywhere, even at the President's levees."

A Northern newspaper editor, Dr. J.H. Van Evrie, claimed during the war that, "The equality of all whom God has created equal (white men), and the inequality of those He has made unequal (negroes and other inferior races) are the corner-stone of American democracy, and the vital principle of American civilization and human progress. We should announce that the grand humanitarian policy of progressive and civilized America is to restore subgenation all over the American continent." Van Evrie changed the name of his newspaper to *The Caucasian* during the War and was one of the most vocal proponents of "white supremacy" in the nineteenth century. He was from New York.

In all Midwestern states in the 1850s, referendums extending voting rights to blacks were defeated by crushing majorities, and in several of these states, blacks were not allowed to establish residency. This was commonplace. Even Northeastern states adopted harsh policies toward blacks before the War. Many of these policies had waned by the 1850s, but their legacy ensured that the free black population of New England would remain low for most of its history. Massachusetts prescribed whipping for any non-resident free black who stayed in the State longer than two months. Connecticut denied blacks residency in the colonial period. There were strict policies regarding black property ownership in all New England states in the colonial period and free blacks had to carry passes to travel. Even into the 1850s, Pennsylvania debated allowing free blacks to settle in the State.

It must also be said that free black Southerners could vote in Southern colonies and some Southern states into the early nineteenth century. The same was not true for the North. Black Northerners could not vote in 19 of 24 Northern states at the end of the War in 1865, and before 1860 Northern blacks could not serve on juries.

Alexis de Tocqueville described the situation for black Northerners as thus in his *Democracy in America:* "So the Negro [in the North] is free, but he cannot share the rights, pleasures, labors, griefs, or even the tomb of him whose equal he has been declared; there is nowhere where he can meet him, neither in life nor in death."

While the situation in the post-bellum period seemed to be better in the North, some of the most brutal race riots and lynchings took place on Northern soil in the early-twentieth century.

The Ku Klux Klan of the 1920s did not wave the Confederate Battle Flag, but instead displayed Old Glory at every rally. The U.S. flag was the only one on parade during a large Klan march in Washington D.C. in 1925. Their dream was a progressive *America* devoid of black residents. The last "grand wizard" of the

1920s Klan was from Indiana. He was later convicted of rape and when denied a pardon by his good friend the Governor of Indiana, he exposed several leading Indiana politicians as members of the Klan, many of them Republicans.

The lynching of Will Brown in Nebraska in 1919 was one of the most brutal and heinous in American history. He was beaten, hung, shot, and burned by a mob. This lynching was part of a series of race riots in Northern cities during the summer of 1919, often called the "Red Summer Race Riots."

The infamous photo of the lynching of Thomas Shipp and Abram Smith was taken in Indiana in 1930, many miles from the Mason-Dixon.

The worst of the 1968 race riots were in the Northern cities of Chicago and Detroit.

Race riots broke out in Boston in the mid-1970s over forced busing, a policy Bostonians gladly accepted for their Southern brothers but violently rejected in their own backyard.

Last time I checked, none of these States were part of the old Confederacy, and none has a history of "Confederate imagery."

The most iconic image from one of the 1976 Boston race riots was of a white Bostonian beating an unarmed black attorney with the U.S. Flag.

I don't recall the Confederate Battle Flag ever being used as a physical weapon against black Americans.

Rally around the U.S. Flag, boys!

Of course, anyone could reasonably claim that the U.S. flag in these instances was being used out of context, that its meaning was hijacked by the Klan and other Northern racists. Some even admit that the U.S. flag has flown over far more racist events than the Confederate Battle Flag—even over slavery for ninety years—but because that flag today represents something else to most Americans, it should not viewed as a symbol of "hate."

That is the same claim made by the vast majority of those who currently fly the Confederate Battle Flag. Isn't it ironic?

To these Southerners, the flag's meaning has been distorted, abused, and stolen by "white supremacist" groups like those who showed up at Stone Mountain. The leader of the Brazilian group dedicated to the preservation of Confederado history (relocated Southerners after the War) calls the Battle Flag a "symbol of love," meaning a love for his family, its traditions and history, and its people. To other Americans, the flag is a symbol of self-determination, of the Jeffersonian tradition of self-government and resistance to tyranny, a distinctly *American* tradition. The Battle Flag was displayed in Europe during waning days of the Cold War as a dissident gesture to the Soviet Bloc governments. A modified form has been adopted by the leaders of the Ukrainian separatist movement today.

The opening quote by proslavery advocate George Fitzhugh may seem odd to the modern reader. Fitzhugh did not believe white and black Southerners to be equal—far from it—but there is a touch of humanity that a modern American would not expect to find from such a "hate filled" man. Hate would be the incorrect word to use to describe the white antebellum Southern attitude toward black Americans. Superiority, yes, but not hate. By the eve of the War in 1861, Southerners commonly recognized the humanity of slaves. The preeminent historian Eugene Genovese wrote in his seminal *Roll, Jordan, Roll,* "The white South, almost with one voice in the late antebellum period, denounced cruelty to slaves and denied that much of it existed. Here and there, yes, one could find it; to a significant or noteworthy extent, no. Northerners who knew the South well often agreed." Following the War, Alexander H. Stephens of Georgia, infamously known for his "Cornerstone Speech," urged the State of Georgia to accept black Southerners as equal before the law as a sign of "gratitude."

In fact, Southerners realized that they lived in a much more racially diverse region than the North. That is why Fitzhugh could claim that the Southerner was "the negro's...only friend." The historian Jennifer Weber noted in her study of Northern Copperheads that "no prominent Copperheads ever discussed or even acknowledged the fact that racial mixing was well established in American life, having taken place for generations on Southern plantations." Northern Republicans labeled the Democrat Party the "Mulatto Democracy" because they believed Democrats favored "bleaching the darkies...the best blood of the Democracy [ran] in the veins of the 'peculiar property.'" Indeed, the free black population of the South was larger than that of the North in 1860, even though the Northern population, counting the Midwestern states, was nearly twice the size of the South. Many of these Southern "free people of color" were mulattoes.

White and black Southerners had lived together for over two hundred years by 1854, and nearly four hundred years by 2016. Their common history has not always pretty or peaceful, it was even exploitative (so was nineteenth-century Northern industrial wage labor) and unfortunately sometimes brutally violent, but there was a familiarity between these groups of people that escaped Northern Americans, both then and now, a familiarity that Northerners wished to avoid. "Free Soil, Free (white) Labor, Free (white) Men!" De Tocqueville again noted in his *Democracy in America,* "In the South, where slavery still exists, less trouble is taken to keep the Negro apart: they sometimes share the labors and the pleasures of the white men; people are prepared to mix with them to some extent; legislation is more harsh against them, but customs are more tolerant and gentle." This is why in 1895 Booker T. Washington could ask white and black Southerners to "cast down your buckets where you are," and why he characterized his white "mentor" as a typical "Yankee woman." Washington was a Southerner first and foremost. He never complained about voting in Macon County, Alabama.

One of the more interesting pictures from the "white supremacist" rally at Stone Mountain was of a black protestor, identified only as "Miss Black Woman," wrapped in a Confederate flag. Ostensibly, she did this to thumb her nose at the white power crowd, perhaps even to incite their rebuke. The people I know who honor the Confederate flag would have given her a hug and invited her to supper. Just as with the Confederadoes in Brazil, their support for the flag is one of love.

Genovese wrote in *Roll, Jordan, Roll* that, "Blacks and whites in America may be viewed as one nation or two or as a nation within a nation, but their common history guarantees that, one way or another, they are both American." Genovese was correct, but he missed one important point. Most black Americans were and are not just American, but Southern. Many are moving back to the South after years in Northern cities for that reason. The South is home.

Racial reconciliation is a laudable and desirable goal, but removing, renaming, or re-contextualizing Confederate symbols, or worse outright vandalism, is not going to achieve any type of resolution to the *American*—not just Southern—legacy of racism. Fully understanding the complex relations and history of white and black Southerners including the good, not just the bad and the ugly, could be better achieved without a Reign of Terror style purge of anything deemed "racist" by the self-appointed gatekeepers of "truth" in America today.

There are many Northern symbols and heroes that would need a thorough re-contextualization as well. When that process begins, perhaps more Southerners would be open to a discussion of their symbols, but I have yet to see a call for the renaming of Yale or Brown University, of Faneuil Hall, of the removal of the Lyman Trumbull statue from the Illinois Statehouse, the furling of the U.S. flag, or a "re-contextualization" of the Lincoln memorial with information about his support for colonization or with an added inscription of his own words: "I am not in favor of making voters or jurors of negroes, nor of qualifying them to hold office, nor to intermarry with white people..." or "I am in favor of the race to which I belong, having the superior position."

For those who need interpretation, that would be called "white supremacy."

AHA Revisionism

ON 28 AUGUST 2017, the American Historical Association (AHA) issued a "Statement on Confederate Monuments" that presumed to speak for the entire American historical profession on the issue of whether these monuments should remain or if they should be removed from public spaces.

Unfortunately, this "statement" is little more than historical establishment claptrap disguised as highbrow intellectual discourse—par for the course in the modern profession—replete with distortions, exaggerations, half-truths, and presentism myths.

The "statement" opens by suggesting that the AHA "welcomes the emerging national debate about Confederate monuments..." but suggests that "Much of this public statuary was erected without such conversations, and without any public decision-making process."

The "statement" later concludes by asserting that "Nearly all monuments to the Confederacy and its leaders were erected without anything resembling a democratic process. Regardless of their representation in the actual population in any given constituency, African Americans had no voice and no opportunity to raise questions about the purposes or likely impact of the honor accorded to the builders of the Confederate States of America."

Both arguments are disingenuous at best. The "public statuary" in question did involve conversations both North and South, not just about Confederate monuments, but about general American iconography, and every monument involved some type of "public decision-making process."

Nearly all of the funds raised for Southern monuments came from private donations. Women's organizations sought pennies to help fund relief enterprises, including finding artificial limbs for Confederate veterans. They also hoped to erect monuments for the dead. Republican controlled governments, military occupation, and lack of capital put off many of these projects until the several years after the War, but by the 1870s, monuments to Confederate soldiers began appearing in towns and cities across the South. One of the first was constructed of wood in Columbus, Georgia's Linwood Cemetery. In fact, the vast majority of these monuments were erected in cemeteries until the turn of the twentieth century, but even as the monuments began to be placed in public locations, most were dedicated to the common Confederate soldier, not individuals.

But this was not just a Southern movement. Across the United States during the Gilded Age and Progressive Era, Union veterans organizations began constructing monuments as well, and these, like their Southern counterparts, focused on the heroism and sacrifice of the Union dead. There was no animus between erstwhile foes. New Yorker Cornelius Vanderbilt, at the insistence of his Southern wife Frank, funded several charitable causes that benefitted exclusively Confederate veterans. By the early twentieth century, some Northern monuments had the financial backing of the federal government. The now vilified Stone Mountain carving in Georgia had to rely on private donations while the more famous Mount Rushmore carving in South Dakota had federal funding. Northern and Southern taxpayers subsidized the Lincoln Memorial in Washington D.C. while the monument to Jefferson Davis in Richmond was built by private donations. All were part of public beautification projects in a progressive effort to reconcile the sections.

Booker T. Washington thought these memorials and monuments were worthwhile. In 1914, he agreed to help find funding for the Confederate monument in Opelika, AL, saying that, "We all realize more and more that men like him [Confederate Veteran George Paul Harrison, Jr.] are true friends of our race, and that any monument that will keep the fine character of such heroes before the public will prove helpful to both races in the South." Washington was African-American and both had a voice and "an opportunity to raise questions about the purposes or likely impact of the honor accorded to the builders of the Confederate States of America." He made clear he thought such monuments would "prove helpful to both races in the South." Black Americans often attended unveiling events and when Jefferson Davis and John B. Gordon traveled through Alabama and Georgia after the cornerstone ceremony for the large Confederate sculpture in Montgomery, thousands of black Southerners lined up to see the procession.

The AHA "statement" contends that, "History comprises both facts and interpretations of those facts. To remove a monument, or to change the name of a school or street, is not to erase history, but rather to alter or call attention to a previous interpretation of history." Curiously, the "statement" then argues, "A monument is not history itself; a monument commemorates an aspect of history, representing a moment in the past when a public or private decision defined who would be honored in a community's public spaces."

Part of this is true. History is interpretation, and the AHA is willfully engaging in a bit of historical revisionism in its "statement." The AHA correctly states that most of the monuments were built in the decades after the War, but then claims, "this enterprise was part and parcel of the initiation of legally mandated segregation and widespread disenfranchisement [sic] across the South. Memorials were intended, in part, to obscure the terrorism required to overthrow Reconstruction, and to intimidate African Americans politically and isolate them from the mainstream of public life." For an organization that insists all statements like this should be "rooted in evidence and disciplinary standards," they fall far short of meeting their own objectives.

In the hundreds if not thousands of memorial address, dedication ceremonies, and public events held to unveil a monument or commemorate the Confederacy in the postbellum South, very few, if any, spoke of "white supremacy" or the attempt to "terrorize" and "intimidate African Americans politically and isolate them from the mainstream of public life." Memorial addresses spoke of the heroism and sacrifice of the soldier, the dedication of Southern women, and the principles of liberty and independence, and most expressed satisfaction that slavery had been abolished for the good of humanity.

For example, at the 1915 cornerstone ceremony for the Stonewall Jackson monument in Richmond, VA, William A. Anderson, a Lexington, VA native, Confederate veteran, and member of the Stonewall Brigade, said that the Jackson statue would memorialize "The example which he [Jackson] gave the world of self-sacrificing devotion to principle and to country, of loyal obedience to duty, and unquestioning faith in God, the unsurpassed manifestations of courage which he exhibited, and the radiance with which his genius illumined the fields of his triumphs...." Anderson believed these traits would "compel the admiration alike of friend and foe, and constitute a part of the patrimony of glory, not of Virginia and the Confederate South alone, but of the American people and the human race." The hate for anyone other than white Southerners clearly seethed from Anderson's pores.

As to the statement that such monuments are "not history," that defies the value of such monuments as works of art. Is the Lincoln Memorial only a "monument?" What about Mount Rushmore? Or the Washington Monument? Do they not constitute something other than a monument? The AHA stands behind the Washington Monument and would not want to see it removed to "a museum or some other appropriate venue" as in the case of Confederate monuments. The AHA further thinks "Americans can also learn from other countries' approaches to these difficult issues, such as...Memento Park in Budapest, Hungary." Most Americans would not recognize the loaded symbolism of this statement. Memento Park is filled with statues and monuments to the Soviet Union and communism. In other words, Confederate monuments are as illegitimate as the Soviet empire, as bloody as Marxism, and constitute a foreign part of American history. They are not American. No bias there.

Perhaps the most bizarre section of the "statement" is where the AHA contends that, "Decisions to remove memorials to Confederate generals and officials who have no other major historical accomplishment does not necessarily create a slippery slope towards removing the nation's founders, former presidents, or other historical figures whose flaws have received substantial publicity in recent years." This is simply not true. See attacks made on the George Washington and Andrew Jackson statues in New Orleans, the attempt to rename James Madison High School in Wisconsin, the vandalism of a Christopher Columbus statue in New York, calls for the removal of the Thomas Jefferson statue at UVA, or the actual removal of the Richard Stockton bust at Stockton University. And this is only the beginning. No slippery slope? The AHA is delusional or maybe just overtly political. This part of the statement could have been written by "distinguished" historian Annette Gordon-Reed, whose pseudo-history of the (debunked) Jefferson-Hemings affair earned her a Pulitzer Prize. See the Jefferson Hemings Scholars Commission. Gordon-Reed laughs at the idea that the founding generation is next because "We can distinguish between people who wanted to build the United States of America and people who wanted to destroy it...." Never mind that many of the prominent leaders of the Confederacy were descendants of Southern founders and that the United States continued to exist in 1861 even without the Southern states. To Reed and other "distinguished" members of the AHA, Confederate leaders and veterans are not worthy of recognition.

I have never joined the AHA, and I would encourage other historians who take issue with their recent "statement" to reconsider sending another dime to a historical organization that clearly cares little for "evidence and disciplinary standards" in its own publications.

A Cautionary Tale on Monument Protection Laws

When Jefferson County Circuit Judge Michael Graffeo issued a ruling on the Alabama Memorial Preservation Act just minutes before his term expired last week, he upended the entire understanding and meaning of the original Constitution and the relationship between the States, the cities, and the general government. More importantly, though Graffeo's decision will probably–not definitely–be overturned, the ruling provides a cautionary tale in ongoing efforts to pass similar legislation across the South.

But first, a brief history of the controversy is in order. The City of Birmingham began discussing plans to remove the Linn Park Soldiers and Sailors Confederate Monument in 2015 after the Emanuel A.M.E. Church massacre in Charleston, SC. Just one week later, then Governor Robert Bentley ordered that all Confederate flags be removed from the Alabama Confederate Monument on Capitol Hill in Montgomery. In response, the Alabama legislature began crafting the Memorial Preservation Act aimed at protecting all monuments and memorials across the State, not just those dedicated to Confederate history. Bentley was eventually forced to resign for corruption and the Act was signed into law in April 2017 by Governor Kay Ivey.

Four months later, the City of Birmingham, at the direction of former Mayor William Bell, covered the Linn Park Confederate Monument in plastic and erected a tall, black plywood barrier around its base after Ohio resident James Alex Field murdered Heather Heyer following the 2017 "United the Right" rally in Charlottesville, VA. Bell stated he did so because, "This country should in no way tolerate the hatred that the KKK, neo-Nazis, fascists and other hate groups spew." How that related to an inanimate object dedicated over one hundred years earlier by the United Daughters of the Confederacy (not the KKK) and nearly thirty years before the rise of fascism was unclear. This was political grandstanding at its finest.

The State then sued the City of Birmingham for violating the Preservation Act, and as per the law, began demanding a $25,000 daily fee as long as the barriers remained around the Linn Park monument. The City refused to pay, hired the Southern Poverty Law Center to help defend it in court, and kept the "plywood screen" in place for over a year.

This seemed to be a certain victory for the State. The cornerstone for the Linn Park monument was dedicated in 1894 and the monument was finally completed in 1905, making it more than forty years old. The "barrier" clearly "altered" and "disturbed" the monument because it prevented people from seeing most of the memorial or reading the inscriptions on the base. The State also contended that the City lacked standing in the case because as cities are "creatures or instrumentalities of their state of origin" they are not private citizens and therefore have no individual rights.

The City argued that the law violated its right to freedom of speech and right to due process as outlined by the First and Fourteenth Amendments to the Constitution and because corporations (cities) are persons, the State was denying fundamental civil liberties.

Graffeo, in a thinly veiled political ruling, sided with the City. He reasoned that, "It is undisputed that an overwhelming majority of the of the body politic of the CITY is repulsed by the Monument." Graffeo argued that the city has a "right to speak for itself, say what it wishes, and select the views that it wants to express," and that by forcing the City to accept a monument with a message it finds "repulsive," the state of Alabama was infringing on that right. He also contended that the State violated the Fourteenth Amendment by prohibiting the City from moving or altering an object on city property, thus preventing proper due process.

His entire ruling is a distortion of federalism, due process, the Bill of Rights, and the Fourteenth Amendment.

Both the Tenth and Eleventh Amendments to the Constitution make clear that the States are the building blocks of the general government. States retain all powers not delegated to the central authority and cannot be sued without their consent. The general government, then, is the creation of the States or the people thereof, as are cities and municipalities. While Graffeo did not deny that States have extensive powers over cities, he believes that those powers are limited by the Constitution because cities are somehow "persons."

The notion of "corporate personhood" is a relatively recent creation of the federal court system. No one in the founding generation considered corporations to be "persons," and more importantly, the ability to charter corporations is not a delegated power of the general government, Alexander Hamilton's opinion notwithstanding. Only sovereign entities (States) can charter corporations, and as such the State of Alabama could revoke the charter for the City of Birmingham and confiscate all city property. In other words, the City does not technically "own" the property under the Linn Park monument; the State does.

Moreover, a city having "free speech rights" would have been an anathema to the founding generation. Individuals could certainly protest the Linn Park Monument. They could stand in front of it all day with bullhorns and signs as long as they did not prohibit others from expressing their own view of the obelisk, disturb the peace, or incite violence. That is protected by Section 4 of the Alabama Constitution, the Constitution Graffeo should have referred to in his decision. But a city is not a person and therefore does not have "free speech rights," unless, that is, you agree with the 2010 Supreme Court decision in *Citizen United v. Federal Election Commission,* which did more than any other decision to craft the "corporate personhood" argument in modern American jurisprudence. Graffeo sounds a lot like John Roberts.

The legal relationship between the general government and the States also illustrates that the States are sovereign, and thus, as the Attorney General of Alabama noted, the City of Birmingham had no standing in the case. Graffeo disagreed, but the historical evidence does not support his opinion. The United States general government cannot legally revoke the status of a State. In fact, when Hamilton proposed that the States be reduced to mere corporations of the general government at the Philadelphia Convention in June 1787, he was entirely ignored and his plan rejected. The "friends of the Constitution" insisted that the States retained all "police powers" and that the general government possessed only the powers *expressly*–the word was used in public defense of the document– delegated to it *by the states.* In other words, the States weren't giving up their control of the federal system, nor were they surrendering their sovereignty. The Constitution would not have been ratified under any other meaning. The Congressional Radical Republicans during Reconstruction certainly insisted they had the power to do so, and by passing the 1st Reconstruction Act in 1867 followed through on their "state suicide" and "conquered provinces" theory, but this idea is inconsistent with the original understanding of the document. Critics barked loudly about this radical theory during Reconstruction.

Additionally, Graffeo's contention that the Memorial Preservation Act denies the City due process is a distortion of the term. The founding generation, and even the authors of the Fourteenth Amendment, understood due process to be procedural, meaning that the State (or the general government) could deny an individual their property as long as proper legal procedures were followed in a court of law and the legislation authorizing the move legally promulgated. But Graffeo applied a substantive due process model to the legislation. Essentially, substantive due process means that a legislative body cannot pass any legislation that *might* infringe on the right of property–or any other civil right or liberty. This rationale and definition of due process was used by Southerners in the 1850s to combat congressional attempts to legislate for slavery in the territories. They argued that barring the ability of a slaveholder to bring his slave property into the common territories of the United States through legislation denied him his due process under the law because such laws would essentially prohibit him from using (moving or altering) his property the way he saw fit. Graffeo and the SPLC will, of course, find solace that the legal reasoning behind Graffeo's decision would be supported by those slaveholders who championed *Dred Scott v. Sanford* in 1857, the first time this novel approach to due process was codified in American law.

Considering the City as a person with "free speech rights" also twists the meaning and intent of the Bill of Rights and the Fourteenth Amendment. Incorporation of the Bill of Rights against the States is the greatest legal coup of the twentieth century, and it was made possible by, ironically enough, a former Klan member from Alabama, progressive Supreme Court Justice Hugo Black. Through a series of rulings in the 1950s and 1960s, the Supreme Court decided, against the historical record of both the Bill of Rights and the Fourteenth Amendment, that the civil liberties protected by the First Amendment also applied to the States. Black wanted to do so, in part, to prevent Catholic schools from using taxpayer funded buses to transport children to school. His incorporationist dream has eventually been applied to every other Amendment in the Bill of Rights, but that does not make it legal or proper.

Ultimately, Graffeo's ruling is interesting because if anyone follows his logic, and the appellate courts sustain his decision, a city or municipality could prohibit pornography or saggy pants, for example, under the cover that these things are "repulsive" and that the local government could "select the views that it wants to express," or deny those views it seeks to censure for the welfare of the "overwhelming majority of the body politic." That would be democracy in action, but it would certainly be opposed by the same progressives who are now championing this outrageous decision. Regardless, those crafting current monument protection legislation in various States should consider Graffeo's decision as a warning that progressive justices and their legal allies will use any method–including hypocrisy, historical amnesia, and blatant distortion of the law–to advance their agenda. Legislation only offers so much protection when the two sides aren't playing on the same field. They aren't even in the same game.

Ashley Judd Gets Nasty

"Treat a woman like a lady, And your lady like a queen…." Charlie Daniels

ASHLEY JUDD'S RECITATION of "I'm a Nasty Woman" at the "women's" march on Washington D.C. splashed across every media outlet in America. Judd proudly proclaimed to be a feminist and then launched into a verbal diatribe against "racism, fraud, conflict of interest, homophobia, sexual assault, transphobia, white supremacy, misogyny, ignorance and white privilege." To Judd and the poem's author, a sweet little Tennessee donut shop employee named Nina Donovan, the symbol of all this mischief and oppression are "Confederate flags being tattooed across my city. Maybe the South actually is going to rise again, maybe for some, it never really fell."

Somehow being a strong woman today requires both a high level of "ignorance" and the desire to get in the gutter. Getting nasty with Ashley were Madonna and a host of other leftist activists who think the only way to get a man's attention (and isn't that the point?) is to grab their crotch and act like a spoiled teenager. Being a man is another thing, something Southerners of both sexes know something about.

Take Augusta Jane Evans of Mobile, Alabama for example. Neither Judd, nor Madonna, nor Donovan would consider her a feminist. She proudly waved the Confederate flag and watched hundreds of men suffer for the cause as a nurse. For her, the South never fell, because an America without the Southern tradition would have been an America without its soul. She was highly intelligent. Her books require the reader to have a level of education I'm sure Ms. Donovan—and for that matter both Judd and Madonna—lacks. She never voted, did not think it was proper for women to vote, and never jumped around on a stage grabbing her crotch and gyrating to "express yourself." But she did express herself, quite well in fact.

Evans was one of the best-selling authors of the 1860s. Her novel *St. Elmo* lined bookshelves across the United States, no small feat for an unreconstructed Southern belle. Women often required their daughters and granddaughters to read it. It might be a stretch, but one could probably assume that no nasty pink hatted woman at the Washington D.C. rally has ever cracked open the book. Their loss, for they are missing one of the more important feminist novels of the nineteenth century.

Evans held the cause of women's suffrage in low regard and scoffed at "blue-stockings," educated women who shunned the traditional role of wife, mother, and care-giver for politics and speaking engagements. Her anti-suffrage position puts her at odds with modern society, but she was not alone in the nineteenth century. While the modern reader may laugh at her quaint provincialism, her reasoning, made clear in *St. Elmo*, stemmed from her faith and her dedication to "womankind."

Edna Earl, the main character in *St. Elmo*, is a devout, pious, pure, well-read, beautiful, and intelligent young woman, the model of Christian virtue. She falls in love with an immoral scoundrel, St. Elmo, but does not allow herself to express her interest because he is unworthy of her love. She pities him and prays for him, and though her heart is his, she never betrays her feelings. As a result, she spends much of her young life engaged in study, in nursing sick children, writing critically acclaimed books and articles, and fighting off suitors who boast high social status and money but who cannot win her pure heart. In the end, Edna is able to reform St. Elmo. He returns to Christ, becomes a minister, and marries Edna. While it is a great romance, *St. Elmo* is also a political tale interwoven with social critique.

For example, Evans, through Edna Earl, argued that women should "jealously [contend] for every woman's right which God and nature had decreed the sex. The right to be learned, wise, noble, useful, in woman's divinely limited sphere; the right to influence and exalt the circle in which she moved; the right to mount the sanctified bema of her own quiet hearthstone; the right to modify and direct her husband's opinions . . . the right to make her children ornaments to their nation . . . the right to advise, to plead, to pray; the right to make her desk a Delphi, if God so permitted; the right to be all that the phrase 'noble, Christian woman' means." But she cautioned her fellow woman against involving herself in anything that might "trail her heaven-born purity through the dust and mire of political strife...."

In *St. Elmo*, Evans described her heroine's writing career in words that could just as easily be applied to her own:

The tendency of the age was to equality and communism, and this, she contended was undermining the golden thrones shining in the blessed and hallowed light of the hearth, whence every true woman ruled the realm of her own family. Regarding every pseudo "reform" which struck down the social and political distinction of the sexes, as a blow that crushed one of the pillars of woman's throne, she earnestly warned the Crowned Heads of the danger to be apprehended from the unfortunate and deluded female malcontents . . . and to proud happy mothers, guarded by Praetorian bands of children, she reiterated the assurance that "Those who rock the cradle rule the world." Most carefully she sifted the records of history, tracing in every epoch the sovereigns of the hearth-throne who had reigned wisely and contentedly, ennobling and refining humanity; and she proved by illustrious examples that the borders of the feminine realm could not be enlarged, without rendering the throne unsteady, and subverting God's law of order.

Politics, Evans pointed out, has never proved to be the salvation of the human race. This is still true today. Women, most importantly mothers and wives, had long been the calming factor, the guiding hand, and the nurturing vessel of a prosperous and peaceful people. Evans believed neither voting nor political office were necessary when women already held such power over men.

Every nasty feminist at the Washington rally failed to understand that the "misogyny" of the nineteenth century was in fact a manifestation of a *respect* for the fairer sex, a realization that men were, and are, fragile creatures that need a soft hand and a moral compass that often only women can provide, and that women were, in fact, superior members of society. "Women and children first" had real meaning. Acting "nasty" appeals to the animalistic side of man, but it debases rather than elevates womankind. Women might as well put up a sign in neon lights: "Bring out your clubs and procreate, caveman. No conversation nor courtship necessary."

This isn't about voting. It's about manners and refinement, of culture. Edna Earl would be a much more enjoyable challenge than Ashley Judd. But maybe that is old fashioned. Real ladies did not show up in Washington. Treating your woman like a lady and your lady like a queen is too "Old South." Then again, maybe that is exactly what America needs from both sexes.

BATTLE FOR THE OLD DOMINION

WITH THE RECENT triumph of the Democrat Party in the 2019 statewide elections in Virginia, it will only be a matter of time before an effort is made to rewrite Virginia law concerning "memorials for war veterans." Progressive efforts to topple these monuments have been thwarted by legal obstacles, and now, with a majority in both houses of the Virginia legislature, Democrats will undoubtedly include a potential revision to any monument protection law as part of a larger "social justice" legislative package. The culture war will consume Old Virginny.

Part of the problem, of course, rests with the modern education system. The minds of mush who run around demanding an end to symbols of "white supremacy" are encouraged by an academic establishment more interested in activism than understanding and knowledge. Two recent pieces on Virginia history, written or influenced by professors at the University of Virginia, underscore the problem.

The first by Professor Elizabeth Varon–"UVA and the History of Race: The Lost Cause Through Judge Duke's Eyes"–places Confederate monuments in Charlottesville entirely within the context of "white supremacy," an argument that violates even the basic tenets of Logic 101. The second is a new book by Professor Alan Taylor which considers slavery to be the heart of the UVA experience. Jefferson may have thought otherwise, but according to Taylor, you can't train "despots" to be good republicans. In other words, republicanism could never exist in the South, but racism could. Harvard Professor and Jefferson-Hemings myth-maker Annette Gordon-Reed, who scribbled the review, couldn't agree more.

That this drivel drips from the pens of University of Virginia "scholars" shows the depths of the problem of activism masquerading as scholarship. It also exemplifies why Virginia will undoubtedly expunge everything Confederate–

and perhaps everything truly Virginian–from its historical record in the coming years. And while these professors continue to blame traditional Virginia for every problem afflicting the people of the Old Dominion, the people piling in to Jefferson's country will lap up the academic crusade against the Southern tradition and vote for their political accomplices in Richmond and elsewhere. Demographic displacement is not and has never been kind to tradition.

On the other hand, educational material like the documentary from Kent Masterson Brown on the Virginia origins of the Confederate Battle Flag won't be listed on any university syllabi. Why? Because he doesn't talk about race and slavery, and he displays respect for the men who fought and died under the "Southern Cross." This would have been the standard interpretation just thirty years ago. Unfortunately, seeking to understand rather than condemn or disparage has become the real "lost cause" in the historical profession. And the ghosts of the Old Dominion weep.

Randall and McWhirter

The PC police have found a new target. Not satisfied with monuments and flags, the Maryland general assembly recently voted to alter the lyrics to the official State song, James Ryder Randall's "Maryland, My Maryland." Lincoln apologist Christian McWhirter penned a piece for *Time* magazine that labeled the song "dissident." This is true if using the standard definition of the word, opposition to official policy, especially that of an authoritarian state. Anti-Hitler Germans were dissidents. George Washington, Thomas Jefferson, Sam Adams, and the rest of the founding generation were dissidents. Anti-Lenin and anti-Stalin Russians were dissidents. Demonstrators at Tiananmen Square were dissidents. It seems dissidents are those usually on the right side of history. Obviously McWhirter disagrees.

He also opined that because the song was "pro-Confederate," it is also "pro-slavery and pro-secession." I would agree that "Maryland, My Maryland" is pro-Confederate and pro-secession. Randall openly advocated Maryland secession, but pro-slavery? Not a word in the song is dedicated to the institution. As for pro-secession, so what? It seems McWhirter not only opposes free-thinking but self-determination. Even McWhirter's hero Abraham Lincoln thought secession was perfectly acceptable in 1848, "...Any people anywhere, being inclined and having the power, have the right to rise up, and shake off the existing government, and form a new one that suits them better-- This is a most valuable, -- a most sacred right -- a right, which we hope and believe, is to liberate the world...."

McWhirter also wrung his hands in angst that the poem expresses "patriotism" to the "failed Confederacy," classifies Lincoln as a "despot," and calls Northerners "vandals." This is heresy in modern America, and to McWhirter it cannot be silenced quickly enough. Of course, Lincoln was a despot and Northerners did vandalize the South, so both statements are true.

As for Randall, "Maryland, My Maryland" made him famous, but he claimed one of his other poems written shortly after the war, "At Arlington," to be his best. This work is both a denunciation of military reconstruction and a moving eulogy for the Confederate dead buried there. It is also a stirring call to action. The annotation at the beginning of the poem could have been written in 2016. Gone are the actual bayonets, but make no mistake, current efforts to cleanse the American landscape of all things Confederate is a modern reconstruction. As McWhirter unknowingly illustrated--I am giving him benefit of the doubt--this will also erase self-determination and opposition to authoritarianism from American political discourse. We might as well start toasting "God Save the Queen." At least then Americans would be consistent in their disdain for all things "dissident."

*****

My recent piece on James Ryder Randall, "At Arlington", touched a nerve, at least with Christian McWhirter. I spent some time in "At Arlington" discussing his March *Time* magazine piece, and thus he was compelled to reply.

McWhirter begins by wondering when the "neo-Confederate crowd" would respond to his article. It only took him one sentence to use the tired pejorative "neo-Confederate" to try to undermine my position (one comment on his article wondered why it only took me six sentences to compare Lincoln to Hitler, which I did not do). To people like McWhirter, anyone who disagrees with the modern pogrom against all things traditionally Southern has to secretly pine for a return to the 1860s.

He takes issue with my labeling him a "Lincoln apologist" by arguing that he "barely mention[s] Lincoln in my [McWhirter's] article." According to his byline at *Time*, McWhirter is an Assistant Editor for The Papers of Abraham Lincoln and Editor of the Journal of the Abraham Lincoln Association. He also uses Lincoln as his avatar on his blog. I think that would constitute a Lincoln apologist regardless of how many times you "mention Lincoln" in your "article."

From there, McWhirter jumps into a discussion of the term "dissident," which was featured prominently in his piece. He agrees that the term "is often used to describe opponents of authoritarianism," but then contends "that obviously wasn't my meaning in the article." To whom was it not obvious? He directly called Ryder's *Maryland, My Maryland* "dissident" and complains that the song is "pro-secession." That would be "dissidence." What magical and hidden definition of the term is he using? Perhaps he needs a better thesaurus or dictionary.

He then states that I suggest "all such action"–meaning dissidence–"is good." Reading comprehension is a problem here. From my piece: "It seems dissidents are those *usually* on the right side of history [emphasis added]." When did "usually" become synonymous with "all"? That new thesaurus would come in handy again.

The real crux of his argument in this paragraph is that the state of Maryland should not use *Maryland, My Maryland* as the official state song because:

> *Maryland didn't secede during the Civil War and thus has never claimed to be independent from the United States. Thus, it makes no sense for an obviously loyal state with deep ties to and clear benefits from the American union to have a state song that openly calls for the dissolution of that union.*

True, Maryland did not secede from the Union in 1861. It did declare its independence from Great Britain separately in 1776, making it a "free and independent state" legally independent from both Great Britain and the United States which had yet to be created. Maryland acceded to the Union in 1781 and again in 1788, but the state of Maryland preceded the Union of the States. And how loyal was Maryland? It is fairly well established that Maryland may have seceded in 1861 had not Benjamin Butler had the entire pro-secession faction of the legislature thrown in jail. That is not my definition of "obviously loyal." And what about John Merryman and other citizens of the state, including the Baltimore police chief, who were arrested for their opposition to the Lincoln administration? Did these men have a "clear benefit from the American union"?

McWhirter then claims I argue "that the Confederacy has nothing to do with slavery." I never said that in my article. Again, reading comprehension. I did say, "I would agree that "Maryland, My Maryland" is pro-Confederate and pro-secession. Randall openly advocated Maryland secession, but pro-slavery? Not a word in the song is dedicated to the institution." That was in response to McWhirter's position that because the song is "pro-Confederate" it is "thereby pro-slavery." That is a logical fallacy. Randall only penned the poem in response to the federal invasion of the state. How is that a defense of slavery? And I will repeat, not a word in the poem is dedicated to slavery.

McWhirter also takes issue with my classification of Lincoln as a despot, stating, "There are more than enough places online and elsewhere to find eloquent and convincing refutations of those *long discredited Lost Cause positions* [emphasis added]." Finally the "Lost Cause" rears its pejorative head. He had already knocked out "neo-Confederate" so it was only a matter of time before "Lost Cause" entered the fray. Lincoln was classified as a despot *during the War* by many prominent *Northerners*, including abolitionists Lysander

Spooner and former Supreme Court Justice Benjamin Robbins Curtis. In fact, more mainstream historians and legal scholars are coming to this conclusion. This is not a creation of the "Lost Cause" and it has not been "long discredited." McWhirter is obviously blinded by his adherence to the Lincoln myth, the real "Lost Cause" in American history.

McWhirter displays his inconsistency and dishonesty in the next paragraph:

> First of all, McClanahan can't possibly know my opinion on the removal of Confederate monuments because I've made no public statements on the matter. Indeed, I go out of my way in my original article to set the two issues apart.

He then cites these lines from the *Time* piece:

> Unlike current dialogues about Confederate monuments, there's really no room for debate here. We might hesitate to move or destroy marble monuments for fear of permanently losing them, but if Maryland leaves "Maryland, My Maryland" behind, the song will still exist—it will just go back to the historical record where it belongs.

But he fails to mention these sentences from the first paragraph of *the same piece:*

> Yes, after decades of failed attempts, we finally have a compromise that might work—replacing the original 1861 lyrics by James Ryder Randall with a milquetoast but inoffensive 1894 rewrite. It's a big step and part of the broader movement to remove, replace, or re-contextualize public displays of pro-Confederate (or Lost Cause) memory across the nation. Up to this point, these efforts have paid more attention to monuments and building names, but "Maryland, My Maryland" certainly deserves such scrutiny.

That is only setting the "two issues apart" by about 500 words.

As for the quotes, "hesitate" is the key word in the first. A hesitation is a pause before an ultimate action, the action in this case being the purging of Confederate symbols. I have seen no such "hesitation" on the part of anti-monument people in the last year. It can also mean a reluctance to do so, but from his opening paragraph, it is clear that McWhirter is not reluctant to take part in a "broader movement to remove, replace, or re-contextualize public displays of pro-Confederate (or Lost Cause) memory across the nation." How do I know that? He calls Maryland's decision to alter the state song "a big step," and he lumps changing the song together with removing and replacing monuments. That is a "public statement" on the issue. And by the way, the original title of the piece when it ran at the History News Network was "What Took Maryland So Long." No hesitation there.

He closes with a poor attempt at humor coupled with a concurrent display of unwarranted hubris:

> *Apparently, if his imaginary version of me and my PC buddies change the song and remove these monuments, we won't just alter the country's historical landscape, we'll erase the very ideas of "self-determination and opposition to authoritarianism." I had no idea I (or "Maryland, My Maryland," for that matter) wielded such enormous power. It's like McClanahan's the Uncle Ben to my Peter Parker. Who knew I had the strength to obliterate democracy itself? Here, I just thought I was pointing out how absurd it is for a loyal state [sic] to have a song defying the existence of the federal government, but I'm actually summoning a horrifying Orwellian dystopia of political correctness and blind deference to authority. My God, what have I done?*

I never said McWhirter himself "wielded such enormous power." I never placed such high emphasis on his work. Hubris, even if it was an attempted joke. But I think McWhirter unknowingly admits why these symbols are under attack. It is not "racism," of which the North was in no short supply, or slavery, for as the ardently neo-Confederate "Lost Cause" partisan James McPherson has pointed out, the vast majority of Confederate soldiers did not fight for the institution. No. Confederate symbols are under attack because they represent resistance to authoritarianism and centralization, the true definition of "dissidence." After all, the inscriptions on many of these monuments erected long after the conclusion of the War say as much. They also exemplify non-conformity with Lincoln's America and a belief in self-determination. By default, removing them finally, permanently, and shamefully confers the slander of "traitor" and "treason" to their cause, the same cause which created the American states in 1776. You will be assimilated. McWhirter takes issue with *Maryland, My Maryland* because it is "dissident." Even if he wants to, he cannot alter the definition of the word or his original line of attack.

Ultimately McWhirter's piece is an example of the current political climate and as such should be discussed and refuted. Confederate symbols and monuments are the low-hanging fruit for the modern PC crowd. But what happens when they are gone? Where does the mob go next? No one can rightly believe that political correctness will end there. If they do, they are not paying attention. Simply writing "Trump" in chalk on a college campus is now viewed as a violation of a "safe space."

I would recommend, however, that McWhirter keep writing for such an esteemed publication as *Time*. They have a fine track record of being on the right side of both history and political issues in general. And yes, I am having a bit of fun with the one or two people who actually read his blog and comment on it ("It is not political correctness. It is historical correctness"), because as you know, all of us "neo-Confederate," "Lost Cause," Tom Woods and Tom DiLorenzo "shrill" partisans believe Lincoln's secret middle name was Adolf.

GOD BLESS AMERICA

JEFFERSON DAVIS AND Robert E. Lee were only the beginning. For anyone that believed American iconoclasm would stop once Confederate statues were removed or "contextualized," they were rudely awakened last week after the Philadelphia Flyers decided to remove the Kate Smith statue in front of the Wells Fargo Center in Philadelphia due to her "racist" recording history.

They first bagged it, then removed it. This action came on the heels of the New York Yankees banning her rendition of "God Bless America" from the seventh inning stretch. The team had been playing her version since 2001 following the September 11 attacks.

Smith, who died in 1986, was clearly another low hanging fruit. After all, she was born in Virginia and was called the "Songbird of the South" at the height of her popularity during World War II. She must be a racist. Smith recorded one "offensive song" in 1931, "That's Why Darkies Were Born," and another for the 1933 musical *Hello, Everybody*, "Pickaninnay Heaven." She also posed in an advertisement for a "mammy doll" in the 1940s. This was enough to boot her from public spaces and polite conversation, or more importantly, to lose the ability to enjoy her beautiful contralto voice at Yankee or Flyer games.

Not everyone bought the latest social justice crusade with even some traditionally leftist voices saying this went too far, but once the Reign of Terror begins, all vestiges of the *ancien regime* have to go. It's almost as if these Dantonists are slandering Robespierre before they lose their heads, too.

One New Jersey town offered to take the statue, but the Flyers refused. Just like Confederate statues bulldozed by city governments, they must be removed from public site, or better yet placed in a junkyard.

We can shake our heads at the destructive tendencies of these social justice morons and their useful idiots in the public sphere, but the lesson is that reconciliation is no longer fashionable. The American education system has succeeded in in its goal of making presentism the dominant "historical" lens. Judge everything by fashionable present standards or off with your head!

It used to be that Northerners of all races and backgrounds would sing and write about the South in glowing terms. They weren't duped into this position. They experienced it themselves and sought to capitalize on the dominant view of the American South, and black Americans loved the South as much as white Americans. Louis Armstrong's "music video" for "When It's Sleepy Time Down South" would be panned today for its "overt racism," but Louis Armstrong and every actor in the video are African-American. They loved their home. Armstrong wasn't forced to record this tune, and it was, in fact, one of his standards. Does that make him a racist?

Moreover, Smith wasn't the only person to record "That's Why Darkies Were Born." African-American Paul Robeson performed the tune as well, and his version is perhaps better than Smith's. Does that make him a racist?

Or how about the any other African-American musician that performed antebellum plantation tunes in the early to mid-twentieth century? Does that make them racist?

The point of reconciliation was to heal the wounds of the War and Reconstruction. Music had that effect, and because all American music is Southern music, Louis Armstrong's South, not the modern interpretation of the region, is what dominated popular opinion in the mid-twentieth century. The Kate Smith disaster is what should be expected in our modern Orwellian society. American history cannot begin until about 1975. Everyone before that needs to be "contextualized" according to modern standards, if not marginalized or removed.

The point of history is to understand through the context of the time in which the actors lived. That cannot be done in our current political and social climate. But that is the objective. Slogans, chants, and platitudes have replaced real scholarship and understanding, and Kate Smith's "God Bless America" is the latest victim. It doesn't matter that Smith helped raise truck loads of cash for the war effort in the 1940s, or that she was instrumental in getting female African-

American artists air time, or that African-American artists performed the same "racist" songs as Smith, or that her version of "God Bless America" was used in both the 1940s and early 2000s as a cathartic release, or that she was awarded the Presidential Medal of Freedom in 1982. Kate Smith committed the sin of being a woman of her time and for that she and her legacy must be punished or banished.

Unfortunately, this won't end any time soon.

The Southern Political Tradition is Winning

NATIONALIST JEFF SESSIONS gets canned and a nullifier takes his job.

This is actually an odd twist of fate. A friend of mine knows Sessions personally, and he continually expressed disappointment at Sessions's actions as AG. Jeff Sessions is from Alabama and is named after two famous Confederate heroes, Jefferson Davis and P.G.T. Beauregard. His replacement, Matthew Whitaker, hails from that great bastion of federalism, Iowa. But Whitaker said he supported nullification not once, but twice in 2014. Sessions never took such a stand.

You almost couldn't make this up. The North is out "constitutioning" the South.

Of course, the Twitter legal scholars jumped all over Whitaker after CNN published a November 10 hit piece. So did the "actual legal scholars," most of whom just regurgitate the same tired nonsense about the supremacy clause, racism, and slavery. Middle school students could get more creative. And most probably know more history.

One Twitter legal scholar said that nullification was acceptable for weed, but anything else should be off the table. This passes for deep thought in 2018.

You see, according to the "actual historians" and "legal scholars," Whitaker is nothing more than a "hack." Why? Because he also had the nerve to criticize *Marbury v. Madison* in addition to saying that the founding generation supported nullification.

He is right on both issues, but to our modern intellectual overlords, Whitaker exemplifies everything they hate, namely people who think independently and have the nerve to say it.

Of course, the Left (and some neoconservatives as well) are challenging Trump's temporary appointment as unconstitutional. They don't want a man who won't bend to their will to have such power. The vanilla Eric Holder was so much better. To be honest, Whitaker probably couldn't get through the spineless weasels in the Senate, so his time as AG will be short-lived, but even so, this is the first time since the middle of the 19th century that a man with even marginally supportive views of nullification held that position.

The most important takeaway from the Whitaker appointment is that the Southern political tradition is gaining traction and the agents of the state can't stand it.

Take, for example, the hit piece Think Progress published about the Abbeville Institute's recent conference on "The Revival of Secession and State Nullification." I could have written it before the event took place. The "reporter" probably did.

Mention white supremacy and the Confederacy: check.

Mention the SPLC: check.

Mention segregation and slavery: check.

Mention John C. Calhoun and George Wallace: check.

Media outlets like Think Progress really think throwing out these bogeyman comparisons works on anyone with more than a quarter of a brain. That says a lot about their readers.

The "reporter" who attended lied about what organization he represented and only relented after speaker Michael Boldin pressured him into giving up the ghost. What transparency. One Think Progress acolyte wanted to let them know he has been "tracking" the Institute for years if they needed any further information. This makes it seem like the Institute hides in dark corners of the web and holds secret conferences with secret papers that only its secret participants can read. Let me help. The Institute has a FREE website that contains virtually every lecture from every conference FREE of charge along with a FREE podcast, FREE articles, and a YouTube channel with FREE videos. The organization has so much to hide.

This "reporter" understated attendance at the conference, failed to mention that two of the seven conference speakers were Leftists, and conveniently omitted that Boldin used Rosa Parks as an example of nullification. Yes, these speeches were seething with George Wallace inspired white supremacist rage.

Most people who read the Institute's material or attend its conferences walk away with the impression that the Southern tradition is the *American* tradition, that so much of what makes America great was born and bred in the South. The Institute's message is a positive affirmation and academic exploration of what is true and valuable in the Southern tradition. That includes a rich cultural heritage of music, food, literature, and art as well as people (Calhoun, Upshur, Taylor of Caroline, Randolph of Roanoke), symbols (Confederate monuments and flags), and ideas (state nullification and secession) that many in the mainstream political class and media find deplorable. The South is a beautiful mosaic, or better, as Dr. Robert Peters called it, a bountiful garden in need of cultivation.

The Southern political tradition is finding currency in the age of Obama and Trump because unlike the drones at Think Progress and other "mainstream" media outlets, thoughtful people across the political spectrum are seeking solutions to modern problems that don't involve Washington D.C. They are being distinctively *American*. But according to the SPLC, that makes them "political extremists." I wonder if they would use the same classification for Hillary Clinton, or better yet Jefferson and Madison? Clearly not, but the examples of Whitaker and Clinton also means we are winning.

Think Progress and CNN just don't want you to know it.

Section Five
Yankees, Republicans, and Nationalists

Colonial Slavery

IN 1715, COLONIAL Governor Charles Craven remarked that his front-line troops in the fight against a hostile American Indian tribe comprised "two hundred stout negro men."

Just five years prior, Indian agent Thomas Nairne wrote that the colonial militia in this same colony possessed "a considerable Number of active, able, Negro Slaves; and the Law gives everyone of those his Freedom, who in the Time of an Invasion kills an Enemy."

In 1708, when threatened by a potential invasion, newspaper reports from the colony had nearly "1000 good Negroes that [know] the Swamps and Woods, most of them Cattle-hunters...."

When the "two hundred stout negro men" were not enough to defend from Indian raids, Craven asked a neighboring colony to send extra "stout negro" slave manpower. The colony responded by asking for one female slave for every male slave it supplied for the fight. Craven and other leaders refused, for they found it "impracticable to Send Negro Women in their Roomes by reason of the Discontent such Usage would have given their husbands to have their wives taken from them which might have occasioned a Revolt."

It seems that no one in this colony viewed African slaves as inferior or dangerous. They were well armed and were an integral part of colonial defenses. They even refused to break up families, fearing that such a move was might not only lead to a "Revolt" but that it was inhumane to do so. These men were not considered "chattel," and by serving in the militia they were guaranteed their freedom.

The same racial attitudes were not held by those in another British North American colony.

In 1701, John Saffin, a man who made considerable wealth in the lumber, tobacco, fish, and fur trade, penned the first known defense of slavery in North America, one that would outline the "positive good" defense later used in the nineteenth century.

Saffin dabbled in the slave trade and owned several indentured servants. When the term of one his African servants named Adam ended in 1701, Saffin refused to give him his freedom.

A local clergymen penned a pamphlet both condemning Saffin and slavery, to which Saffin replied with a piece entitled *A Brief and Candid Answer*.

Saffin argued that God intentionally "set different Orders and Degrees of Men in the World…" while equality would "invert the Order that God had set." Saffin considered slavery to be a Biblically ordained institution, for nature proved that some men were to be "High and Honourable, some to be Low and Despicable; some to be Monarchs, Kings, Princes and Governors, Masters and Commanders, others to be Subjects, to be Commanded; Servants of sundry sorts and degrees, bound to obey; yea, some to be born Slaves, and so to remain during their lives." This was God's law.

Saffin believed that the colony would be better off without African slaves, but if they could not be "all sent out of the Country…the remedy would be worse than the disease." Saffin thought that free Africans would be a "plague to this Country" and thought the African was better off as an American slave. "It is no Evil thing," he wrote, "to bring them out of their own Heathenish Country, [to] where they may have the knowledge of the One True God, be Converted and Eternally Saved."

Later, Saffin scribbled a bit of poetry about "the Negroes Character," where he labeled them "Cowardly and Cruel," and "Prone to Revenge, Imp of inveterate hate." They had "Mischief and Murder in their very eyes," and were "Libidinous, Deceitful, False, and Rude/The Spume Issue of Ingratitude."

He thus considered slavery to be a benefit to both races, for whites could use their slaves as needed and Africans would be lifted up from barbarism.

Quiz time:

What colony called Charles Craven governor?

What colony did John Saffin call home?

If you answered South Carolina for Craven and Massachusetts for Saffin, you would be correct.

The Massachusetts courts eventually forced Saffin to free Adam, and following the Stono Rebellion of 1739, racial attitudes stiffened in South Carolina, but in the early eighteenth century, African slaves in South Carolina possessed at least a modicum of liberty and were free from the racial stereotypes that Saffin noted in his *A Brief and Candid Answer.*

In fact, the Carolina Charter required every *man*–including slaves–to be able to defend the colony from foreign invasion. This was not the case in Massachusetts.

History, and the history of American race and slavery in particular, is a complex mosaic. Southerners did not invent proslavery ideology. Much of it came from Northern theological instruction. Saffin was tutored by Puritan minister Charles Chauncy, the future President of Harvard. Such history does not neatly fit with modern conceptions of social justice and Northern self-righteousness, but when many Americans are simply taught platitudes and slogans, it is almost too much to expect anything more.

Grant's Failed Presidency

A review of *U.S. Grant's Failed Presidency* (Shotwell Publishing, 2019) by Philip Leigh

THERE WAS A TIME in recent memory when thoughtful people consistently ranked U.S. Grant's presidency as one of the worst in history. The scandals, military Reconstruction, the mistreatment of the Plains Indian tribes, and the poor economy during the 1870s wrecked his reputation. That all began to change when "social justice" took center stage in the historical profession and Republican Party partisans sought to revitalize the dismal reputation of one of their most important presidents. After all, Grant was a *Republican*, and men like Karl Rove and Dinesh D'Souza will never grow tired of telling people it was the Republicans who saved America from those evil Southern traitors.

More importantly, historians like Ron Chernow, whose critically acclaimed biography of the 18th President sits on bookshelves across the United States, have sought to refocus attention on Grant's "successes" rather than failures. Chernow places special emphasis on Grant's attempts to protect former slaves during Reconstruction rather than the scandals which rocked not only his administration, but which destroyed the United States economy and smacked of crony capitalism and the corruption that undergirds the practice. This type of feel good revisionism is part of a broad push to revitalize the reputations of the "active" presidents in American history, men like Polk and Jackson, those that embody the antithesis of what the founding generation designed for the executive branch.

This new love for U.S. Grant is unfounded. Philip Leigh provides a quick and punchy rebuttal to this hagiographic Grant revisionism in his *U.S. Grant's Failed Presidency*.

Using the same sources as the revisionists, Leigh takes apart the thesis that Grant wanted to "protect" minorities in the United States. Leigh conclusively illustrates that like most Republicans at the time Grant's sympathy for freedmen had to do more with winning elections than moral obligation or chivalry. Grant would not have won in 1868 without the freedmen vote, and both he and the Republican Party knew it. Leigh points to Republican policy toward American Indians and Chinese immigrants as proof of Republican hypocrisy on the issue of "civil rights."

Leigh also argues that Grant had more to do with the economic corruption of the period than most realize. He gladly pursued both physical and economic reconstruction, promoted the interests of the Republican monied class and turned a blind eye to the rampant corruption among Northern "carpetbaggers" in militarily occupied Dixie. There is a reason Grant was shown in an infamous political cartoon as a conquering emperor riding on the back of the barefoot South in a carpetbag supported by United States troops. Leigh considers that to be the real Grant, not the trumped up image pushed by Ron Chernow.

This nicely illustrates that the protectors of the American empire on both the left and the right have a vested interest in promoting the imperial presidency as a sort of good tyrant king. To them, Grant could be a Pericles riding to the rescue of the American experiment, the great citizen general who rid America of the backward agrarian Southern Spartans.

Except Grant was never that magnanimous or heroic, and his presidency was little more than a political rubber stamp for the revolutionaries who were radically remaking American society in the 1860s and 1870s. Leigh contends that you can't understand Reconstruction without understanding Grant. That is certainly true.

It might be easy to have a tinge of sympathy for Grant, the uncouth general who never cared for politics, voted Democrat, but through war was elevated to the presidency in one of most bitterly partisan eras of American history. Grant, according to this interpretation, was a "Victim," (as opposed to a "victim") an unwilling participant in a larger drama over the spoils of war. Leigh paints a different picture, a Grant that understood the stakes and actively pursued a partisan agenda with Republican victory more important than principles or the Constitution. In other words, Grant was like every other "active" president in the imperial era, and like Lincoln chose party over union and the Constitution.

There had to be winners and losers, and Grant ensured the South was not only defeated but punished. That was Grant's decades long legacy south of the Mason-Dixon, and even in the North, his adherence to the radical Republican agenda helped give rise to the populist revolt of the 1890s.

The original historical presidential rankings with Grant near the bottom may be the only time I agree with the "establishment" assessment of the American executive. Grant should be perpetually buried at the bottom.

Leigh has added a nice counterweight to the modern attempt to portray Grant as some type of righteous cause acolyte deserving of fawning praise.

If you're looking for a concise history of the Grant administration without the modern propensity for over-saturated "presentism," skip Chernow and read Leigh. It is by far the best summary of his administration in the last half-century.

Reconstruction and Recreation

2019 MARKS THE 150th anniversary of U.S. Grant's inauguration as President of the United States. It also has sparked a renewed interest in Reconstruction, particularly the notion that America failed to capitalize on an "unfinished revolution" as the communist historian Eric Foner describes the period.

This general description of the 1860s has been used by both radical leftists like Foner and neoconservative historians and pundits, meaning that the postbellum period in America has received an establishment consensus. If only America had followed the Radical Republican agenda in 1868, the United States would have been a better, more tolerant place.

Take for example an upcoming PBS documentary produced by Henry Louis Gates, Jr. based on his forthcoming book, *Stony the Road: Reconstruction, White Supremacy, and the Rise of Jim Crow.* The tone of both the documentary and book are clear: Reconstruction was a missed opportunity for a radical restructuring of American society with freedmen being the central actors in a great struggle for "true citizenship" as Adam Gopnik argued in a recent piece in *The New Yorker*.

Gates's collection of characters includes former New Orleans Mayor Mitch Landrieu and of course Eric Foner. It will undoubtedly be hailed as a seminal moment in American film making, a truly objective and tragic view of a violent and repressive period, and both leftist and neoconservative politicians and talking heads will praise Gates for his courage in denouncing Southern racism and violence and for championing equal justice. The Republican Party, after all, has carried on a concerted effort in recent years to attach the modern GOP to the radicals of the 1860s. It was the Democrats, not the Republicans, who rode as Klansmen and authored Jim Crow legislation. Neoconservatives like Dinesh D'Souza and Bill O'Reilly are, in essence, attempting to out social justice the social justice warriors. Even their tepid response to the toppling of Confederate monuments has shown that they are receptive to the Foner narrative on Reconstruction, meaning they agree that Southerners were traitors who deserved punishment, and the South would have been better off if former Confederates were permanently disfranchised and prohibited from holding political office.

That is the Grand Old Party line from 1869. But is this true? In short, not really.

Certainly, it is easy to sympathize with former slaves clinging to newfound political power and general rights of citizenship, to recoil at the racial violence of the Reconstruction period. But this is only part of the story. No one has ever bothered to ask Gates or Foner if they were to be disfranchised and governed by a newly created and at times foreign ruling class because of a crime (treason) no one in the South ever faced trial for if they would simply concede and capitulate. This is what was asked of the vast majority of white Southerners in the 1860s and 1870s. They deserved it is not a valid rebuttal. The Anglo-American tradition rests on the rule of law, and while blacks were being abused by extra-legal and unjust means (lynching, mock-trails, and terrorism), white Southerners faced illegal, unjust, and unconstitutional property confiscation, the suspension of *habeas corpus*, and disfranchisement. Two wrongs don't make a right, but it is the modern "American Way" to pick a sympathetic winner and believe the loser earned the punishment.

And this was an era of violence. Not only did the Klan and other paramilitary organization ride at night to intimidate and at times kill black political leaders and their white Republican allies, but black militias, the Union League (a militant arm of the Southern Republican Party), and the United States Army did their share of killing and plundering. In a logical world divorced from the emotivism and guilt that marks modern identity politics, a rational person could understand how this type of political and social climate would produce two armed camps, one fighting to maintain newly granted liberties, the other determined to regain the same. It's almost as if the Republican Party created this dysfunctional climate, was "shocked" by the results, and then asked for absolution for any complicity in the violence. Neo-Puritanism can never be held accountable.

It only got worse. As Lincoln said when asked by Alexander H. Stephens what would would happen to the freedmen, they could "root, hog, or die" for all Lincoln cared. But they had to vote Republican. The first African-American elected to the United States Senate, Hiram Rhodes Revels, eventually sniffed this out and in a scathing letter denounced the Republican Party as a collection of dishonest politicians only interested in gaining and maintaining power. Black Southerners were useful pawns in a longstanding game for the spoils of political victory.

Clearly the South alone did not create this mess. As C. Vann Woodward pointed out in *The Strange Career of Jim Crow,* the South did not invent Jim Crow legislation. Northern States dominated by the Republican Party can be pegged for that. "Free [white] Soil, Free [white] Labor, Free [white] Men!" as the Republican slogan went in the 1850s. The social transformation eventually extended to every leftist driven "ism" that plagues the modern era, and the Republican Party eventually led the chorus for unlimited immigration in the 1860s and 1870s.

Reconstruction governments at both the federal and State level were known for their corruption and mismanagement. That corruption led to several major scandals, the abuse of the American Indian Tribes–"the only good Indian is a dead Indian"–and the establishment of American imperialism. If you don't have Southerners to abuse, focus on the Indian tribes (they can't vote, either), and if your egalitarian goals fail in the South, help your "little brown brothers" in the Philippines. As a McKinley campaign poster emphasized in 1900, the United States flag had only been planted on foreign soil for "hummanity's sake." That boilerplate material originated during Reconstruction. Gates won't have much to say about that, I'm sure.

The Republican Party of the 1860s finally had the reins of power, and they used it to codify their version of the American empire. Big banks, big business, high tariffs, an aggressive foreign policy, and a newly established North American economic colony (the South) propped up the Republican nationalist vision. Alexander Hamilton once opined that corruption made the British Constitution the best in the world. Had he lived to the 1860s, he could have said the same thing about the United States model.

William T. Sherman insisted during the War that the Southern people had to be wiped out in order to gain a total victory in the War. "War is hell," but so was Reconstruction. It used be called a tragic era, a time of lawlessness, depraved and selfish political acts, and the finest example of American political corruption. All of that has been sacrificed at the altar of political correctness. If, as Gopnik suggests, Southerners should have been treated as Nazis following World War II, then that opens the door to the modern movement to exterminate any vestige of traditional American culture by any means necessary, from Washington to Lee and everyone that admires either man or the traditional South. After all, even the "founding racists" were problematic.

The Social Justice Conservatives and Reconstruction

A slightly different version of this essay was originally published in the February, 2020 issue of *Chronicles: A Magazine of American Culture.*

FOR DECADES, AMERICAN conservatives rightly viewed the Reconstruction period as a "tragic era" rife with corruption, scandal, mismanagement, and unconstitutional power at both the state and federal level. Radical leaders of the Republican Party orchestrated the entire process by which the United States was "recreated" rather than "reconstructed." The Constitution ceased to be the anchor of the federal republic, and dangerous utopian ideals of "equality," political centralization, and mass democracy that had been incubated in the beer halls and socialist clubs of central Europe crossed the Atlantic and took root on American shores. European "Red Republicans" like Carl Schurz found common cause with American bred reformists Thad Stevens, Benjamin Wade, Charles Sumner, Schuyler Colfax, and Henry Winter Davis, all leaders of the radical faction of the Republican Party. These discontented souls thought America needed to be remade in a righteous cause to eliminate Southern influence in the general government.

Abraham Lincoln's pithy 1863 Gettysburg Address allowed both the "Red Republicans" and Radical Republicans to work under the false premise that they were continuing the work of the founding generation. These 272 words allowed Lincoln to "revolutionize the Revolution" as the historian Gary Wills wrote. More than anything, Lincoln had unknowingly provided the intellectual basis for what passes as establishment conservatism today, for his "proposition nation" served as the origination point for a strange transition in the American conservative tradition.

Conservatives would no longer be hidebound to defend traditional order or "well-constructed institutions" as Edmund Burke called them. The "ancient constitutions" that for centuries had guarded the liberties of the Anglo-American tradition would be supplanted by a metaphysical "higher law" of American egalitarianism as articulated by Lincoln's future Secretary of State William Henry Seward. To the modern conservatives who subscribe to this position, both the antebellum and postbellum South—as the peculiar other in American history— represented a departure from real "Americanism," the deviation from the "founding principle" of "all men are created equal." Thus, "equality" not tradition or even the Constitution became the foundation of what should be termed "social justice conservatism," and this type of conservatism has been masquerading as American conservatism for the last thirty years. This is almost entirely the result of a distortion of the origins of the Republican Party and the story of the War and Reconstruction.

For example, the social justice conservative online journalist Jarrett Stepman wrote in his recent tome *The War on History* that, "This is what the Civil War was about. This four-year conflict was ultimately over whether the central tenets of the Declaration of Independence was true, or false. Thus, the Gettysburg Address is the perfect summation of a generation of debate over slavery and the nature of the Union."

The social justice conservative historian Forrest Nabors followed a similar line in his *From Oligarchy to Republicanism*. The modern American, he said, "schooled from birth as they are in the general idea of equality," would view the "political character" of the antebellum South as a relic of "another continent in a far-distant age." Nabors surmised, "At their first encounter with the ruling class of the Antebellum South, the same Americans who proudly wave the Confederate flag today would likely feel their American blood boil, hoist the Stars and Stripes, and reach for their guns." More importantly, Nabors believed they would run out and take a sledgehammer to the Confederate monuments they so proudly defend.

Compare Nabors to a foreign-born Union officer described in Confederate General Richard Taylor's memoirs, *Destruction and Reconstruction*. Taylor was the son of President Zachary Taylor, and following the War he told of an unnamed German who in 1865 attempted to comfort and assure him "that we [Taylor and other Confederates] of the South would speedily recognize our ignorance and errors, especially about slavery and the rights of States, and rejoice in the results of the war." Taylor responded that he appreciated the effort and "apologized meekly for [his] ignorance." After all, because Taylor's ancestors had emigrated from England to Virginia in 1608, they "no time to transmit to me correct ideas of the duties of American citizenship." Taylor then sarcastically remarked that his grandfather, "commanding the 9th Virginia regiment in our Revolutionary army, had assisted in the defeat and capture of the Hessian mercenaries at Trenton, and I lamented that he had not, by association with these worthies, enlightened his understanding." The German simply smiled and told Taylor he would help him if requested.

This German seemed more civil than the "offensive brute—a foreigner of some mongrel sort" Ambrose Bierce encountered as a fellow Union prisoner during the war, but neither immigrant seemed to be able to avoid voicing their opinion on Southern society. Bierce admired his Southern enemies more than he did his foreign comrade. He praised the culture and refinement of his Southern captors but bemoaned that his alien companion had "just sufficient command of our tongue to show that he could not control his own."

What should be clear is that Nabors and other social justice conservatives have adopted the imperial rhetoric of these foreign revolutionaries and have made their reformist agenda the so-called conservative cause of the twenty-first century. To modern social justice conservatives, the Radical Republicans and their socialist European companions are the good guys. But social justice conservatives are nothing more than the Girondists in a culture war that will ultimately consume them. None will be spared the guillotine.

Yet, perhaps the more important issue for these social justice conservatives, at least in the last two decades, has been a mission to salvage the reputation of the Republican Party. Social justice conservative historians such as Allen Guelzo at Princeton University have developed a cottage industry around the myth that the Republican Party has been *the* force of good since its inception in 1854.

In a recent mass market video for Prager U., Guelzo argued that Reconstruction should have been a "glorious chapter in America's story" but instead became a "shameful one." Republicans missed an opportunity to remake the South. His better "conservative" plan would have included "a *real* occupation" of the South "until a new political generation grew up in the South which learned a newer lesson about race and rights than white supremacy," and a program of land confiscation and redistribution to former slaves and economic diversification to rescue the South from backwardness. Guelzo might as well have channeled Sumner or Stevens who both insisted that the South needed to be fearfully punished for her sins.

And it doesn't stop with professional historians. Pseudo-intellectual pundit and social justice conservative Dinesh D'Souza has wrongly argued that no Republican ever owned a slave while championing the Party as the real home for American values and institutions. D'Souza has called the Republican Party the historical party of "nice guys" only to insist that they should really be following Lincoln's example of violence. When someone asked him after a speech how he would respond to Antifa thugs, D'Souza invoked Lincoln's actions during the War, suggesting that such strong measures were the only way to oppose the "racist" goons in the antebellum and postbellum Democrat Party. He may have a point. Lincoln started a war that led to nearly a million dead American soldiers and thousands of civilians, both black and white. That is the real legacy of the Republican Party, but to D'Souza, this was a necessary and righteous cause, the original Constitution (and historical accuracy) be damned.

Unfortunately, neither Guelzo, Nabors, nor D'Souza are alone. They have simply echoed a growing chorus of social justice conservative voices who saw the War and Reconstruction as a righteous cause to fulfill a romantic destiny of liberty and equality. Karl Rove has openly called Confederate soldiers "the enemy" and bemoans the supposed failures of Reconstruction the South. Newt Gingrich, the G.O.P. establishment historian turned politician, championed "the combination of white Republicans and African Americans that sustained the Reconstruction of the South along [democratic] lines...." And Bill O'Reilly—neither an historian nor an intellectual heavyweight—has sided against the "slaveowners rebellion" and falsely claimed in his *Legends and Lies: The Civil War* that Lincoln believed that slavery "violated the constitutional declaration [sic] that 'all men are created equal.'" This is little more than the language of the Left. What are these social justice conservatives seeking to conserve? Certainly not the original federal republic or the "ancient constitutions" of the founding generation.

Barack Obama's insistence during his first inaugural address in 2009 that his administration would continue the process of "recreating America" might as well have been written by the establishment social justice conservative intellectuals entrenched in think tanks and conservative institutions across America including the Republican Party and the media.

The real victors in this social justice conservative transition are Eric Foner and the progressive movement. Social justice conservatives like Guelzo and Nabors have adopted Foner's myopic view of the War and Reconstruction. To Foner, both cataclysmic events were always about race, equality, and democracy. They represented an "unfinished revolution" as he titled his seminal work on Reconstruction but nevertheless represented a "second founding."

This is the key. Foner correctly argues that the Rump Congress led by radicals in the Republican Party rewrote the Constitution during Reconstruction and recreated America in the process. Social justice conservatives who give lip service to "originalism" while concurrently praising the radical transformation of America in the immediate postbellum period are digging their own graves. The paradox should be easily identifiable, but it seems establishment social justice conservatives do not have the capacity to understand that you cannot praise the original Constitution, the founding generation, or the early American order and its adherence to federalism, localism, and decentralization while concurrently hitching your wagon to Abraham Lincoln and the reptiles in the 1860s Republican Party. That Republican Party was by no means conservative.

As Foner points out, the older interpretation of Reconstruction and the radicals that dominated it formulated by the so-called Dunning School of the early twentieth century consistently thwarted progressive efforts at reform. Columbia University professor William A. Dunning and his students crafted a narrative of Reconstruction that blamed the process on overzealous Northern reformers who had little understanding of Southern political or social institutions. Foner insists that the Dunning School has been discredited. This is false. It has simply been reinterpreted with the communist W.E.B DuBois and his acolyte Foner dominating the narrative. Everything is now viewed through the lens of race, though Dunning was far more inclusive in his narrative than even Foner in his monumental tome. Dunning and his students may have been racists, but they did not define their studies by race or racial identity. Foner does, and so do many of the social justice conservatives who write about the era today.

Regardless, the progressive legislative agenda in the late nineteenth century was hamstrung by references to the dark days of corruption during Reconstruction, so much so that before Teddy Roosevelt assumed the presidency in 1901 some American conservatives believed American progressivism was dead. Not so, and with a shift in historical interpretation following World War II, Reconstruction became the gateway to the cultural revolution of the 1960s. Foner and DuBois indirectly led that charge. Would either be considered conservative?

American conservatives must understand that by praising the Reconstruction Republican Party they are indirectly conceding the field. There can be no American conservative consensus while progressivism is mislabeled and repackaged as "conservatism," and that is what these social justice conservatives have unwittingly accomplished. Richard Waver wrote in his *Southern Tradition at Bay* that, "The Old South may indeed be a hull hung with splendid tapestries in which no one would want to live; but from them we can learn something of how to live." American conservatism cannot exist without the Southern tradition, and the Southern tradition cannot exist within modern interpretations of Reconstruction, including those of establishment social justice conservatives. They might as well swear homage to Foner.

The First Congress

A review of *The First Congress: How James Madison, George Washington, and a Group of Extraordinary Men Invented the Government* (Simon and Schuster, 2016) by Fergus Bordewich

AMATEUR HISTORIANS USUALLY write excellent histories. Left unshackled by the latest groupthink of the academy, these historians tend to be independent thinkers and more importantly better writers than their professional counterparts. Shelby Foote used to implore historians to learn to write better. After all, our job is to influence the public, to "interest it intelligently in the past" as G. M. Trevelyan wrote. Popular histories tend to accomplish this needed and worthwhile goal. Most Americans gather their historical knowledge from the amateurs, but when the amateur lacks a comprehensive understanding of the past or has so ingested the propaganda and dogma of his age that his writing suffers from countless mistakes, it brings to mind Polybius's question, "But if we knowingly write what is false whether for the sake of our country or our friends, or just to be pleasant, what difference is there between us and hack writers?" Fergus Bordewich fits that last description.

Bordewich writes well. His style is crisp and lacks the pedantry of an academic work, but that is the only benefit to reading his scribblings. A good history on the First Congress was needed. Bordewich correctly asserts that this was perhaps the most important Congress in American history, but to suggest that the First Congress "invented the government" displays a lack of understanding of American history, and more importantly, Bordewich does not seem to be aware that the Constitution's ratifiers—the proponents or friends of the document—insisted they were not creating a national government but maintaining the federal republic as under the Articles of Confederation. The nationalists that dominated the First Congress perverted the founding. To Bordewich, they saved the "nation" and "breathed life into the Constitution." As James Madison asserted, the public ratification debates gave the Constitution its life and validity, not the First Congress.

Bordewich makes several mistakes in the book, some embarrassing, others subtle. For example, he claims that John Adams wrote the Lee Resolution urging American independence, insists that James Madison's reputation "increased during the long campaign for ratification" as a known author of the *Federalist* essays—he wrote them anonymously and with little overall impact—and portrays opponents of a strong central government as a "small minority." Southerners, particularly those who attempted to retard the headlong rush toward nationalism, are described as "temperamental," "hot-tempered," "stony-faced," and "haranguing" while Northerners are "brilliant," "provocative," "handsome," "elegant," and "tireless."

Bordewich blames Southerners for rampant sectionalism, all to defend slavery, while Northerners get a pass because of their far-reaching nationalist vision and (tepid) commitment for abolition. Of course, Northern nationalism was always a disguise for sectionalism. One of Bordewich's heroes, Fisher Ames, was a leading New England secessionist after he retired from Congress. Bordewich omitted that from his narrative by instead highlighting his experimental Massachusetts farm. How quaint and incorrect.

There is little doubt that the First Congress transformed the United States. I often tell people that the Constitution died in 1789 with Oliver Ellsworth's first Judiciary Act. Bordewich considers that legislation to be one of the crown jewels of the First Congress because it ultimately allowed for the modern activist federal court system. He expresses disappointment in Madison's failure to have his "incorporation amendment" added to the Bill of Rights and argues that Jefferson implicitly approved of such an amendment because of what he later wrote to the Danbury Baptists. In fact, Bordewich fails to understand why the "Antifederalists" insisted on structural amendments, meaning what became the Tenth, while paying very little attention to civil liberties. They did so because they understood without such structural restrictions on central authority, the general government would soon morph into a "national" monstrosity at the expense of the States. This was a more prescient prognostication than anything the "Federalists" proposed during the First Congress. Ellsworth worried his legislation would not last a few years. The Tenth Amendment turned out to a paper tiger while the Judiciary Act became a legal juggernaut.

Bordewich admires Hamilton's financial plan and delights in the ultimate victory of nationalism over State power. This should be expected. The standard narrative of American has the nationalists as the visionaries, the true believers in the original Constitution, while the "Antifederalists" are the thorny, narrowly provincial troublemakers intent on destroying the United States. This is a magical fairy tale. James Madison did not "evolve away from his early Federalist [sic] roots toward an embrace of states' rights…" he simply defended the Constitution as ratified by the States in 1788.

The First Congress is a noble idea born from the twenty volume First Federal Congress Project at George Washington University. In more capable hands, it could have been a valuable addition to the historical canon of the early federal republic. As it stands, Bordwich's tome is better suited to the bargain bin at the local bookstore, a light and at times fun narrative that lacks necessary depth, context, and a comprehensive understanding of the founding period.

Recarving Rushmore

A review of *Recarving Rushmore: Ranking the Presidents on Peace, Prosperity, and Liberty* (The Independent Institute, 2014) by Ivan Eland

THE ANNUAL VENERATION of American monarchy–"Presidents Day"– has passed again. While still officially called "Washington's Birthday" by the general government, the American public has embraced the idea of honoring the executive branch by shopping for furniture, jewelry, or cars. George W. Bush encouraged us to shop after September 11, 2001. He might as well have issued a presidential bull.

This is a curious holiday for Americans, one that is so anti-republican that it would have been universally rejected by the founding generation. But we have grown to love our elected kings. They are supported for life after leaving office, command six figure speaking fees, and are showered with praise at official state funerals when they die. Some get their own action figure. Even our former colonial overlords in Great Britain don't spend this much time worshiping a real monarchy.

Foisting this much attention on the executive branch has led to an unhealthy and distorted understanding of American politics and government. Our collective history is dominated by presidential administrations, the "activity" of the executive office, and the cycle of presidential elections. It has also led to mountains of literature on American presidents, from the banal, pedantic, and trivial, to sweeping generalizations on presidential epochs. Anyone studying the middle of the nineteenth century has to wrestle with "The Age of Jackson." Most of these works are not worth the paper and ink used to print them, and few are groundbreaking or thought-provoking studies that need to be taken seriously. Most modern historians are an incestuous and uncreative lot who simply regurgitate the fashionable opinions of the day. When they tell you to "read a book" as a retort to a serious question, they admit to not having an original thought. And that "book" is typically the one stamped "acceptable" by historical groupthink.

"Presidential rankings" suffer from the same historical ignorance. Historians generally consider the "best presidents" to be those who did the most harm to the United States Constitution, the document each swears to uphold and defend before taking office. That doesn't matter. The ends justify the means. Who cares if Franklin Roosevelt's "Second Bill of Rights" would destroy every vestige of whatever is left of the original Constitution? Does it provide "social justice" or "equality" or "economic security?" More important, both parties often wonder if such a presidential edict can create an electoral advantage. Ideology trumps both restraint and the Constitution itself in the modern era.

Can there be a better way to grade the presidents? Ivan Eland argues absolutely in *Recarving Rushmore*. He judges forty-one of the forty-three men who have held office on a simple formula: how did they maintain or destroy peace, prosperity, and liberty? This is a unique measuring stick to determine effectiveness, one that flips "executive activity" on its head. If we are going to embrace executive government, we should consider what type of activity we want from the president.

Eland's best presidents are not the typical top four. John Tyler, Martin Van Buren, Grover Cleveland, and Rutherford B. Hayes fare well in his study, while Lincoln, both Roosevelts, Jackson, and Wilson are kicked to the end of the list, joining longstanding bottom dwellers in James Buchanan, Andrew Johnson, and Franklin Pierce. Eland ranks Jimmy Carter better than Ronald Reagan, a move sure to elicit the ire of conservative readers, and even George Washington is criticized for his reckless (and unconstitutional) actions during the Whiskey Rebellion. Eland slaughters several sacred cows in the process, and his breezy writing and short chapters allow for a quick and punchy read. One must give him credit for simply venturing to take on establishment group think and for his determination to view the presidency through a different–and unfortunately controversial–prism.

Yet, while Eland's tome is a worthwhile and refreshing departure from most presidential histories, the book suffers from some of the same problems as the "acceptable" studies. The good points of the books can at times be overshadowed by an ideologically driven form of presentism, so while Eland professes to define the presidency as ratified in the original Constitution, his critique of various administrations sounds more like a twenty-first century op-ed then a desire to understand the men and their times.

For example, Eland is critical of Zachary Taylor for doing nothing to "alleviate" the "shameful murder" of the American Indian tribes in California during the California Gold Rush, and he castigates Franklin Pierce for "stealing Indian land" and for his "slave based" foreign and domestic policies which he claims led to the "Civil War." These are opinions best expressed in modern presentist textbooks authored by the deans of the historical establishment. Eric Foner could not have written a better description of the Pierce administration. He praises presidents for executive energy when in defense of "liberty" and criticizes them when they don't but fails to understand that these actions would have (and often did) violated their oath of office. Original restraint sometimes means doing nothing even if doing nothing is politically incorrect or out of step with modern libertarian ideology.

Regardless, everyone with even a minor curiosity for presidential history should read *Recarving Rushmore*. It is a refreshing and novel departure from the mundane, repetitive, and sycophantic presidential biographies that generally occupy space on bookshelves. This isn't John Meacham's *American Lion*. Anyone who has the guts to rank John Tyler as the best president in American history–and I agree–deserves attention.

Two Against Lincoln

A review of *Two Against Lincoln: Reverdy Johnson and Horatio Seymour, Champions of the Loyal Opposition* (University Press of Kansas, 2017) by William C. Harris

IN A SPEECH BEFORE the Senate in 1863, James A. Bayard of Delaware stated that "The truth will out, ultimately...though they may be voted down by the majority of the hour, though they may not be known at first—the great truths will not triumph, with a little energy and a little perseverance." Bayard had for two years relentlessly attacked the Lincoln administration for its legal gymnastics regarding the Constitution, and he believed that in the future, Americans would come to view the Lincoln administration as a watershed in a downhill slide to despotic government. Bayard later resigned from the Senate after taking Charles Sumner's "Iron Clad Oath," a vocal though defeated and marginalized critic of the Republican war effort.

Defeated and marginalized summarizes the entire collection of Lincoln opponents described as "Copperheads" by the Republican press. The reason is possibly tied both to Lincoln's assassination in 1865 and the process of reconciliation after the War. Lincoln was martyred, his constitutional abuses chalked up to wartime necessities, and the burgeoning Lincolnian America solidified by the "Gilded Age." But even long after the War, few historians spent much time studying Lincoln's "fire in the rear" and those that did often regurgitated the partisan attacks leveled against them by the Republican Party both during the conflict and in the more militant phases of congressional reconstruction. For many Americans, men like Clement Vallandigham and illusions to the "Knights of the Golden Circle" conjured up images of "treason" and misguided opposition to a just cause. The Copperhead's principled defense of "The Union as it was and the Constitution as it is" was left to the dustbin of American history, or worse described as the *New York Times* called it in 1864, "Copperhead charlatanry."

Frank Klement resurrected the reputations of the Midwestern "Peace Democrats" in several monographs during the 1960s, but those volumes represented almost the entirety of scholarly research on the Copperheads for most of the twentieth century. Jennifer Weber revived interest in the Copperheads with her 2006 publication of *Copperheads: The Rise and Fall of Lincoln's Opponents in the North*. While this tome has several flaws, notably the emphasis she places on race being the central theme of Copperhead opposition, it nevertheless forced the historical profession to reconsider Lincoln's wartime opponents as a viable and principled collection of men.

William Harris's *Two Against Lincoln* focuses on the actions of two "loyal opponents' of the Lincoln administration: Reverdy Johnson of Maryland and Horatio Seymour of New York. Johnson is a little-known United States Senator who sniped at the administration once taking his seat in 1863. His background as a former Whig and his familiarity with Lincoln adds to the story. Johnson spent much of his time in the concluding years of the War defending his fellow "Northern" conservatives against charges of treason by the Republican dominated Congress, attacking military interference at polling places across the North, but particularly in his home State, and in denouncing Lincoln for his "utter unfitness for the presidency." He also gave one of the more important speeches in favor of the proposed amendment to abolish slavery, one that laid equal blame for the difficulty in ending slavery on virulent abolitionist of the North and staunch pro-slavery "fire-eaters" of the South.

Harris portrays Johnson as a man without a party and a moderate stuck in the middle of a nasty political war that spilled into Reconstruction. Johnson did not believe secession to be legal, nor did he think the Southern States had physically left the Union, but he bristled at the efforts of the radical Republicans to impose their political will on the South. He voted against Andrew Johnson's impeachment and sealed the political deal that kept the president in office. Harris additionally argues that it was Reverdy Johnson's work in defense of five men charged under the Ku Klux Klan acts in 1871 that established federal interpretation of the Fourteenth and Fifteenth Amendments for a generation. Harris concludes that:

> *Like many former Whigs in the border states and elsewhere, Johnson's staunch Unionism was based on his belief in national progress and the greatness of American institutions. Although often opposed to Lincoln's*

policies and conduct of the war, Johnson held a view similar to that of the president on America's future and its transcendent purpose in fighting to prevent the destruction of the republic.

Thus to Harris, Johnson was neither a "Copperhead" nor a secessionist as contemporary critics claimed, but a loyal defender of the Constitution who differed with the Republicans and the Lincoln administration about war powers, the prosecution of the War, and the policies of Reconstruction, but not in the preservation of the "Union."

As a former presidential nominee for the Democratic Party, Seymour has a higher historical profile than Johnson, but as Harris notes, like Johnson he is often little more than a footnote in the War narrative. That should not be so. Seymour was the wartime governor of New York and he worked tirelessly to restrain the wartime objectives of the Lincoln administration and the Republican Party. Seymour blamed the War on Northern fanaticism, the desire for New England to "meddle" in local affairs, and a press that buttressed their wild-eyed claims of a Southern "slave-power" conspiracy.

Harris describes Seymour as a principled conservative Democrat who like Johnson supported the War and never harbored any secessionist sentiment. Seymour sympathized with the Southern position in the 1850s and urged Northerners to adopt the Crittenden Compromise, but when Lincoln called for 75,000 troops to put down the "insurrection" in 1861, Seymour threw his efforts behind raising money and troops for the limited goal of the preservation of the Union. To Seymour and most Northern Democrats (as well as some Republicans including Lincoln), the War was not a righteous crusade to free the slaves but to save the Union. Seymour made that clear in his public pronouncements throughout the conflict.

Harris's chapter on the post-bellum Seymour is a somber though somewhat biased review of Seymour's political activities. Harris confidently asserts that the Republicans never intended to transform the Union, nor did Lincoln want to remake the executive branch. He describes Seymour's speeches as shrill and filled with "typical hyperbole" that were intended to appeal to the paranoid element of the Northern electorate. His description of Republican reconstruction efforts implies that Seymour and the Democrats mischaracterized their motives. Seymour never wavered. He said after the War that "Time will set all that right." Harris concludes "It never did."

Though he has done a service to the reputations of both Johnson and Seymour, Harris's conclusions still seem to maintain the traditional description of both men as little more than a perpetual nuisance for the Lincoln administration with paranoid and false predictions about the future of America. How can he make those claims? Because to Harris, Lincoln was a great politician capable of handling their dissent—something his successor was unable to do effectively—and who, "Fortunately for America," chose to accept a "mighty destiny" to "save the Union." Curiously, Harris believes that it has been "a long-accepted view" that the War led to consolidation and executive abuse. If by long accepted he means never, then one can subscribe to his conclusion. Only recently has the Lincoln legacy come under sustained academic attack by a few hearty souls willing to challenge the now ingrained depiction of Lincoln as the quintessential American hero.

Though his book offers a fresh addition to the field of Northern dissent, Harris discounts his subjects' prescient observations of American society and politics, both then and now. Harris's affinity for Lincoln and for reading history in reverse produces conclusions that will forever maintain the tainted legacy of both Johnson and Seymour. They were wrong, and Lincoln was right. That is a subjective analysis.

The Hard Hand of War

A Review of Joseph W. Danielson, *War's Desolating Scourage: The Union's Occupation of North Alabama,* University Press of Kansas, 2012; Charles A. Misulia, *Columbus Georgia 1865: The Last True Battle of the Civil War,* The University of Alabama Press, 2010.

On Easter Sunday, April 16, 1865, Union forces under the command of General James Harrison Wilson attacked, captured, and sacked Columbus, GA in the last major battle of the War east of the Mississippi. Wilson's campaign began in North Alabama and quickly moved South.

By this point in the War, Alabama could offer little resistance. Even the great Forrest could not stop Wilson at Selma. The "army" defending Columbus–like Forrest's army at Selma–was little more than young boys and old men. Hastily constructed forts on the Alabama side of the Chattahoochee River were unmanned.

The Battle of Columbus began well enough for the Confederate defenders. They duped the Union cavalry into trying to cross a bridge packed with oil-soaked cotton bales. As the Union charged the position, a Confederate battery overlooking the bridge opened fire and the bales were set ablaze. This temporarily halted the assault, but when the rest of the cavalry showed up later that day, Wilson decided on a night attack.

The Union army ultimately overwhelmed their disoriented and disorganized foes and the occupied the city. Much has been made of Sherman's "March to the Sea" in 1865, but very few are aware of Wilson's Alabama campaign and the "hard hand of war" in the Yellowhammer State or the Battle of Columbus.

Historians Joseph Danielson and Charles Misulia have brought this little-known companion to Sherman's swath of destruction to light.

Danielson begins his narrative in of the Union occupation of North Alabama in 1862. His picture of defiant Southern belles and recalcitrant civilians meshes nicely with Gary Gallagher's portrayal of Southern nationalism and morale in his *Confederate War*. Danielson explains that while the Union army initially adopted a conciliatory policy in relation to Southern property and civil liberties, that soon gave way to tough measures after Southern civilians bristled at "Lincoln's hordes." Union soldiers began ransacking houses, stealing goods, and confiscating food. By 1864, one North Alabama woman remarked that Union soldiers had left her "poor children [with] nothing but a little piece of fried middling, and bread and water." Fall harvests were seized while many Union soldiers walked away with clothes and shoes from helpless Southern women.

This story was repeated many times across the hills of North Alabama. Southern women who believed that a chivalric code would protect them from attack soon found out that Union soldiers did not subscribe to the same standards as their Southern men. "Lincoln's hordes" took liberties with Southern women, burned their homes, and subjected them to physical violence. Their crime: supporting their men in the cause of independence. Their resolve was so strong that Union soldiers often marveled that it was the women, not the men, who were the most ardent patriots in North Alabama. If anyone were to read Drew Gilpin Faust's nonsensical *The Creation of Confederate Nationalism*, they would believe that Southern women failed to support the cause and instead took to rioting across the South to find bread that had been confiscated by the Confederate government. Danielson has done much to dispel that myth.

Danielson concludes that "For a region where no major battle had occurred, the Confederate people, towns, and countryside suffered greatly." Women chided their men for surrendering, took to bed out of grief, and refused to write in their journals for months after the war was over.

The hard hand of Union military occupation eventually transitioned to a punishing campaign across the State which culminated in the Battle of Columbus on Easter Sunday 1865.

Misulia provides a thorough blow by blow narrative of the event and its aftermath. Once the Confederate army failed in its defense of the city, the Union cavalry proceeded to loot and destroy anything of value, including almost every mill and factory in town. The only exception was the city's grist mill. Wilson and his men occupied the finest homes in town, destroyed several bank vaults to steal now worthless Confederate money, tore apart storefronts in an effort to secure jewelry and clothing, and walked off with livestock and other valuables. The great conflagration of the city began when careless soldiers began detonating the thousands of pounds of munitions they captured in the raid. Some raiding also took place in the surrounding areas. Present day Phenix City was looted while many slaves looked on in horror as "ugly haired" men raided their plantations. One slave recalled, "they just rambled through the house a-cussin' an' a-carryin' on, an' breakin' up all the dishes. The ole master, he run away."

Alcohol fueled much of this thuggish behavior, and while Misulia argues that most of the soldiers behaved themselves, the simple fact that so much destruction was leveled on the city says more about Union command that the Union soldiers themselves. Wilson not only condoned their behavior, he encouraged it, as did General Ormsby M. Mitchel who oversaw Union occupation of North Alabama. The plundering began at the top.

These crimes are often brushed aside as a regrettable but necessary part of war. George W. Bush era crony Karl Rove praised the Union war effort in a review of Danielson's book, calling the Confederate soldier the "enemy."

Rove's opinion is indicative of a larger problem, one that a careful reading of both Danielson's and Misulia's books can correct. Danielson is not pro-South, far from it, but he honestly portrayed Union actions in North Alabama. Misulia is not a professional historian which gives him an advantage over the academic crowd: he does not have to answer to the overlords of acceptable opinion in American history departments. Both books correct the notion that Southerners were traitors who deserved the beating they took, that the Union army was a virtuous band of moral crusaders, and that the majority of Southerners were duped by the plantation oligarchy into fighting and supporting a war they did not want. Certainly Rove did not gather this from the book, but his Republican colored glasses hid the real tragedy of the conflict.

Antebellum Southerners were Americans who had a different vision of American government and society, and the War set the South back both physically and economically for decades. Did any group of Americans deserve that? And if not, could there have been another way? Perhaps the "hard hand of war" imposed upon the South by "Lincoln's hordes" was unnecessary. At the very least, Americans should consider it barbaric, but that would require a reassessment of the modern American historical narrative.

Yankee Foreign Policy and the Cold War

NORTH KOREAN DICTATOR Kim Jong-un is rattling his sabers and threatening war against the United States. He blew up an American aircraft carrier in one propaganda video and has goaded the Trump administration in several other statements, ostensibly to create the image of manly firmness to his people. Obviously, high profile assassinations and executions along with staged videos showing Jong-un running through crowds of forced applause and mandatory groveling at his feet are not enough. North Korea does this about every twenty years. It is in the ruling family's DNA.

But most Americans don't understand the role North Korea played in the expansion of unconstitutional executive power in the United States nor its importance in the open-ended foreign policy commitments of the twentieth century. That is the real story.

The villain in this narrative is the oft forgotten and, in many cases, unknown Yankee bureaucrat Dean Acheson, a man who once reportedly called Hillary Clinton a "terrific person."

The Connecticut born and bred Acheson helped craft much of the more important foreign policy directives of the twentieth century. As assistant secretary of state, Acheson drafted the blueprint for the Lend Lease Act which, though sold as a measure to avoid war, pushed the United States only inches from armed conflict. That was Franklin Roosevelt's plan from the beginning. As the historian Charles C. Tansill famously wrote at great cost to his career in *Back Door to War*, Roosevelt was uncharacteristically occupied with his stamps during the Pearl Harbor attack while George Marshall conveniently was enjoying the second most famous horseback ride in American history. The first, Paul Revere's, helped Americans prepare for an attack. Marshall's cost the lives of 2000 American servicemen.

Acheson led the American delegation to Bretton Woods in 1944 and was instrumental in the creation of the IMF, the World Bank, and GATT. After President Harry Truman promoted Acheson to Undersecretary of State, he further advanced the cause of globalism by designing the Marshall Plan. This was a great coup for Acheson. In 1933, Roosevelt appointed Acheson to the treasury department, but he was canned because he knew little about economics. Now, the blundering Acheson not only helped establish the apparatus that would drive the world financial sector into the modern age, he involved the United States in an expensive, taxpayer funded open-ended policy of financial assistance for Europe and Asia. Everyone seemingly forgot that Acheson was a financial dolt.

More importantly, the Marshall Plan pushed United States foreign policy in a different direction and Acheson knew it. Truman handed the job of Secretary of State over to the scheming bureaucrat in 1949, and he rewarded the American people with the North Atlantic Treaty Organization, the first time since 1800 that the United States found itself in a permanent peacetime European alliance. Former Secretary of State George Kennan worried that Acheson was trying to militarize the Cold War. He was correct. In 1950, Acheson favored the findings of NSC-68, a paper that called for the massive expansion of both American military spending and the CIA. Until that point, the CIA was a relatively innocuous intelligence gathering organization. That quickly changed in the 1950s as the CIA was given a fresh influx of cash and secret powers. Without Acheson, the Dulles brothers would never have had the power to reshape American foreign policy during the Eisenhower years and beyond.

Acheson, in fact, was the mastermind of the Cold War. He convinced Truman of the necessity of "containment" and the importance of halting North Korean aggression in 1950. This led to the "Truman Doctrine," the Korean War, and Truman's bizarre speech before the Congress calling for Americans to pay more taxes and accept bigger government and less freedom because that would help bring about the fall of communism. The Politburo could not have written it better.

That brings us full circle to 2017. The Korean War was not only unnecessary, it led to a major policy shift for the United States. Vietnam followed Korea, and American meddling in the Middle East was a direct result of Acheson's ongoing fear of globalist communist aggression. We are living in a Cold War world without the Cold War. It is the gift that keeps on giving and Acheson was Santa Claus.

Acheson's story is emblematic of destructive Yankee influence in America. Their "city upon a hill" mentality has permeated every vestige of mainstream political thought, but most conspicuously in the neo-conservative faction of the Republican Party. This is not to say that Southerners were always anti-imperialists or correct in their public positions—far from it—but is always certain that Yankees will pursue the path of obnoxious intervention under the false notion of "humanity" guided by the "treasury of counterfeit virtue." Americans should be divesting themselves of this type of Yankee thinking. Unfortunately, it seems we are rushing to embrace it.

The Latest 18th Century Fake News

THE "FAKE NEWS" pejorative has become commonplace in modern public discourse, so much so that social media outlets have taken it upon themselves to "police" so-called "fake news" stories and warn people about their dangers. This was largely due to the supposed impact "fake news" had on Trump supporters in 2016. To these self-appointed gatekeepers of truth, honesty, and the American way, nothing that contradicts their version of American history can be acceptable.

Their narrative goes something like this: America was created as a singular nation on the principles of "justice" and "equality." You "anti-American" fools that argue the founding generation believed something different need to study Alexander Hamilton, John Marshall, and Abraham Lincoln [sic]. They clearly and correctly argued that the Union predated the States, just read the Declaration of Independence.

There are several holes in this argument, not the least of which is the classification of the original Union from a federation of States to an amorphous mass of "one people."

That would be 18th century fake news.

The earliest proponent of this position was not Hamilton but the Scottish immigrant and future Supreme Court Justice James Wilson of Pennsylvania.

Wilson argued in a 1785 speech supporting the unconstitutional (according to the Articles of Confederation) Bank of North America that:

> To many purposes, the United States are to be considered as one undivided, independent nation; and as possessed of all the rights, and powers, and properties, by the law of nations incident to such. Whenever an object occurs, to the direction of which no particular state is competent, the management of it must, of necessity, belong to the United States in

congress assembled. There are many objects of this extended nature. The purchase, the sale, the defence, and the government of lands and countries, not within any state, are all included under this description. An institution for circulating paper, and establishing its credit over the whole United States, is naturally ranged in the same class.

The act of independence was made before the articles of confederation. This act declares, that "these United Colonies...are free and independent states; and that, as free and independent states, they have full power to do all acts and things which independent states may, of right, do."

This was twisted logic unsupported by history. Wilson somehow believed that Thomas Jefferson intended the phrase "free and independent states" to mean the Union of "United Colonies," not thirteen separate States bound together in common cause against a singular enemy. To Wilson, "they" represented the plural "United Colonies." That would be news to Jefferson or virtually anyone else from the founding generation. "They" clearly meant each State individually as they were at one time "United Colonies" and were now "free and independent States" in the plural form, not as a singular community. If Wilson was correct, then it would have read "a free and independent state."

The 1783 Treaty of Paris confirmed that each State was independent of the others, and Article II of the Articles of Confederation codified that each State "retained its sovereignty and independence."

And the term "state" had real meaning. A "state" in the 18th century was a sovereign political entity, like the "State of Great Britain" as Jefferson calls it in the Declaration.

Wilson knew he had to engage in a grand game of sophistry for anyone to believe him, so to "prove" his point, he had the Declaration of Independence rewritten to reflect his wish to abolish the State designations. Wilson was fabricating history.

In other words, he was promoting "fake news."

Two Harvard researchers uncovered his lie in a little archive in Great Britain in 2015. They have since argued in a paper that this "proves" Wilson was correct, that the Union predated the States and that the state centered approach to the founding period does not fit the record. That would be true if we only listened to Wilson.

His "clever and elegant" lie obviously influenced them, but it is still just a lie, a lie that has now been exposed for the world to see.

If you have to fabricate a document to make your point, then your point is built on a house of cards. It is no wonder this so-called "Sussex Declaration" was never accepted by any of the founding generation except Wilson, or that it never saw the light of day until now.

Had the evidence remained buried in the English countryside historians would still have marveled at Wilson's artful fallacy, but they would never have had proof that he was making things up as he went.

This discovery should finally discredit the "nationalist myth" of American history, but unfortunately, if the current reaction is any sign of things to come, the "one people" myth makers will double down and insist that Wilson's understanding of American history is superior to every other interpretation, evidence to the contrary be damned.

The Stupid Empire

AS THE FIRST LEG of the American invasion force rolled through Iraq in 2003, Sergeant Brad Colbert of the 1st Reconnaissance Battalion of the United States Marine Corps leaned out the window of his Humvee and urged the Iraqi people to "vote Republican." This moment was captured by the embedded reporter, Evan Wright, and made famous in a series of articles that appeared in *Rolling Stone* magazine and later in the HBO mini-series *Generation Kill*. (I recommend this series to anyone who wants a realistic view of the early stages of the war in Iraq. It is not for the faint of heart, however. The vulgarity and violence may turn some viewers off, but it also helps explain why people in other parts of the world hate the United States.) Wright later recounted that Colbert was not making a joke; he firmly believed what he was saying. While this surprised Wright, it typifies the "stupid empire" of the Republican Party and progressives in general.

From the war to "end slavery" to the war to "liberate Iraq," the United States has been waging war for the last one-hundred and fifty years to theoretically bring "liberty and democracy" to "heathen" parts of the world. These are, rhetorically, wars for "humanity's sake," but more than anything they bring a perverted form of empire, one in which United States taxpayers are on the hook for trillions of dollars with nothing to show for it except more war, higher taxes, inflation, and resentment from many of the people the military sought to "liberate." Liberation becomes a relative term, and most of the people "freed" by the United States become dependents of the federal government or are betrayed by the loose promises of "freedom and democracy."

On 18 December 1865, the Radical Republican Thaddeus Stevens of Pennsylvania made the following remark before the House of Representatives: "The future condition of the conquered power depends on the will of the conqueror. They [the Southern states] must come in as new states or remain as conquered provinces." In one sentence, Stevens clearly articulated the intent of the Republican Party during the War Between the States. Southerners were a conquered people subject to the will of the Republican Party. Former slaves, the "liberated," were the pawns by which to keep the South "loyal" to the Union.

It is easy to imagine a Union soldier insisting that Southern blacks "vote Republican," just as Colbert called on Iraqis to "vote Republican." And, of course, most freedmen and their descendants did vote Republican until the 1960s. Grant would have been hard pressed to win the 1868 presidential election without them and the concurrent disfranchisement of most "evil" Southern whites through the illegally passed 14th Amendment. The Republican war machine spent four years destroying homes, property, lives, and infrastructure and now planned on rebuilding, or more accurately remaking, the South with the help of the "liberated." As Radical Republican Lot Morrill of Maine said following the war, "The ballot in the hands of the negro became as much the necessity of reconstruction of the republican States and their restoration as the bayonet in his hands was the necessity of the war."

Abraham Lincoln made the war a "humanitarian" effort with the pithy though incorrect Gettysburg Address in 1863, but where was the humanitarianism of William T. Sherman's army as they plundered their way to the sea in 1864 or Philip Sheridan's army as it commenced with the burning of the Shenandoah Valley in the same year? And how was the Republican Party being "humanitarian" when it used the military to enforce carpetbag rule, higher taxes, and both direct and indirect confiscation of property following the war? It seems the blueprint for the United States Empire was written in the years after the unnecessary carnage of the War Between the States: "liberate" a group of people and make them dependent on your continued rule; disfranchise those who oppose you and destroy their property and culture, but tell the world you are doing this for the good of the "liberated." The South, personified as the woman in the following political cartoon, could easily be any other culture who has faced the burden of the American empire in the last 150 years.

As the Democrats consistently pointed out during the years following Reconstruction, the Republican Party did not change. Without evil Southerners to fight, the Union army turned its attention to the West, and under the direction of Sherman and Sheridan, the western Indian tribes faced the onslaught of the new American foreign policy of "liberty and equality." Tribes that supported the Confederacy during the War Between the States felt the hammer of the federal government or were intentionally deceived in order to secure land for the railroads. Others who opposed the "blessings" of the Republican Party and the Union army were often slaughtered. Lincoln, in fact, ordered the largest mass execution in American history. 38 Dakota warriors were executed in 1862 after a Sioux revolt against Minnesota residents who continually breached treaties between the tribes and the federal government. Republican benevolence had limits, particularly in regard to those who could not help the Party win elections.

The frontier was "closed" during the administration of Republican Benjamin Harrison with the land runs in Oklahoma beginning in 1889. Again, the government, under Republican leadership, mainly through the corrupt Radical Republican Henry L. Dawes of Massachusetts, reneged on promises to the Five Civilized Tribes and seized their land through "re-allotment." The Dawes Act of 1887 divided Oklahoma into small homestead farms, often too small to be productive. Dawes and other Republicans insisted that the re-allotment process would "help" the tribes and provide them with the blessings of liberty and prosperity, but without question, the Act destroyed tribal culture and through corruption and intimidation, most of the tribal members who received land eventually sold it for less than what it was worth or lost it. Dawes had shown a propensity for scheming before—he had been part of the infamous Credit Mobiler Scandal of 1872—and his actions toward tribal lands did him no justice. This should not have been a surprise, however. It was the M.O. for the Republican Party, the same men who pillaged the South following the War in the name of humanity and who ran roughshod over the Constitution during Radical Reconstruction.

The election of Republican William McKinley in 1896 ushered in a new age of American imperialism, but one directly tied to the ideas of Reconstruction. Less than two years after taking office, McKinley asked congress for a declaration of war against Spain. This "Splendid Little War," known as the Spanish-American War of 1898, netted the United States Cuba, the Philippines, Guam, and Puerto Rico. The United States went to war, in part, to "liberate" the Cubans and the Filipino people from evil Spanish rule. Without question, Cuban revolutionaries fighting for independence from Spain before the war began were harshly treated by the Spanish governor of Cuba, but opponents wondered whether that justified American involvement. And, since the United States occupied Cuba after the war and inserted the infamous Platt Amendment into the Cuban Constitution in 1901, what had Cubans gained by cozying up to the United States? Authored by Connecticut Republican Orville Platt, the Amendment made Cuba a virtual protectorate of the United States, and the big brother to the north could intervene at any time to "save" Cuba from itself.

In the Pacific, the United States became involved in a guerrilla war against Filipino insurrectionary forces after they refused to submit to American rule. Teddy Roosevelt, as Assistant Secretary of the Navy, had instructed Admiral

George Dewey to invade the Philippines once war was declared in 1898 (How that related to the poor, downtrodden Cubans no one could answer). Dewey steamed into Manila Bay, defeated a larger Spanish Fleet, and helped protect the American expeditionary force led by Wesley Merritt, a Union War veteran and participant in Sheridan's burning of the Shenandoah Valley in 1864. The Philippines were placed under an American military governor—at first all Republican Civil War vets starting with Merritt—in an effort to bring the blessing of "liberty" their "little brown brothers," but not all of them accepted American gestures of "humanity" and "liberty."

Filipino Emilio Aguinaldo harassed American combat forces for three years. This was the first American Vietnam. William H. Taft was eventually appointed governor of the Philippines by McKinley, and to his credit reluctantly accepted the position because he did not support the acquisition in the first place, but Taft did oversee some of the fiercest combat of the Philippine-American War and ultimately supported American occupation.

Republicans trumpeted American military successes (sound familiar?) and claimed that the war was merited to help the pitiful Cuban and Filipino people.

By the time Teddy Roosevelt assumed the presidency in 1901, the Republicans had firmly established themselves as the Party of international empire, and no better articulation of this principle can be found than Roosevelt's 1904 annual address. In this message, Roosevelt rolled out the principles of the Roosevelt Corollary to the Monroe Doctrine: "Any country whose people conduct themselves well can count upon our hearty friendship. If a nation shows that it knows how to act with reasonable efficiency and decency in social and political matters, if it keeps order and pays its obligations, it need fear no interference from the United States. Chronic wrongdoing, or an impotence which results in a general loosening of the ties of civilized society, may in America, as elsewhere, ultimately require intervention by some civilized nation, and in the Western Hemisphere the adherence of the United States to the Monroe Doctrine may force the United States, however reluctantly, in flagrant cases of such wrongdoing or impotence, to the exercise of an international police power." So, the United States determines good conduct and "decency in social and political matters," and if you fail, the United States will become an "international police power" to keep you in line. This has since been extended to the globe. Ask the people of the Middle East.

Successive presidents used Roosevelt's logic to intervene in Latin American affairs, and interventionism found new flavor under Democrats Woodrow Wilson and Franklin Roosevelt. Imperialism was no longer confined to the Republican Party; progressives had co-opted the message and used it to bring "liberty and democracy" to "unenlightened" or "hopeless" people around the globe. Wilson re-organized Europe after World War I (to the detriment of many cultures in Europe), and Roosevelt helped jump start fifty years of American "police power" by involving the United States in World War II, by appeasing Josef Stalin at Yalta and by insisting on a United Nations. This led to the loss of hundreds of thousands of lives during the Cold War.

All of these actions had their roots in the Radical Reconstruction of the South. Republicans conquered and subjugated the South and found new votes in the Freedmen. They extended their "humanitarian" efforts by crushing the Plains Indian tribes and in the process opened thousands of acres for their railroads. The Party brought "liberty" to the Cubans and Filipinos and became the police force of the Western Hemisphere under Teddy Roosevelt. "Vote Republican!" Of course, by World War I, you no longer had to vote Republican; voting for either major party sufficed.

So, why is the United States the "stupid empire?" Simple. Unlike other empires in history, the United States expects the conquered to love the conqueror. The Romans did not expect their conquered subjects to love them. They ruled and the conquered accepted. The Athenians crushed several attempts to jettison their rule during the height of their empire, and the British did not care for the plight of their "subjects." A subject in each case was part of the best and most free state in the world. Resistance was preposterous (and deadly). Americans, however, believe that our efforts are the result of a simple dichotomy of good vs. evil. We freed you from evil and "gave" you your country back (conditionally), so love us! Reconstruction is taught that way, so is the American push to "liberate" other parts of the world. Certainly, the hypocrisy of the Spanish-American War and the misfortunes of the Plains Indian tribes have been documented, but no one connects the dots between the Republicans who looted the South during Reconstruction and the Republicans who raided the West, the Pacific, and Latin American during the late-nineteenth and early-twentieth century.

History has been unjustly kind to the conquerors and many mainstream historians have defended the conquering under idiotic moralistic pretenses. Slavery was bad so white Southerners deserved a beating; the railroads and western homesteaders needed property and Indians were vicious, so the tribes (somewhat) deserved a beating; the Spanish brutalized the Cubans and the Filipinos so the Spanish deserved a beating; Saddam was bad so he deserved a beating. Of course, Hitler, Stalin, Saddam, and others were brutal madmen, but it had never been American foreign policy to make "corrections" in the name of "liberty and democracy" until after the War Between the States. Like grizzly bears, the Republicans tasted human blood and had to continue their feeding. It has never stopped. Unfortunately, now voting for either major party perpetuates the "stupid empire." Love us or die! [But we'll give you everything back anyway with our strings attached because Americans are the "good guys."]

The Compact Fact

MAINSTREAM HISTORIANS ARE both an incestuous and snarky bunch. They latch on to trends–fads really–and pull those trends like mules lugging a heavy cart to market (where they hope to sell books to their tens of fans). In time, the mules give out, but unlike the mule, these historians never realize they are whipped. They hire more mules like them and cut and snipe at the stallions who bravely defy the yoke.

Unfortunately, these trends become ingrained in the academy and become the catchy slogans and clichés of the "educated" elite. Our history then becomes distorted, often unrecognizable from a traditional viewpoint.

Every now and then a stallion is allowed to run free.

Professor Nathan Coleman's new tome, *The American Revolution, State Sovereignty, and the American Constitutional Settlement, 1765-1800*, is the type of book the mules will hate. He refutes the now cliche nationalist narrative of American history and paints a different picture of the American founding, one that places the States at the center of American government.

The evidence is entirely on his side. From the beginning of the Imperial Crisis in 1765, American colonists viewed the struggle with Parliament as a constitutional crisis over the scope and power of the central government in London. For over one hundred years, the colonial legislatures were able to define taxing and monetary policy within their colonial borders. The central authority in London was charged with defending the colonies and regulating *international* trade. Such regulations were often overlooked, thus leaving the colonies as virtually self-governing societies with different cultures and customs. Benjamin Franklin recognized as much when he complained in 1754 that the prospect of forming a "congress" of all the colonies would be impossible because of colonial "provincialism."

When the Parliament passed the Stamp Act in 1765, American reaction against the act was based on the traditional decentralization of the British empire. Several colonies in fact nullified the law. The Royal Governor of Massachusetts, Francis Bernard, knew that unless the colonial legislatures could be consolidated into one large mega-colony, the British would be facing continual resistance to acts of the central authority, particularly when the colonies were only "virtually" represented in London. Their intransigence and intractability were predictable considering they had been largely left alone during the era of "salutary neglect."

Every step from 1765-1776 showed that the colonies viewed themselves as separate entities with only one common enemy: The Parliament in London. Certainly, they acted in concert at times, but an American "nation" in the traditional sense of the word did not exist. John Adams called the delegates to the Continental Congress "ambassadors," and each were mutually suspicious of the other delegations.

When Jefferson declared that the "states" were now "free and independent"– on equal footing with the "state of Great Britain"–in 1776, he was simply codifying what had already been established by custom and precedent in the previous one-hundred and fifty years.

Coleman expertly moves through the early federal period and explains in detail how a "constitutional settlement" was reached between the nationalists, most conspicuously Alexander Hamilton, and the republicans who favored the traditional role of the "local" over the "national." This settlement did not abridge the sovereignty of the States; rather it strengthened American federalism by forcing the nationalists to recognize the importance of the State governments within the Union.

The Constitution, Coleman correctly contends, was a compact fact between States, not a "compact theory." Suggesting it is merely a "theory" concedes too much to the other side.

Certainly, the settlement established at Philadelphia and in the ratifying conventions faced challenges, and Coleman nicely details how the nationalists attacked the Constitution as ratified in 1788. The First Judiciary Act of 1789, Hamiltonianism, the *Chisholm v. Georgia* (1793), and the Alien and Sedition Laws offered serious challenges to the compact. The Judiciary Act in particular, an often-overlooked law that did tremendous damage to the "settlement," is one area where Coleman offers a fresh perspective. Each of these obstacles were briefly overcome, but the fact that real federalism has been so largely ignored by historians and the public at large shows that the nationalist position won the day, not because it was correct, but because as Coleman concludes the nationalists bludgeoned the other side to death in the great war between 1860-1865. They rewrote the original meaning of the Constitution and created their narrative of American history, one that portrayed "state sovereignty" as nothing more than a quaint outlier, or more accurately a retardant, in the nationalist/progressive futuristic Utopia.

Forward, comrades!

Coleman has done a great service to the prestige of the academic community, though they will not see it as such. For once, an academic book has bucked the groupthink so pervasive in the ivory tower and has given us room to hope. Too bad none of the mules will read it and those that do will inevitably dismiss it as some "originalist" fantasy. That will say more about them than it does about Coleman's skill as a historian or his attention to detail both of which are exemplary, as is his book.

Rethinkin' Lincoln

THE MOST FREQUENT question I have received during promotion of my new book, *9 Presidents Who Screwed Up America and Four Who Tried to Save Her*, has been, "How can you say that Lincoln screwed up America?"

After all, he is the man who saved the Union and who put slavery on the path to extinction.

There should be a qualifier…at the expense of the Constitution.

Lincoln's crimes against the Constitution are not as well-known as they should be, but historians and legal scholars, even mainstream academics, have begun to take a hard look at the lasting legacy of Lincoln's abuse of executive power, particularly in the last decade.

Lincoln was called a dictator and a tyrant by many *Northern* opponents, was publicly castigated by former presidents Franklin Pierce and James Buchanan and famous authors Nathaniel Hawthorne and Herman Melville, and barely squeaked by in the 1864 election even though the war was in hand and he only had to win Northern votes. That should say something about his reputation among his peers, but how did he "screw up" America and the Constitution?

Lincoln unilaterally suspended *habeas corpus*, a power not delegated to the executive branch by the Constitution. This resulted in the incarceration of over 30,000 *Northern* civilians for the crime of opposition to the Lincoln administration and the War. Lincoln's Attorney General, Edward Bates, tried to justify Lincoln's move, but many constitutional scholars were not buying it, and though the Congress later rubber stamped the move by suspending *habeas corpus* themselves, it did not change the fact that Lincoln acted outside the law and suppressed American civil liberties in the name of unconstitutional and imaginary "war powers."

Lincoln also signed into law a slew of unconstitutional legislation, including a shiny new central banking system—long opposed by Southerners and many Northerners as being a clear violation of Article I, Section 8—and the first income tax in American history. If Lincoln believed his oath to "defend" the Constitution, both of these egregious pieces of legislation would have met his veto pen.

Even the War itself was constitutionally dubious. Lincoln did not have a declaration of war. He knew that such a move would have recognized the legitimacy of secession both by law and in fact, so he adopted the position that the Southern States were in "rebellion." The Constitution is clear on federal power in relation to "insurrection" or "domestic violence," in other words "rebellion." Article IV, Section 4 allows for the federal government to protect the States against "domestic violence" only through the application of the State legislature or through the State executive. Lincoln had neither. Article I, Section 8 allows the *Congress* to call forth the militia to "suppress Insurrections," but that power is qualified by Article IV, Section 4, and Congress did not call forth the militia; Lincoln did. Another unconstitutional move by the "Great Emancipator."

And speaking of emancipation, Lincoln is given credit for putting slavery on the path to extinction. But did he do it constitutionally? No, says Massachusetts abolitionist and former Supreme Court Justice Benjamin Robbins Curtis. In a stinging rebuke to Lincoln's Emancipation Proclamation, Curtis wrote: "If the President, as commander-in-chief of the army and navy in time of war, may, by an executive decree, exercise this power to abolish slavery in the States, which power was reserved to the States, because he is of opinion that he may thus "best subdue the enemy," what other power, reserved to the States or to the people, may not be exercised by the President, for the same reason that he is of opinion he may thus best subdue the enemy? And, if so, what distinction can be made between powers not delegated to the United States at all, and powers which, though thus delegated, are conferred by the Constitution upon some department of the Government other than the Executive?" Good question, and one that Northerners answered with "nobody cares whether it is constitutional or not."

As for Lincoln, he said, "as commander-in-chief of the army and navy, in time of war, I suppose I have a right to take any measure which may best subdue the enemy." Curtis and the founding generation disagreed.

The glorification of the Lincoln administration by those who profess to be "constitutional conservatives" exposes a glaring problem in American politics, namely the blatant hypocrisy of the American right. Conservatives often whine when Barack Obama abuses power through executive orders, signing statements, illegal bombing raids in Syria, non-recess recess appointments, and the like, but turn a blind eye to George W. Bush's abuse of power through executive orders, signing statements, and illegal bombing raids in the Middle East. Obama has said many times Bush did it, too. And he is right. Executive abuse didn't start with Obama.

And it didn't start with Bush as the Left would suggest.

There are countless examples in American history of executive abuse, many from the "sacred cows" of American politics. If Americans want to be honest stewards of good government, and by good government I mean constitutional government, we need to hold every president who abused power accountable, even "Honest Abe." That is the only way we can truly resurrect the federal republic the founding generation created when they formed the Union. American can be made "great again," but it is going to take a concerted effort by the American people to hold the next president accountable to his oath of office.

The Nationalist Myth

Dave Benner, *Compact of the Republic: The League of the States and the Constitution* (Life and Liberty Publishing, 2015).

James Ronald Kennedy, *Uncle Seth Fought the Yankees* (Pelican Publishing, 2015).

Jack Kerwick, *The American Offensive: Dispatches from the Front* (Stairway Press, 2015).

ONE OF THE RESULTS of the Northern victory in 1865 was the codification of Lincolnian nationalism and its resulting effect on American society and the interpretation of the Constitution. All issues that had long been decided by the States were thrust into a "national" spotlight and by default fell under the purview of the "national" government in Washington D.C. Real federalism vanished in a rush to punish the South and remake the entire United States in a Northern image, one that was expressly refuted during the ratification of the Constitution and then rejected by the majority of the American public—both North and South—in the eighty years before the War.

Much of our modern political "conflict" is a result of this shift from a federal republic to a "national" government. Education, healthcare, social welfare, and a host of other issues that were once decided solely by the States have taken a "national" tone with prospects for "national" solutions. Only one thing continues to work against this modern narrative, the Constitution itself.

Lincolnian nationalism relies on a "common law" approach to the American political order, that is the courts and legal decisions become more important than the language of the Constitution or the original intent of the document. Unfortunately for these common law proponents, the Constitution has changed little since 1861, and even the fifteen amendments ratified after 1861 did not alter the nature of the delegated powers in the document. This has opened an opportunity for American traditionalists to slice away at Lincolnian nationalism using the language of the founding generation to buttress their claims that original intent is still the most acceptable method of interpreting the Constitution. Lincolnian nationalism is built on a "myth," one might call it the "Nationalist Myth," of American history.

Americans have never been "one people," and the federal republic was designed to absorb and respect differences in section and culture. Lincoln and the War changed that.

Dave Benner's *Compact of the Republic* is a very good summary of the "compact fact" of the United States Constitution. Benner is an "amateur" historian, in other words a very good one, so no peer reviewed journals would even contemplate reviewing his work. That doesn't matter. His approach to the Constitution and American law is simple: what did the founding generation say the Constitution would mean when the document was ratified in 1788? He correctly concludes that the facts point to a limited federal republic of "expressly" delegated powers. This type of reasoning does not require a law degree or a Ph.D. but simple common sense and the willingness to comb through public domain resources readily available online. The end result is a thorough dismantling of the "Nationalist Myth" in American history.

James Ronald Kennedy's *Uncle Seth Fought the Yankees* takes a similar approach to the Constitution through folksy homespun tales told by an elderly "Uncle Seth" to his young decedents many years after the War. The Kennedy's are well known for their *The South Was Right!* and here one of the Kennedy twins takes a stab at historic fiction with great effect. In 107 short stories, Kennedy tells the tale of Southern valor and Yankee atrocity, of Southern heroism and Yankee lies, and most importantly of the "compact fact" of the United States Constitution. This is a full-throated assault on the "Nationalist Myth" of American history, one designed to rescue the American public, particularly Southerners, from their misguided attachment to the recreated "Union" after the War.

Jack Kerwick's *The American Offensive* does not address the Constitution or the original federal republic, but is a collection of essays that confronts the symptoms of the larger disease of the "Nationalist Myth," namely one-size-fits-all policies from the general government. Kerwick is a good writer and as a professional philosopher presents a well-reasoned case for traditional American conservatism. Unfortunately, this case is made more difficult by the "Nationalist Myth." Many American conservatives, Kerwick excluded, fail to equate the triumph of the Union in 1865 as the true turning point in limited government in America. Certainly, there are examples of resistance to the progressive assault on traditional American culture well into the twentieth century, but without the "Nationalist Myth," progressives never get their agenda off the ground. Kerwick's outstanding discussion on cultural issues—immigration, race, religion, conservative philosophy—mirrors that of Pat Buchanan, but it would not be necessary had the "Nationalist Myth" not triumphed through war and Reconstruction. These issues would be locally handled and would be out of the scope of the "national" government in Washington D.C. As Kerwick states in his introduction, "It has been my hope in bringing to bear clear thinking upon the Politically Correct juggernaut that dominates our culture—*including both national parties and virtually every ideology*—that we can expose its cognitive and moral bankruptcy for what it is [emphasis added]." Lincoln opened Pandora's Box, and closing it has proven nearly impossible.

But there is hope. The "Nationalist Myth" is facing more of a challenge today than at any point in post-bellum American history. And the "armatures" are leading the way. Even Kerwick has dedicated much of his young career to reaching a popular audience. Discussions of real federalism, State's rights, nullification, and secession are taking place not only on the Internet but publicly in statehouses across the country. That would have been impossible twenty years ago. The "Nationalist Myth" made possible by the election of "Honest Abe" in 1860 may finally be meeting a real challenge to its century old dominance of American political discourse. All three books prove that the real myth in America is not the "Lost Cause" but Lincolnian nationalism.

Made in the USA
Las Vegas, NV
20 October 2021